WISDOM IN THE HEBREW BIBLE

EXPLORING GOD'S TWILIGHT ZONE

WISDOM IN THE HEBREW BIBLE

EXPLORING GOD'S TWILIGHT ZONE

T. A. PERRY

HENDRICKSON PUBLISHERS

Wisdom in the Hebrew Bible: Exploring God's Twilight Zone

© 2008 by Hendrickson Publishers Marketing, LLC
P. O. Box 3473
Peabody, Massachusetts 01961-3473

ISBN 978-1-61970-491-6

Previously published in 2008 as *God's Twilight Zone: Wisdom in the Hebrew Bible*.

Printed in the United States of America

First Printing New Hendrickson Publishers Edition — May 2014

Cover Art: The cover artwork entitled "Dream of Joseph" was produced by He Qi in 2005 using gouache on rice paper. The work depicts Joseph, wearing the colored coat from his father, looking toward the heavens as his jealous brothers watch and plot. Photo Credit: Copyright Dr. He Qi (www.heqigallery.com). Used with permission.

This book is dedicated to my beloved grandchildren
Adin and Abigail Bracha.

עטרת זקנים בני בנים

Prov 17:6

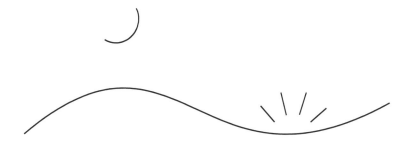

TABLE OF CONTENTS

PART ONE

CREATING AND MAINTAINING A RIGHTEOUS WORLD

PART TWO

INTERPRETING IN THE TWILIGHT ZONE

PART THREE

THE REBIRTH OF VULNERABILITY AND WONDER

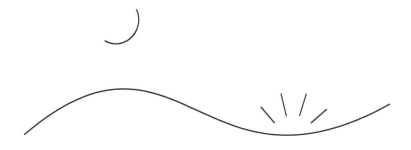

Preface

This book offers a series of close literary studies, all previously un-published, on key moments in the Hebrew Bible that deal with wisdom themes and methods. The two are closely connected, since wisdom writers loved to tell their stories and expound their values through methods long familiar both in the Bible and in world literature: proverbs, riddles, *mashal*-comparisons, and say-ings, especially when attached to narratives. Their champions in the Hebrew Bible include Noah, Abraham, Judah and Tamar, Jo-seph, Solomon, and the often anonymous sages who coined prov-erbs about King Saul, longed for righteousness, and exalted the importance of life and family values.

Special emphasis is placed on the Bible's very beginnings, on Genesis, where much of wisdom's later message is compacted and previewed, especially in respect to righteousness as the world's foundation. The ensuing decline of classical prophecy gave new importance to methods already in evidence in Genesis, as God's message was viewed as increasingly accessed through a twilight zone of ambiguous oracles and signs, dreams, riddles, and an ideology that was seen to spring from the Bible's earliest moments.

At twilight things become blurred, open to multiple interpre-tations, and there are not one but two twilights to each day, the one going from day to night and the other, the reverse. Taken together, they express the dynamism, the changing fortunes of human existence, perpetually shifting from happiness to misery, ignorance to clarity. Far from being moments of rapid passage, the twilights become the very image of human existence. For the text does not focus on stable entities like night and day, but rather on their perpetual flux and connectedness: "And it was evening and it was dawn," two twilights, one single day.

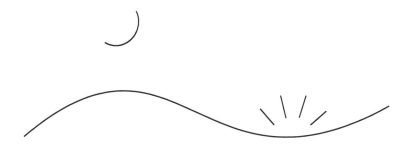

ABBREVIATIONS

AB	Anchor Bible
Abot	*Pirkei Abot* [*Ethics of the Fathers*]
AJS	Association for Jewish Studies
b.	Babylonian Talmud
BDB	Brown, Francis, S. R. Driver, and C. A. Briggs. *A Hebrew and English Lexicon of the Old Testament, with an Appendix Containing the Biblical Aramaic.* Oxford: Clarendon, 1906.
BibInt	*Biblical Interpretation*
BSac	*Bibliotheca Sacra*
ch(s).	chapter(s)
FOTL	Forms of the Old Testament Literature
Gesenius	Gesenius, Wilhelm, E. Kautzsch, and A. E. Cowley. *Gesenius' Hebrew Grammar.* Oxford: Clarendon, 1906.
HTR	*Harvard Theological Review*
HUCA	*Hebrew Union College Annual*
ICC	International Critical Commentary
JBL	*Journal of Biblical Literature*
JETS	*Journal of the Evangelical Theological Society*
JPS	The Jewish Publication Society
JSOT	*Journal for the Study of the Old Testament*
Midr.	*Midrash*
MT	Masoretic Text (the standard Hebrew version)
n./nn.	note/notes

NCB	New Century Bible
NIB	*New Interpreter's Bible*
NICOT	New International Commentary on the Old Testament
NJPS	*Tanakh: The Holy Scriptures: The New JPS Translation according to the Traditional Hebrew Texts*
NRSV	New Revised Standard Version
OTL	Old Testament Library
OtSt	Oudtestamentische Studiën
Qohelet / Kohelet	The book of Ecclesiastes
Rashi	Rabbi Shlomo Yitzhak (1140–1105). See *Torat Hayyim.*
RSV	Revised Standard Version
SBLDS	Society of Biblical Literature Dissertation Series
v(v).	verse(s)
VT	*Vetus Testamentum*
VTSup	Supplement to Vetus Testamentum
WBC	Word Biblical Commentary
ZAW	*Zeitschrift für die alttestamentliche Wissenschaft*

Biblical books are abbreviated according to the guidelines published in the *SBL Handbook of Style.* All references to the Bible and to classical texts give chapter followed by verse or appropriate sub-division. I cite Hebrew Scripture according to the chapter and verse of the MT and give the English enumeration when different. All biblical and other translations are mine unless otherwise noted.

For the transliteration of Hebrew, since in all cases the goal is less to reproduce the exact spelling of MT than to recall the shape of the Hebrew words, vowels are transliterated as they would sound in an English reading. Consonants are transliterated according to the "General Purpose Style" in the *SBL Handbook of Style* with the exception of the *aleph* and *ayin* which follow the "Academic Style."

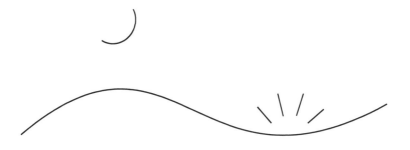

INTRODUCTION

If God's mind is rich beyond comprehension, our world's origin—which God is said to have conceived—is not. Intended to be full of divine glory, the universe depicted in the Book of Genesis begins in an environment of *tohu va-bohu* (Gen 1:2), a desolation and confusion that might be imagined today as a nuclear holocaust, or the continued enslavement and destruction of entire peoples such as in the Bible itself were periodically reproduced, whether as a global flood, the incineration of Sodom, or the descent into Egyptian slavery. From this perspective, Genesis is less about beginnings than about how to avert the need for a new start.

Put differently, just as humans are themselves dust and to dust shall return, Genesis is a survival handbook in a world originating in desolation and threatening destruction. The heroes of the story, those that legend qualifies as Mothers and Fathers, survived conditions of extreme hunger and famine, endless wandering and homelessness and exile, in brief, all the dangers (rape, murder, enslavement, robbery, guile) associated with their existence as aliens. Instead of succumbing, they dreamed of better lives and tried to include others—indeed, the entire human race—in their own dreams. They dreamed those dreams as God's own plan for the universe, but their ways were those clear and *un*mysterious ones that still work today: human liberation, family and community building, labor, friendliness, justice and assistance for all, but with special attention and care for the weak and unprotected. Why these were included rather than left to their own devices is because all people were, as the saying goes, felt to be family (Gen 12:3).

The dreamers par excellence were Abraham and Sarah, our parents, and their plan was focused: to keep *tsedaqah* and *mishpat*, righteousness and justice;[1] to behave decently towards *all* creatures so that the world can be saved. This still leaves room for God, of course, and throughout Genesis God is a major player in a field of dreams. But leadership is gradually handed down or over, so that while God is dominant at the start and rules supreme, by the end it is mainly Joseph ("Mr. Adding-on") and Judah ("Mr. Thankful" or, "Mr. Contrite") who run things. And God also learns a thing or two, so to speak, mainly how to deal with humans. For one thing, He learns tolerance for their evil and waywardness: what a transformation from the God of the Flood to the God who forgives even the Ninevites in the book of Jonah! For another thing, the venue of communication with humans has become enmeshed with their own projects. I refer again to dreams, to those nightly visions that speak ambiguously, perhaps about God's plans but also about the strength of our hopes, the complexities of our character. Genesis is a book bracketed by dreams: at one extreme, Adam's erotic dream of Eve and their one flesh; at the other, Joseph's visions of personal power but also of sustenance for the masses in need.

The main protagonist is God, but a God whose powers are regularly questioned and tested and who, through constant dialogue and debate with humans, reveals other Names. As humans expand and create, He projects a personality both richer and more withdrawn. Readers of the biblical text are mistaken when they infantilize a complex deity or complicate God's simple directives. Thus, on the one hand, the statement, "And God said to Abram" (Gen 12:1), seems so compelling that we wonder whether Abraham could possibly have refused God's direct command, forgetting that the normal human way is to refuse and having no possible idea of what or how God speaks to us anyway. Maybe He spoke "directly" as in those old days of what Rabelais called "the Good Old God of Hosts (Armies)." But since there is no

---

[1]Gen 18:19; Isa 5:7; 9:7; 56:1; Amos 5:7, 24; 6:12; Pss 33:5; 72:1; Prov 21:3.

clear prophecy today, how do we even begin to imagine? And if God, out of respect to human freedom and intelligence and initiative, draws tighter into himself, how is human contact to be maintained?

The complex relationship between God and humans emerges at the very beginning of the Bible, and its development unfolds within the dominant theme of creation and creativity. Since the transfer from divine to human creativity occurred very early, however (Gen 2:4), access to the divine patterns and prescriptions became paramount. These were traditionally apportioned to three different groups:

> For instruction shall not perish from the Priest,
> Nor counsel from the Sage,
> Nor the word from the Prophet. (Jer 18:18)

When direct prophetic revelation expired with Malachi and the priestly duties with the destruction of the Temple, however, the vacuum was taken up by the third and only remaining category, the sages, whose duty was first and foremost to govern things down here in accord with the original plan.

This study examines how this transfer from divine to human creativity was recorded from the very beginning of the Hebrew Bible and remained a focus throughout. The texts discussed in this book are presented in the order in which they appear in the canonical Hebrew Bible. What follows is a brief synopsis of their contents.

The opening part of this book, "Creating and Maintaining a Righteous World," is a study of the righteous and the wicked in Genesis and Exodus. The antithetical pair of *tsaddiq* and *rasha*ᶜ, of righteous and wicked people as central concepts in the description of humankind's purpose and possibility, is found in Ps 1 (see ch. 7). In the portions of Genesis and Exodus explored here, we learn that just as the *tsaddiq* is the human agent of the world's existence, the *rasha*ᶜ is seen as its destroyer.

The two chapters on Genesis bring new light to the dominant theme of righteousness. Across the spectrum of wisdom literature the Tsaddik is regarded as the "foundation of the world," but it is difficult to find a critical and clear analysis of this concept. While current notions of "charity" and "freedom from guilt" remain pertinent, the righteousness materials of Genesis focus on the earliest commandments of the Bible: being fruitful and multiplying, filling the earth, generating and saving families and entire peoples, and keeping families together. This is an important refocusing of this central wisdom concept.

In Exodus, Pharaoh's fear that the Israelites will "rise up from the land" (Exod 1:10) remains a crux. Through a renewed and expanded analysis of this expression, the central pillar of Pharaoh's counter-ideology of genocide is laid bare. Egypt's monarch is a self-confessed *rashaᶜ* or wicked person (Exod 9:27), the very antithesis of the righteous *tsaddiq*.

In the second part of this book, "Interpreting in the Twilight Zone," we study some of wisdom's literary methods as they are used in the composition and interpretation of central wisdom figures and texts. In the first of these chapters, we examine Samson, quite possibly the least beloved of Israel's judges, but for reasons that may have to do more with his critics than himself. The focus here is on debate through riddles (Judg 14), since it epitomizes the conflict of civilizations between the Israelites and one of their enemies, the Philistines. The issue is one of interpreting wondrous signs that occur and become reflected in the riddles: are they natural or sent by God? Such signs are ambiguous, as are other literary devices that were of interest to the sages: proverbs, dreams, oracles, and sayings. Samson's expertise in riddle-making alone qualifies him as a sage, no less perhaps than Solomon in the company of the Queen of Sheba. Add to this his innovative pay-as-you-go approach to warfare with neighboring ethnic groups, based not on petty vindictiveness, but rather, as God does on countless occasions, on the universal principle of measure for measure (see, for example, Judg 1:7). Set in the text between the extremes of Joshua's intended decimation of entire populations, at one end, and Saul's failure to wipe out only the really dangerous Amalekites, at the other, Samson's is a live-and-let-live policy regulated by a measured retaliation for wrongdoing. If that solution failed, this was due not to Samson but rather to those who were not up to his standards.

Just as the Samson story gives a privileged peek into the twilight zone of riddle formation and interpretation, so too does the Saul story in the related field of proverb creation. The famous proverb about Saul in 1 Sam 10 and 19 ("Is Saul too among the prophets?") may provide insight into what has remained a puzzle for proverb research since Archer Taylor's resistant question "where do proverbs come from?" Specifically, do proverbs originate among sages or the common people? Here Samson's debate in riddles is replicated as a "dialogue in proverbs," suggesting an evolutionary model for the origins of wisdom itself. The dialogic model operates at another level as well, in the depiction and evaluation of Saul's changing character and persona. For the narrative line is repeatedly challenged by a proverb that "perspectivizes" Saul from various points of view, from that of the local populace that longs for a king to the proverb's particular external focus, that of prophecy. The Saul story can thus be characterized as a narrative in search of a proverb. For it is through the interplay of narration and proverb formation that Saul's career is evaluated, modeling a dialogic relationship between sages and common people mediated by a wisdom perspectivism reminiscent of wisdom's dual track in Qohelet. For is not one of wisdom's chief interests to investigate how proverbs respond to and evaluate evolving contexts?

Unlike any other human being, Solomon was given a "wise and understanding heart" (1 Kgs 3:12), with the famous story of the split baby as proof (1 Kgs 3:16–29). We rush to a hagiographic reading (what a sage!) but without knowing why, and the typical "Because it was sent by God" only begs the question, because we still must understand how it was given, if only for pedagogical reasons. The narrative presents a case that cannot be solved by the usual means because of an intended total lack of evidence, and the woman's cry ("Give her the baby!") likewise gives no clear indication of guilt or innocence. The judge's only and last resort then becomes one of wisdom's ideology. Readers will be interested in exactly what that is.

There is consensus identifying Ps 1 as a wisdom text, and since it serves as an introductory prologue to the entire Psalter, its focus on righteousness is of particular importance. This psalm also introduces themes of central significance for the development of wisdom practice, notably pedagogy and a dialogue with God that is distinct from cult and prayer. The focus becomes a person's "ways," or daily behavior.

In the final part of this book, "The Rebirth of Vulnerability and Wonder," we focus on vulnerability and then on wonder and its role as intermediary between heaven and earth. Since this sense of wonder arises particularly in later life, its connection to the vulnerability of old age presents an important aspect of wisdom's optimism. In chapter 8 we focus on the famous "allegory on death and dying" found in the closing section of Qohelet (12:2–7), which is not only a literary masterpiece in its own right but also, paradoxically, the centerpiece of the book's optimistic theology: a realistic optimism, based on what things really are rather than on what we would like them to be. This pedagogical text is intended to teach a youth two facts of life: that life is transient and to be enjoyed. This apparent paradox is not dissolved but rather theologically reinforced by reference to the Creator-God who has ordained the world so. The standard epicurean thesis of carpe diem, however, is of little value for those later years, when the youth will say, "I have little pleasure in them." More pertinent are the wisdom concepts of life's seasonableness and *puer-senex,* which aim to provide joy throughout one's entire life, as per Qoh 11:8: "Even those who live many years should rejoice in them *all.*" And, in fact, the so-called "Allegory on Death and Dying" gives concrete descriptions of the joys to be anticipated from aging and even death.

Near the end of the book of Proverbs (30:18–20), an intriguing reflection is offered on four things that exceed human understanding and provoke wonderment, most notably the "way of a man with a woman." The puzzle is compounded by a focus on the incomprehensible wonder of sexuality, including both that of the woman of valor and the adulterous woman.

At the heart of the matter, in all cases, is the meaning of the biblical text, not what we would like it to mean but what in fact it does mean. One crucial focus in this debate is whether it is possible to reach such a "primary meaning." In John J. Collins's opinion, postmodernists deny that such a meaning exists, and he implies that others—historical critics and especially religious folks—allow for and pursue such a possibility.[2] Between these ex-

---

[2]John J. Collins, *The Bible after Babel: Historical Criticism in a Postmodern Age* (Grand Rapids: Eerdmans, 2005), 14.

tremes lies a complicating but realistic compromise, and it is explored in this book. It involves a study of those texts in which the Bible itself speaks ambiguously and polyvalently, not merely for the esthetic purpose of making interesting reading or delightful literature but rather to make basic claims about the nature of discourse and the human condition.[3]

Just as the focus on the interpretation of wisdom's ways was viewed as a special skill by the sages, may our focus on both their life-supporting values and methods of textual interpretation help us recover their access to the twilight zone!

---

[3]For a recent example see T. A. Perry, "Cain's Sin in Genesis 4:1–7: Oracular Ambiguity and How to Avoid It," *Prooftexts* 25 (2006): 259–76.

PART ONE

CREATING AND MAINTAINING A RIGHTEOUS WORLD

Genesis, Book of the Righteous, or What Is a Tsaddik?

> The righteous person [*tsaddiq*] is the
> foundation of the world.
>
> (Prov 10:25)

There is general scholarly accord on viewing the concept of Tsaddik[1] as central to the wisdom enterprise.[2] The question remains as to precisely what a Tsaddik is. Although discussions typically center on "wisdom" texts, notably on the book of Proverbs,[3] the theme exists from the very start of the Hebrew Bible and in a most definitive way. Here we shall explore the evidence of the prologue, as it were, to the entire Bible: Genesis, the Book of Creation, also known as the Book of the Upright.[4] This is perhaps a reference to God, since "Tsaddik and upright is He" (Deut

---

[1]Frequently found spelled Tzaddik or Zaddik and brought into English from Yiddish.

[2]There remains some disagreement on exactly which psalms are to be included in the wisdom listing and, thus, on the precise themes that constitute their allegiance to wisdom literature in the first place. See chapter 7.

[3]For a quick overview see Leo G. Perdue, "Cosmology and Social Order in the Wisdom Tradition," in *The Sage in Israel and the Ancient Near East* (ed. John G. Gammie and Leo G. Perdue. Winona Lake, Ind.: Eisenbrauns, 1990), 457–59.

[4]See Josh 10:13; 2 Sam 1:18; *b. ʿAbod. Zar.* 25a.

32:4), thus making the Tsaddik's ideal coincident with God's own. But in establishing the synonymy of the Upright (*yashar*) and the Tsaddik, this verse places the Tsaddik at the center of the entire book of Genesis, a thought repeated in Prov 10:25, "the righteous person [*tsaddiq*] is the foundation of the world."[5]

Noah the Tsaddik (Gen 6:9; 7:1)

Walking with the Creator-God (Gen 6:9)

In the Masoretic liturgical apportionment of *parshiyot,* or weekly Torah portions, Noah is ushered onto the scene with the Bible's first epithet, and in true epic-style: Noah *'ish tsaddiq,* Noah-The-Righteous-Man. The broader context of his presentation gives important clues to this concept. First of all, unlike the entire world around him Noah avoided violence and did not sin.[6] The entire world is precisely intended, since even the plants had sinned, as it were. This is certainly a possible, though admittedly literalist, reading:

> The earth became corrupt before God, and the earth was filled with lawlessness. . . .
>
> And God said to Noah: "The end of all flesh has come up before me. Since [even] the earth is filled with lawlessness because of them, behold I will destroy them along with the earth." (Gen 6:11, 13)

One might assume that plants too have some level of free will and awareness of right and wrong;[7] or, much more likely and as the verses seem to suggest, the humans who tended them (Gen 2:5, 15) mixed the plants' seeds in unnatural ways. So too with the animals, misled by human corruption:

---

[5]This is the Targum's understanding of the verse. Alternatively, "The righteous person is an everlasting foundation." On this subject see Perdue, "Cosmology and Social Order," 457–78.

[6]Avoidance of evil precedes doing good in a striking way at the start of Ps 1, a wisdom psalm; see chapter 7.

[7]Or perhaps feeling. Philip Roth gives a tragic parody of this same phenomenon in his portrait of Swede's daughter in *American Pastoral* (Boston: Houghton Mifflin, 1997).

For all flesh had corrupted [its ways upon the earth]. Even animals, beast and fowl mated with other than their kind. (Rashi [1140–1105], citing *b. Sanh.* 108a)

The notation of everything being *filled* with lawlessness (Gen 6:11) adds ironic contrast to the violation of God's wish and explicit command to "be fruitful and multiply and *fill* the entire earth" (Gen 1:22, 28).

Before Noah, Mr. Tsaddik, can save the world, however, he must produce a world to be saved, must himself become fruitful:

These are the generations of Noah: Noah-The-Righteous—he was pure in his generations, Noah walked with God—Noah begot three sons: Shem, Ham, and Yaphet. (Gen 6:9)

ᵓ*elleh toledot,* "These are the generations." This formula occurs ten times in Genesis, sounding its major theme of fruitfulness: "these are the children to whom X gave birth."[8] Related to the root *yld,* "child," and the verbal meaning "to give birth," the term reaches far beyond human re-production. Proverbs 27:1 speaks of what a *day* (re-)produces, applicable in the first instance to the works of the six days of the original creation. Its first use in Genesis is particularly significant:

Such is the story [*toledot*] of the heaven and the earth in their being created. . . . On the day that the Lord God made earth and heaven . . . the Lord God formed man from the dust of the earth. (Gen 2:4, 7)

As if to project both of its possible functions in Genesis, the formula here does double duty. First it gives closure to the narrative of God's creation, thus a story or history. Secondly, it also projects further details and even creations, thus generations, what X generates.[9] In the case of Noah, we prefer "generations" to "story"— although, to be sure, it is a story as well—because it serves to introduce his progeny: the three sons that he begot (*yalad*), his proximate descendants.

---

[8]Gen 4:2; 6:9; 10:1; 11:10, 27; 25:12, 19; 36:1, 9; 37:2.

[9]In consonance with Gen 4:2, Renaissance author Leone Ebreo referred to the heavens and the earth as the "parents" of creation. See his *Dialoghi d'amore,* Part II; for a synopsis see T. A. Perry, *Erotic Spirituality: The Integrative Tradition from Leone Ebreo to John Donne* (University: University of Alabama Press, 1980), 15.

The time specification is curious, however, as is the rabbinic exegesis that it inspired: Noah was righteous *in his generations,* but had he lived at the time of Abraham-The-Righteous, either a) he would have accounted as nothing; or b) how much more righteous would he have been![10] The rabbis here focus on the central wisdom concept of righteousness by the comparative method, evaluating Noah according to the model standard of Abraham and measuring his relative merits. One wonders about the plural form, though: "in his generation*s*." Surely, even though he and everyone else in those days had prodigious longevity, "his generation" (in the singular) would have been more appropriate, as the NRSV and others translate and as it occurs later in the same narrative (7:1). The plural may thus suggest a different meaning of "generations," no longer temporal ("in his *age,*" NJPS) but rather generational, thus also rendering the preposition *b-* no longer as temporal but rather causal:

> These are the descendants (NRSV) of Noah (Noah was a righteous man *because of* the generations [*dorot*] that he produced): . . . Noah begot three sons: Shem, Ham, and Yaphet.[11] (Gen 6:9–10)

This passage can now also be viewed as definitional: a Tsaddik is one who begets progeny, a fruitful person. Such a reading gives a different perspective to the other details of Noah's description:

> Restorative [*tamim*] through his posterity, Noah walked with God [*ʾelohim*]. (Gen 6:9)

Noah was, like the Torah of Ps 19:8[19:7], *tamim;* he restored life, thus walking with and fearing *ʾelohim,* the Creator-God of Gen 1.[12]

This reading puts the social background into bold relief. Noah was busy producing for the future at a time when the rest of the world was either wasting its seed,[13] or destroying those already liv-

---

[10]See Rashi ad loc.

[11]For the meaning of *dorot* as referring to one's posterity, see Num 9:10; Job 42:16; cf. BDB, 190. I view the causal *b-* as *pshat* or simple reading here. A famous midrashic use is identified in the very first word of Genesis: *bereʾshit,* "Because of, for the sake of the beginning" (see Rashi ad loc.).

[12]"The Lord's Torah is *temimah,* it restores the soul" (Ps 19:8[19:7]).

[13]Onan's wasting his seed (*shikhet,* Gen 38:9) echoes the world's perversity: "all flesh had corrupted (*hishkhit*) its ways on earth" (Gen 6:12).

ing through *khamas,* violence and lawlessness. His subsequent story is of a piece with this introduction. For what does a Tsaddik do after generating offspring? He protects and maintains them, taking them into his "ark" and tending them.

Feeding the Animals

The twelve-month onslaught of the flood is depicted from the outside, measured out in terms of duration and amounts of water. What happened to the escapees, what daily life was like in the ark, is left to the imagination. And oblivion, perhaps, for who remembers the pains of birth and child-rearing, the long nights of infant colic and illnesses, once the child has arrived to full-blown personhood? Midrashic reconstruction is valuable, however, in its attempt to flesh out the nitty-gritty chores with which a Tsaddik spends most of her/his time. For example, the midrash speculates that Noah brought along all diets appropriate to each species, spending his days and nights tending to their individual needs.[14] The expression in Prov 12:10 also expresses this nitty-gritty, but crucial, tedium of tending to life, "the Tsaddik knows (*yodea*[c]) the feelings [*nefesh*] of his animal."[15]

Of the examples in the Hebrew Bible of the daily grind of a Tsaddik, several focus on the difficulties of administering justice.

---

[14]Aviva Gottlieb Zornberg's brilliant discussion of the midrashic materials deserves to be carefully pondered (Aviva Gottlieb Zornberg, *Genesis: The Beginning of Desire* [Philadelphia: JPS, 1995], 59–62).

[15]"Feelings"is Roger N. Whybray's rendering of *nefesh* (*Proverbs* [NCB; Grand Rapids: Eerdmans, 1994], 193). The literal meaning is "soul," also meaning "throat," thus the animal's hunger and needs (see Bruce K. Waltke, *The Book of Proverbs: Chapters 1–15* [NICOT; Grand Rapids: Eerdmans, 2004], 90). More radically, *nefesh* refers to the "self" (as in Arabic), thus "the individuality" of each of his animals, again referring to the differing needs of each. "To know" (*yodea*[c]) means "to have regard for"; Exod 23:9 uses identical language for the regard one is required to show to the stranger. Thus, animals are entitled to Sabbath rest (Exod 23:12) and are protected from cruelty in their daily labors (Deut 22:10; 25:4). Rabbinic legislation prohibited one from eating anything until his animals are fed (*b. Ber.* 40a). This attitude runs deep in some traditional cultures. Breton peasants honored workers in accordance with their contribution to family labors, thus giving the largest bowl of food at the table to the horse. See Pierre-Jakez Hélias, *The Horse of Pride* (trans. June Guicharnaud; New Haven: Yale University Press, 1978), 13. According to 1 Sam 6:7, the Philistines also lodged their animals in their houses (see also Exod 9:19).

Take Moses's "heavy" daily task of judging the entire people from dawn to dusk (Exod 18:13–26). Or the prophet/judge Samuel, who used to make the rounds to all the places in Israel, so as to judge them in their own cities (1 Sam 7:16–17).[16] The nexus linking the Tsaddik's dispensation of justice with the restorative powers of *tamim* are elsewhere attributed to God himself:

> The Creator/Rock, His work is restorative (*tamim*),
> for all His ways are justice. . . .
> Tsaddik and upright is He.[17] (Deut 32:4)

Noah's feedings, though not depicted, do have verisimilitude, from the mere fact that after the long siege all animals did survive and exit the ark. We are thus prepared, at the other end of Genesis, for Joseph-The-Righteous' salvational actions of feeding (Gen 41:49) and, in juxtaposition, his own fruitfulness (Gen 41:50). For both Joseph and Noah had the task and the merit of ensuring the survival of many people (Gen 50:20).

Who then was Noah? The remarkably succinct synopsis— where his name is repeated no less than four times—shows the genesis of his personality, his and also that of all *bney-Noah*, all subsequent generations:

> These are the generations of *Noah. Noah The-Righteous:* he was restorative in his generations, *Noah* walked with God, *Noah* begot three children. (Gen 6:9–10a)

Noah produced what the new world would require, what would confront the Creator and change His mind about the creation. Noah would first create, transform himself into a Tsaddik: *Noah-The-Righteous.* And what is that? A *Noah* who would clean up the mess and cooperate with the Creator-God; and a *Noah* who would beget and care for others. This defines the individual as we know her/him in the biblical tradition down to this very day: a caring person. Yet, as Aviva Gottlieb Zornberg explains, it was all

---

[16]See the commentary in *b. Šabb.* 56a. This daily need was exploited by Absalom against his father David (2 Sam 15:1–6), who, according to him, failed to provide it.

[17]"Creator/Rock" is an attempt to render both the plain meaning of *tsur,* "rock," with its usual association, in rabbinic exegesis, with *tsayar,* "to create."

for Noah's benefit as well, defining not only what a Tsaddik is but also who Noah *was:*[18]

> All the feeding, the storing of foods, the exquisite concern and attentiveness, are ultimately functions of Noah's relation with his own needs.[19]

For the ark is also the workshop of maturation and character formation: of the children and animals to be cared for, to be sure, but also of the care providers. As Emmanuel Levinas put it in a philosophical context, "the Other individualizes me through the responsibility that I have for him."[20]

Tamar the Greater Tsaddik and the Rise of Judah

Psalm 92:13[92:12] in the RSV states, "The righteous flourish like the palm tree, and grow like a cedar in Lebanon." But this can also be read, "The *tsaddiq* will flourish like Tamar."[21] One should carefully ponder why it does not say *ke-tamar,* "like a palm tree," as it goes on to say, *keʾerez ballebanon,* "like a cedar in Lebanon" Because it is like "*the* Tamar" that we know, the person. This should not be discarded as a cute midrash, since Tamar's righteousness is central to the plot of Genesis, which is the birth of a righteous people.

The Insertion of Gen 38 into the Joseph Story

The extended story of Joseph from chapters 37–50, the very end of Genesis, is curiously interrupted by chapter 38, the story of Judah and Tamar. To Nahum M. Sarna, this anecdote "seems to be entirely unconnected to what precedes and follows it," and Gerhard von Rad is even more emphatic:

> Every attentive reader can see that the story of Judah and Tamar has no connection at all with the strictly organized Joseph story at

---

[18]See Zornberg's (*Genesis,* 59) discussion of the midrash on *was:* he was and will be, through all subsequent generations, a sustainer of life.

[19]Ibid., 62.

[20]Emmanuel Levinas, *Dieu, la mort et le temps* (Paris: Grasset, 1993), 21.

[21]*Tsaddiq kattamar yifrakh,* "a righteous person will flourish *like Tamar.*"

whose beginning it is now inserted. This compact narrative requires for its interpretation none of the other Patriarchal narratives.[22]

It has nonetheless been possible, in order to save the appearance of an integrated narrative, to list connections between this episode and the encompassing story, mainly on the basis of linguistic and thematic echoes. I shall promptly refer to the most famous of these, the *hakker-naʾ* repetition.

More substantially, there is an important strain of older scholarship (Hermann Gunkel, Otto Eissfeldt, etc.) that sees Gen 38 as a tribal history which deals with the claims of Judah.[23] Indeed, since the end of Genesis is focused not only on the descent into Egypt but also the rise of Joseph and his house, it would seem strange, at least after the fact, if Judah's rise were not also chronicled.[24] In his brief but penetrating analysis of our narrative, Benno Jacob gives the point a theological twist by noting that "the hero of the following story is Joseph, but salvation will come from Judah."[25] This notation is crucial to explaining both the presence of the Judah/Tamar episode and its location at this juncture, for the rise of Joseph and Judah must be seen as in some sense parallel. Benno Jacob's analysis, however, through its fine but unique focus on the moral elevation of Tamar—he calls this story the crown of Genesis because Tamar is even higher than the matriarchs—does not help us understand what it claims, namely Judah's own qualifications, why salvation must come through him.

Judah Goldin takes the argument a step further by studying analogical developments, in Genesis and elsewhere, of the theme of a younger brother's triumph over an older.[26] This interesting

---

[22]Nahum M. Sarna, *Genesis. The Traditional Hebrew Text with the JPS Translation* (Philadelphia, Jerusalem: JPS, 1989), 263; Gerhard von Rad, *Genesis, A Commentary* (trans. John H. Marks; rev. ed.; Philadelphia: Westminster, 1972), 356–57.

[23]See Susan Niditch, "The Wrong Woman Righted: An Analysis of Genesis 38," *HTR* 72 (1979): 143–49.

[24]And, in fact, the relationships between the two ascensions have given rise to some interesting scholarship. See, for example, Aaron Wildavsky, "Survival Must Not Be Gained through Sin: The Moral of the Joseph Stories Prefigured through Judah and Tamar," *JSOT* 62 (1994): 37–48.

[25]Benno Jacob, *The First Book of the Bible: Genesis* (trans. Ernest I. Jacob and Walter Jacob; New York: Ktav, 1974), 263.

[26]Judah Goldin, "The Youngest Son or Where Does Genesis 38 Belong?" *JBL* 96 (1977): 27–44.

approach has several weaknesses, however. Goldin is on more solid ground with either Judah's children or father, either Perez's bursting forth in front of his older brother Zerach, or Jacob's grabbing on to Esau's heel. Judah himself exercises no such active, unfriendly takeover of his three older brothers (Reuven, Shimon, and Levi), who are retired entirely through their own mischief and independent of Judah's participation. Goldin must therefore take refuge, like Benno Jacob and others, in the theory of divine election: that is the way God wanted it. This notion can of course quite plausibly be applied to a number of cases in the Hebrew Bible, such as Joseph and his reversal of Manassah and Ephraim (God directed Jacob's hands during the final blessing and transfer of primogeniture, Gen 48:14). I submit, however, that this explanation is out of place for the Judah of Gen 38, who acts entirely on his own and without any visible sign of divine prompting or selection whatever.

Judah's Sin and Levirate Marriage

Let us bring to mind the portrait of Judah as sketched out by the biblical narrative. At his birth his mother Leah exclaims, punning on the name Judah: "Now I will *praise* the Lord" (Gen 29:35; also 49:8). Judah next appears at the attempted slaying of Joseph, where he shows his authority over his brothers by persuading them not to kill their brother but instead to sell him to the Ishmaelites: "and his brothers listened" (Gen 37:27). Judah's next appearance is in the scene that is our focus here, where it is said that "he went down from his brethren" (Gen 38:1). Three meanings have been proposed for this notice: 1) he went to live elsewhere; 2) he "lowered himself" (Benno Jacob) by marrying a Canaanitish woman; or 3) he went down in his brothers' esteem. In Rashi's version:

> His brothers degraded him from his high position. For when they saw their father's grief, they said to him: "you told us to sell him; if you had told us to send him back to his father, we would also have obeyed you."

This interpretation—bordering on the midrashic, to be sure— assumes, not implausibly, that the three older brothers have already been disqualified from leadership, and it gives a strong reading of the chapter's opening formula, which until now has not been sufficiently explained: "And it was at that time," i.e., it was at the time of the sale of Joseph, that Judah went down in their esteem, thus implying a causal connection between these actions.

Such an understanding seems inconsistent, however, with the subsequent Judah who nobly assumes leadership of his brothers when he asks to take Benjamin to Egypt and offers himself as a pledge (Gen 43:3–5), and who becomes the fearless spokesman in the face of Joseph (Gen 44:18–34). The Midrash even pictures Judah threatening Joseph: *ki kamoka kepar*c*oh,* "if you provoke me I will slay you and your master" (Gen 44:18). And it is Judah's noble self-sacrifice that leads Joseph to tears and the disclosure of his real identity. The pathway from the one Judah to the other is the narrative burden of chapter 38.

Whether Judah's "going down" can be explained by his marriage to a Canaanitish woman or not, that is in fact what Judah does, producing three sons: Er, Onan, and Shelah. Er is married off to Tamar and dies, whereupon Tamar is given the second son in levirate marriage, in order to "perpetuate the name" of the first husband. This second son dies in turn, and the levirate responsibility again devolves upon Judah and his remaining son Shelah. However, Judah temporizes and Tamar remains in widowhood. When it becomes clear that the marriage with Shelah will never take place, Tamar disguises herself as a whore, waylays a Judah recently bereaved of his wife, and conceives a child by him. When her pregnancy is discovered, she is ordered to court and condemned to death.

We must take a close look at Judah's meeting with the disguised Tamar. From the text it seems that, after producing three sons from a Canaanitish wife, Judah is having no further children. The reasons are not given—he is certainly not infertile, since he has already produced and will do so again. His wife dies and, after a period of mourning, he seeks out a prostitute. Note carefully that he does not take up a wife but instead goes to a prostitute. Is this merely a passing need for sex, as some have speculated? Perhaps, though one is hard put to find other examples of such motivation in the biblical text, and the weakness does not really correspond to the total abstinence he later demonstrates. More likely is the explanation that Judah's going to a prostitute signifies his decision to have no further children.

Once Tamar's pregnancy becomes known, it is possible that, despite his efforts, Judah cannot prosecute his daughter-in-law because when he came to her she was still a virgin! How else can we explain his most unusual procedure of sending her back to her father's house?[27] Moreover, the text states that both Er and Onan die because they refused to give her their seed. For Er, the text pointedly omits the usual "and he came in to her" and it even states that it was not he that took her but his father took her for him. As for Onan, note the unusual hypothetical "and it was, *if* he came in to her, that he would let it spill."[28]

Tamar's Education of King-Messiah

In order to "save" our tale of Judah and Tamar as an integral part of Genesis and the Joseph narrative, some scholars have suggested secondary purposes in the narrative, for example, "the desire it exhibits of impressing the duty of marriage with a deceased brother's wife" (although doubt is expressed as to whether the Bible can be interested in "such a general principle").[29] While it seems to me that the Bible is certainly interested in promoting levirate marriage here, such a concern must then be seen as related to a much more general principle yet, to a theological argument that dominates Genesis from start to finish: be fruitful and multiply, and keep the thing going.

Before continuing our sketch of this theological argument, however, let us approach the matter by way of Judah's grand admission of guilt concerning Tamar: "She is more righteous than I" (Gen 38:26). Some translations avoid the moral dimensions of the term "righteous" and focus on the immediate, legalistic implications: "She is more in the right than I" (NJPS). While such a version is faithful to the grammatical comparative, it creates the impression that Judah is partially in the right. However, Judah is now aware of his guilt:

---

[27]Niditch ("The Wrong Woman Righted," 146) states that "she is no longer a virgin and does not belong in her father's home." The fact that she can be sent back there, however, may indicate precisely that she still is a virgin.

[28]The verb is alternatively explained as expressing a repetitive action, thus "whenever he came in." Cf. Steven D. Mathewson, "An Exegetical Study of Genesis 38," *BSac* 146 (1989): 377.

[29]Ibid., 388.

a) since he impregnated Tamar, she is now innocent of adultery and
   he is "guilty" by contrast;

b) in lying to Tamar by leading her to believe that she will in fact be
   wedded to Shelah;

c) in withholding his son from levirate marriage.

In this regard, he is and has been aware that Tamar is guiltless, indeed that she is righteous precisely in respect to that action in which
Judah is not righteous in any degree. His admission that "she is
more in the right than I" (Gen 38:26) does not establish relative
right, therefore, but rather asserts that she was right and he wrong
(Benno Jacob). At best, the curious comparative seems to express
a lingering suspicion that Judah felt himself justified to some degree in withholding his son. When faced with the possibility of
sacrificing an innocent person, one might say that he yields to the
lesser of two evils and accepts the embarrassment while maintaining some reserves. Although such a suspicion was originally quite
likely, however, at the moment of his total recognition of guilt it is
entirely out of place. In brief, this scene portrays Judah's full recognition of his sins—the blocking of Tamar's levirate marriage
with his youngest son Shelah—both against Tamar and against
his deceased son.

In the grand court scene of Gen 38 we thus witness the com-
ing into being of *two* sublime characters. First of all, Tamar, who,
having done what she had to do about getting impregnated, compromised that very initiative, preferring to be burned alive rather
than embarrass Judah in public. But we also witness Judah's con-
quest of his own personality, of an additional dimension of himself that makes him worthy of leadership. The *Tosefta* views this as
the re-conquest of his name, Judah:

> Through what merit did Judah earn kingship? Because he admitted
> [*hodah*] in the case of Tamar.[30]

Rashi picks up on this theme. In *b. Ber.* 32a it is said:

> It is better for a man to cast himself into the fiery furnace than to
> embarrass his fellow in public. Where do we learn this? From

---

30 *Tosefta Ber.* 4:17.

Tamar, as it is said: "I am pregnant by the man who owns these. Recognize, I pray thee, whose these are."

Rashi comments:

> But she did not say explicitly: "These tokens are Judah's"; rather, "I am pregnant by the man who owns these. If he confesses he confesses; if not, I shall be burned, but I shall not embarrass him publicly."[31]

At this point Judah rises up and says, magnificently:

> With your permission, my brethren, I make it known that with what measure a man metes, it shall be measured unto him, be it for good or for evil, but happy is the man that acknowledges his sin. . . . It is better that I be put to shame in this world than I should be put to shame in the other world, before the face of my pious father. . . . Now, then, I acknowledge that Tamar is innocent. By me she is with child, not because she indulged in illicit passion but because I held back her marriage with my son Shelah.[32]

Through his action Judah demonstrates his strict impartiality even towards himself and is therefore worthy to be a king and a judge.[33] A character that began in thankfulness to God is now rounded out by a confession, two shapes of the etymological Yehuda.[34] We can now reject von Rad's wish to sever Gen 38 from its frame narrative, for we do very much need our story in order to plot what Robert Alter called Judah's "moral education."[35]

---

[31]ʾim yodeh yodeh, ["if he admits, then he is truly 'Judah'"], veʾim loʾ, ʾesaref veloʾ ʾalbin panav.

[32]Louis Ginzberg, *The Legends of the Jews* (6 vols.; Philadelphia: JPS, 1968), 2:35–36.

[33]*Tosefta Ber.* 69.

[34]It would of course be fruitless to speculate as to why the text chooses to explain name-derivations in some ways and not others, thereby neglecting possibilities heavy with theological promise. But it must be noted that such an etymological possibility is not only rabbinic midrash:

> He who covers over his sins will not succeed; but one who confesses [*modeh*] and leaves them will find mercy. (Prov 28:13)

> I have sinned and admit it; my sin I have not covered over. I said: "I admit [ʾodeh] to my sins to the Lord." (Ps 32:5; also 1 Kgs 8:33, 35)

[35]Robert Alter, *The Art of Biblical Narrative* (New York: Basic, 1981), 11; von Rad, *Genesis*, 356–57.

Among critics this entire question has been much neglected, first of all because of Tamar's magnificence and, later, Joseph's as well. Joseph and Tamar are heroes, to be sure: Joseph, overcoming strong feelings of revenge against his brothers; Tamar because she refused to defame another human being in public and, like Ruth, opted to stay within the camp; both, because they used great effort and ingenuity to further creation and continuity through the family.

Beyond their moral heroism, Tamar and, as we shall soon see, Joseph, are pedagogical heroes as well.[36] Because of their respect for the opposition, they seek not the destruction of the sinner but that the sinner, through repentance, may again live. Tamar and Joseph are prophets in the grand tradition of Nathan before David: great moral teachers who, disregarding thoughts of personal safety (or, in Joseph's case, personal vengeance), pursue the welfare of both the individual sinner and the peace and future of the entire community. But in education glory must also come to the students, although it seems to me an understatement that both Judah, and later David, "are embarrassed into admitting their guilt."[37] Despots have no fine feelings (Judah even speaks like one: *sarof tissaref,* the equivalent of "off with her head!").[38] Indeed, although Tamar can prove beyond doubt that Judah made her pregnant, even were she to accuse him publicly, Judah still has the power to punish her misdeed; and, since the pledges were extracted in private, it would simply be a case of her word against his. However, like David with Nathan later on, Judah listens to Tamar, confesses his guilt, and acknowledges her superior righteousness. The Bible is telling us that this is education that qualifies one for leadership. How it can be asserted, in the face of this,

---

[36]According to Rashi (on Gen 6:14) so was Noah: "Why did God burden Noah with the building of the ark? So that the people of the flood generation would see him working at it for 120 years and would ask him: 'What do you need this for?' And so that he would reply: 'The Holy One Blessed be He is going to bring a flood upon the world.' Maybe they would repent."

[37]Gary A. Rendsburg, "David and His Circle in Genesis xxxviii," *VT* 36 (1986): 442.

[38]I suspect that the intensive *sarof tissaref* means "let her be burned alive," literally "let the burning one be burned." Less likely would be the moralistic reading: "Let the one who burned with illicit passion be literally burned." Compare *tarof toraf Yosef* (Gen 37:33): "the torn one has been torn" = he was torn up alive, and not merely as a dead corpse.

that Gen 38 is "entirely unsuited to homiletical use" or that "certainly few people would choose this chapter as a basis for teaching or preaching," or that the tale should have been "laundered out," strikes me as one of the curiosities of biblical scholarship, not to say of theological orientation.[39]

We can thus no longer abide the impression that in Gen 38 "Judah is portrayed in an unfavorable light."[40] It is indeed possible that by the end of Gen 38 Judah may not yet get the point about his father's pain, but he has learned an important lesson: the ability to place impartial justice based on truth over his personal comfort and prestige, and to confess his sins publicly. What public figure does that today?! He is thus worthy to rule over others.[41] It remains to be seen whether he is worthy to rule over his own brothers, whether his evolved rights of primogeniture can be acknowledged. Just as his wronged daughter-in-law Tamar helped him through the first stage, his wronged brother Joseph will assist him through the second.

Joseph the Pedagogue, the Completion of Judah's Repentance, and Keeping the Family Together

In a real sense, the unity of Jacob's sons is due to the efforts of Judah, first under Tamar's tutelage, as we have seen, but also under Joseph's. And in fact the two are related. How so? The Ginzberg passage quoted above ("With your permission, my brethren . . .") adds an interesting motive to Judah's confession:

> *Because I took the coat of Joseph and colored it with the blood of the kid and then laid it at the feet of my father, saying, Know now whether it be thy son's coat or not,* therefore must I now confess before the court to whom belong this ring, this mantle and this staff.[42]

---

[39]Quoted in Mathewson, "An Exegetical Study of Genesis 38," 373, 388n5. For how the Judah/Tamar story relates to salvation history, see Harold Fisch, "Ruth and the Structure of Covenant History," *VT* 32 (1982): 425–37. Fisch also posits (p. 436) that Ruth is the redeemer of Lot's daughter. It is now apparent that she saves Judah as well.

[40]Mathewson, "An Exegetical Study of Genesis 38," 388.

[41]The Talmud (*b. Sanh.* 18–19) relates the two: a king judges and is judged, which is taken to mean that he is empowered to judge others because he himself submits to judgment. In rabbinic halakah, however, this is said to apply only to exceptional kings, namely those of the House of David.

[42]Ginzberg, *The Legends of the Jews,* 2:35–36.

Whether Judah's sin against his father is brought to mind during the courtroom scene is unclear in the biblical text, but it is certainly not improbable. In fact, this incident is related by the rabbis to the scene when the brothers return with Joseph's coat, stained with the blood of a kid, and ask their father whether he recognizes the coat. For in both scenes the Bible uses the same expression: *hakker-naʾ*:

> "Please acknowledge [*hakker-naʾ*]: Is this your son's tunic or not?" (Gen 37:32)

> "Please acknowledge [*hakker-naʾ*]," says Tamar to Judah, "whose seal and cord and staff are these?" (Gen 38:25)

And from this unusual repetition—these are the only two instances of the expression in the entire Hebrew Bible, and they occur back to back—the rabbis perceived a divine judgment of measure for measure:

> Because Judah had deceived his father through a kid of the goats— for he had dipped Joseph's coat in its blood—therefore, he too was deceived. (Rashi on Gen 38:23)

The importance of this verbal similarity can be viewed from another perspective, so that what is highlighted is less God's justice than the evolution of Judah's moral consciousness. Alter is surely correct in his insistence that Tamar could not have known to speak these words in repetition of Joseph's brothers, but rather that the unusual repetition is a narrative trick which Tamar only happens to voice.[43] But the trick may have a theological point as well, namely that "the answer of the tongue is from the Lord" (Prov 16:1). From other examples in Genesis itself, we know that what "just happens" is not always viewed by the text as mere happenstance. Some call it narrator; others speak of God.

The search for themes in the Joseph narrative has yielded multiple results: the fruitfulness of the sons of Jacob, their descent into Egypt, their formation of a nation and projected triumphant return from slavery, and—closer to our present topic—the rise of Joseph and also of Judah. At another level are important political questions, such as whether a brother should rule over his brothers, i.e., should Israel pass from amphictiony

---

[43]Alter, *The Art of Biblical Narrative*, 9–12.

(tribalism) to monarchy? At yet another level of analysis is what Claus Westermann calls "theological reflections which belong to a different realm of thought."[44] The reference is to those pervasive patterns of thought in Hebrew Scripture that saturate individual texts and sponsor individual "themes" or topics, what may be called the work's arguments.[45] With our heightened sense of the Tamar episode in its connection with the rise of Judah, it becomes easier to posit at the start that a dominant argument of the Joseph story—at the very nucleus of its theological concern—is the theme of repentance.

The main issue may be briefly sketched as follows: In their sibling jealousy over their father's favoritism of Joseph, the child of the favored wife Rachel, his brothers sell him into slavery and contrive evidence that he is dead. Their father Jacob's grief is such that he resolves upon a living death. Later, during the famine and at the height of his power, the wronged brother has the chance to avenge himself; his goal, however, is not the destruction of the brothers but their reinstatement, not the dissolution of the family of Jacob but rather its continuation and stability. He has a single question and condition: would the brothers make the same choice today? He thus devises a situation as similar to the original one as possible, the only real change being the substitution of one brother for another, of Benjamin for himself. However, this replacement is not substantial, or, rather, it goes to the heart of the issue, since it is clear that Benjamin represents Joseph in the issues that really matter. He is the only other son of the favored mother Rachel, he is the son of Jacob's old age and, because of these, he is, as was Joseph, the father's reigning favorite child.

Being newly subject to Joseph, the brothers now experience a pain somehow similar to the pain he experienced in the past:

> And they said to one another: "We are truly guilty concerning our brother, for we saw the anguish of his soul when he beseeched us, but we did not listen. That is why this anguish has come upon us." (Gen 42:21)

---

[44]Claus Westermann, *Genesis: An Introduction* (trans. John Scullion; Minneapolis: Fortress, 1992), 243.

[45]For the distinction between a work's thematic substructure and its argument, see Alexander A. Parker, *The Allegorical Drama of Calderón: An Introduction to the Autos Sacramentales* (Oxford: Dolphin, 1968), 59.

But the focus of interest is on that brother who acts as a guarantor of Benjamin's safe return to his father. Now Judah does not have to sacrifice himself for Benjamin, he can simply leave Egypt, along with his other brothers and their provisions, and return to Jacob. This would solve the problem of Benjamin in a way similar to their selling Joseph into Egyptian slavery, and the consequences, both positive and negative, would be the same: on the one hand, they would experience relief from what they feel as sibling incursion and oppression; but, on the other, they would again authorize their father's pain and undying grief. In other words, confronted with a situation identical to the one he experienced when deciding what to do with Joseph, Judah now chooses differently, thus achieving a repentance[46] that allows family reconciliation, and thus also proving his worthiness as leader of the sons of Jacob.[47]

Joseph-The-Righteous: like Tamar who teaches Judah how to keep the family going, Joseph teaches him how to keep the family together.[48]

---

[46]Moses Maimonides (ca. 1135–1204) states, "What is perfect repentance? A person has the chance to repeat a sin that he has already committed, and he desists and doesn't do it a second time out of repentance." ("Laws of Repentance," in *Book of Knowledge [Mishneh Torah, Book I]* [trans. Moses Hyamson; New York: Bloch, 1937], 2:1).

[47]In this understanding of the repentance of the sons of Jacob I am in essential agreement with Nehama Leibowitz, *Studies in Bereshit (Genesis) in the Context of Ancient and Modern Jewish Bible Commentary* [Hebrew] (trans. Aryeh Newman; 4th rev. ed.; Jerusalem: World Zionist Organization, 1981), 457–61, except that I stress more clearly the leadership of Judah, due to his greater risk and sense of responsibility.

[48]For the idea of the human family as the workshop of Genesis and the basis for all further forms of community, see Westermann, *Genesis: An Introduction,* 115. For recent praiseworthy efforts to identify family values as central to Genesis, see David L. Petersen, "Genesis and Family Values," *JBL* 124 (2005): 5–23. In Genesis larger family reunifications are adumbrated as well. Fisch alludes to what he calls the Ruth corpus, which consists of "episodes in the history of a single family. Lot is the father of Moab and thus the ancestor of Ruth, whilst Judah is the father of Perez and thus the ancestor of Boaz. Another way of putting it would be to say that we have here the story of a single clan (that of Abraham and his nephew Lot) which separates (Gen. xiii 11) at an early stage and is then reunited in the persons of Ruth and Boaz" (Fisch, "Ruth and the Structure of Covenant History," 427).

TWO

GENESIS, BOOK OF DREAMS, AND JOSEPH THE TSADDIK

> You can be in my dream if I can be in yours.
>
> (Bob Dylan)

Dreams of Power, Power of Dreams

Joseph is the dreamer, the one who can get into people's dreams, and who can also dream even beyond Jacob and in both directions: back to the place where the family is again one.

At age seventeen Joseph had a dream and told it to his brothers:

> Hear this *dream* that I have dreamed. (Gen 37:6)

Their reaction:

> And they hated him even more because of his *dreams*. (Gen 37:8)

The shift to the plural is curious and, indeed, has prompted the unlikely suggestion either that it "anticipates the second dream or implies a previous, unreported history of similar vainglorious dreams."[1] Actually, the text itself may provide an easier way out, since Gen 37:5–6 refers *twice* to a dream:

---

[1]Sarna, *Genesis,* 257.

> Now Joseph dreamed a dream and told it to his brothers. . . . And he [later] said to them: "Now hear this [other] dream that I have dreamt."

However, the very ambiguity of the number of Joseph's dreams has its own message, as we shall see.

Later, when in prison, Joseph discovers that Pharaoh's cup-bearer and baker are depressed and asks the reason.

> *They* said to him: "We dreamt *a dream* and there is none to interpret *it*." (Gen 40:8)

The notion of two people having a single dream is so strange that translations typically resort to the plural, unauthorized by the text: "We had dreams" (NJPS); "we have had dreams" (RSV). However, on the issue of singularity or plurality, Joseph prudently leaves out the direct object ("Kindly tell me," Gen 40:8), which translators too willingly supply. For, surely, the issue of whether the dream(s) are singular or plural will prove to be a crucial aspect of interpretation (Gen 41:32), and at this point in the narration Joseph has not reached the interpretative stage. Curiously, when the cupbearer later reports the event to Pharaoh, he retains the ambiguity or, rather, the ambivalence:

> And we dreamed *a dream* on the same night. . . . A Hebrew youth was there with us, . . . and he interpreted *our dreams* for us. (Gen 41:11–12)

In the final dream sequence of the Joseph story, the narrator remains uncommitted on the issue before us:

> And it was that, after two years, Pharaoh was dreaming, and behold. . . . (Gen 41:1)

Here the present participle is not followed by a direct object, which would of course specify a singular or plural event. Again,

> And he dreamed a second time . . . and Pharaoh awoke and behold it was a dream. (Gen 41:5–7)

The latter sentence remains unclear as to whether the reference is to the totality of two dreams or merely to the latter one, and this ambiguity is preserved in the summation:

And Pharaoh told them his *dream,* but there was no one to interpret *them* for Pharaoh. (Gen 41:8)

This final dream sequence is the easiest to understand in the sense that the doubling issue is decided by the dreamer himself and confirmed by his interpreter. First of all, Pharaoh states to Joseph:

I dreamed *a dream.* (Gen 41:15)

And, when he comes to recount the second incident, Pharaoh states that he saw "in my dream" (Gen 41:22), which surely means, as Nahum M. Sarna interprets, that "Pharaoh himself now realizes that the two dreams are really one."[2] In his interpretation, Joseph explicitly addresses the two related issues:

It is one single dream. (Gen 41:26)

And as for Pharaoh's having the same dream twice, . . . (Gen 41:32)

We are thus brought full circle, having seen all the possible combinations of singularity and plurality, of one dream and two (the minimum plural). For in the third dream sequences, two separate dreams by the same person turn out to be a single dream, whereas the single dream of the cupbearer and baker (they at least report it as such), yields two opposite meanings. Introducing both and perhaps also paradigmatic of such doubling or ambiguity is the first sequence, where Joseph's first dream is perceived as a plural, perhaps because both dreams yield the same meaning: the younger's rule over the other brothers.

These situations speak volumes about the permeability of dreams, not only one with another but also with the waking reality from which they originate and to which, in complex ways, they speak. If, according to Pedro Calderón de la Barca's famous play, *la vida es sueño y los sueños sueños son,* "life is a dream and dreams are dreams," this last mention of *sueños* must surely refer to life

---

[2]Sarna, *Genesis,* 238. See also Sforno (1475–1550) on Gen 41:7: "*And behold: a dream:* He sensed that it was all a single dream in itself. For it seemed to him in his second dream that he was still in the same situation as in the first dream, and thus did he interpret afterwards: 'And I looked into my dream'" (Gen 41:22), *Torat Hayyim. Chumash,* 2, 182.

itself as per the opening definition equating dreams with life. But our text itself gives astounding confirmation, for when Pharaoh wakes up, "behold, it was a dream" (Gen 41:7), something he did not know until waking up! One is led to think of a twilight existence, where reality is dreams and dreams reality, distinguishable only by opposition. We shall later see how God accesses this twilight zone and to what purposes.

As to the content of the dreams, Gerhard von Rad has argued that such figures "contain no profound, possibly mythological, symbolism or anything of the sort. They must be considered quite as they are, and they say neither more nor less than what is openly expressed in them; they are quite simple, pictorial prefigurations . . . only silent pictures."[3] While such an approach is helpful in its avoidance of pitfalls, it will not get us far in understanding the complex psychological reactions of the brothers, for beyond the pictorial and the symbolic, the words themselves carry ominous interpersonal and dramatic overtones that must be specified. Since Joseph proves to be the expert at such dream interpretations, his verdict will obviously carry greater weight. However, it is important to know *what the brothers were hearing,* what were the natural preoccupations and fears that led them to speak of more than one dream. Especially in such dramatic circumstances, characters in the Bible are intensely aware of the dialogic possibilities of their situation.[4]

Beyond the complex question of hearer-reception, there is a yet more problematic issue to be put forth, the ambiguous dimension of the words themselves. In the matter of dreams, the rabbis posited that "there are no dreams which don't contain some useless words."[5] Could this also mean "misleading words," and is Joseph trying to deceive his brothers over the meaning of his dreams? If so, he is quite unsuccessful. Or, more likely, does the young upstart, son of the favored wife, choose words calculated to upset his brothers? Or, even more likely, but hovering in the background, is the whole matter of God's plan to bring the Israelites down to Egypt.[6] In such stories there are surely high levels

---

[3]Von Rad, *Genesis,* 351.
[4]On ambiguity, see Perry, "Cain's Sin," 259–76.
[5]See Rashi on Gen 37:10 (*Torat Hayyim,* 2, 146), citing *b. Ber.* 55b.
[6]See below, "God in Human History?"

of verbal ambiguity, embedded in the very ambivalence of language, metaphor, and overtones of language. Joseph's first dream begins by describing a common effort, the gathering of sheaves or food that presumably would become part of the family possessions. The point is made that the brothers all participate in the family work of shepherding (Gen 37:2), although Joseph is for some reason exempted from that labor later (Gen 37:12–14). During this mutual endeavor a strange event occurs: the brothers' sheaves "surround" Joseph's sheaf.

> Your sheaves gathered around [*tesubbenah*] [my sheaf? me?] and they bowed down to my sheaf. (Gen 37:7)

Recalling the same expression in Num 36:7, this is what the brothers think they are hearing:

> Your sheaves passed over to my sheaf.[7]

Let us look even more closely at Joseph's first dream, perceived by his brothers as dreams in the plural:

> Behold, we were binding sheaves in the midst of the field and, behold, my sheaf arose and also stood erect. And, behold, your sheaves gathered around and they bowed down to my sheaf. (Gen 37:7)

From two kinds of evidence, one can readily understand how the brothers postulated two distinct dreams. There is, first of all, two sets of binary details:

> arose / stood erect

> gathered around / bowed down

Secondly, the description is actually divided into three portions, each introduced by *hinneh,* "behold." This perception of multiplicity is expressed in the brothers' dual response:

> Will you indeed be king over us? Will you indeed rule over us? (Gen 37:8)

The two sets of binaries have been condensed, as it were, into the brothers' own binary response: be king / rule over. In brief, in

---

[7]See also 1 Kgs 2:15; 1 Chr 10:14.

addition to the fear that Joseph may become king, there is the fear of dominion, of his taking possession of their property as well. This would explain their belief that Joseph had two dreams, since his usurpation over them will have two distinct levels.[8]

Joseph's qualifications for being a sage extend—beyond his expertise in dream(s) interpretation—to a power perhaps more awesome still, the power of words. For, as the proverb reminds us, "Death and life are in the power of the tongue/language" (Prov 18:21):

> His brothers said to him: "Do you mean to reign over us? Do you mean to rule over us?" And they hated him even more for his *talk* about his dreams. (Gen 37:8 NJPS)

If this means that their anger was increased because, in addition to the content of the dreams (rulership), Joseph had the indiscretion to tell his brothers about it, this would be most curious, since without such a report they would have had no basis to hate him whatever! Perhaps, therefore, it means that Joseph also bragged about his dream(s) to others, and such boasts would then constitute a separate basis for hatred. We know from Gen 37:2, for example, that Joseph was a tattle-tale. However, rather than collapsing the binary talk/dreams, we should translate more literally, along with the RSV: "his dreams *and* his words." The text would then allow a more precise understanding of the *two* threats that the brothers heard:

> "Do you mean to reign over us? Do you mean *to spin out proverbs against us?*" And they hated him even more because of his dreams *and* his words. (Gen 37:8)

Rather than read *mshl* ("to be king") as a mere synonym of "rule," we can hear quite different overtones altogether. "To invent proverbs or parables," for example, is a quite frequent meaning of this verb, and one used, as here, in contexts of verbal abuse:

---

[8]Events connected with Joseph's mother come to reinforce their suspicion. There is Jacob's explicit mention of Rachel as his (only) wife (Gen 44:27); also Rachel's stealing her father's *terafim*, "idols" (Gen 31:34), perhaps signifying her attempt to take over the leadership. See Ilana Pardes, *Countertraditions in the Bible* (Cambridge, Mass.: Harvard University Press, 1992), 71.

Show mercy upon your people, Lord!
Do not give your inheritance over to *reproach*,
that the nations should *rule* over them with a *byword* [*mashal*]!
Why should it be *said* among the nations: "Where is their God?"
(Joel 2:17)

Like Marvin A. Sweeney and James L. Crenshaw, I think that
mashal in Joel is a pun, concealing behind its frequent political/
military meaning of "rule" the verbal aggression of "byword."[9] In
the Genesis context the brothers would then complain not only of
the message of Joseph's dream, his projected rule over them and
their property, but also of his going about inventing prophetic
parables to sell his message: "Do you plan to be king over us? Are
you telling parables at our expense?"

One might then say, exploiting the metaphor of a "two-
edged sword," literally a "two-mouthed sword" (Ps 149:6), that
the brothers have read Joseph's dream(s) as two-edged swords
describing the two ways of killing a human being: with one's
weapon and with the chastisements of one's tongue (Ps 149:7).
For, as we have seen in the case of Tamar, public embarrassment
of another human being is worse than murder, and that may be
why the sage reversed what, for us at least, is the logical order:
"*Death and life* are in the power of the tongue" (Prov 18:21).
Fortunately for their survival, Joseph-The-Righteous was able to
change these horrific possibilities into blessings.

Planning Survival, Feeding the Masses

The Joseph narrative discloses, quite after the fact, the complex inner workings of this remarkable story:

---

[9]See James L. Crenshaw, *Joel: A New Translation with Introduction and
Commentary* (AB 24C; New York: Doubleday, 1995), 142–43; Marvin A. Sweeney, *The Twelve Prophets* (2 vols.; Berit Olam. Collegeville, Minn.: Liturgical,
2000), 169; also Ezek 12:23; 18:3. Note the parallel between *mshl* and *kherpah,*
"reproach, also found in Ps 44:14." Jeremy Schipper ("Narrative Obscurity of
Samson's *hidah* in Judges 14:14 and 18," *JSOT* 27 [2003]: 345) raises this possibility of a double reading in the Samson story, which occurs "at the time when
the Philistines were ruling [*moshelim*] over Israel." The second meaning fits
perfectly with the ensuing proverb contest between Samson and the Philistines,
although it must be noted that it is Samson and not his Philistine hosts who
launches the contest.

Joseph said to them [his brothers]: "Do not be afraid. Am I a substitute for God [*ʾelohim*]? Besides, though you intended me harm,
God intended it for good, in order to bring about the present result—
the survival of many people. And now, fear not: I will sustain you
and your children." Thus he comforted them and spoke kindly with
them. (Gen 50:19–22)

The first and immediate purpose of this speech is to reassure his
brothers that, contrary to their aborted plans against him, he will
not take their lives in revenge. That, even were he to have every
desire and reason to kill them as they tried to kill him (measure
for measure), and although he has the power to carry it out, they
have no cause to be afraid, since he refuses to substitute God's
function for his own. Here the sense of God's name *ʾelohim* is that
of judge. As Sarna puts it, "Man dares not usurp the prerogative of
God to whom alone belongs the right of punitive vindication."[10]
As Joseph says in another context and using the same measure for
measure language of substitution, why should I "substitute good
with evil" [*raʿah takhath tobah;* Gen 44:4)?

Our text put forth a second sense in which Joseph could not
possibly have taken over God's work. Concerning the seven-year
drought, Joseph (and everyone else) needed God's providential
disclosure about the long years of the upcoming drought, for who
could have predicted such an event, let alone caused it to happen?
The answer is that we just do not know; all we know is that there
are no other such events recorded. But if not the timing of these
events, surely their possibility must have been known. What then of
the future? If this narrative is paradigmatic of future happenings—
as the following Exodus story surely is—then the question "Am I
a substitute for God?" has an obvious answer: no, not in the circumstances just traversed.

But our text also gives a strong answer in the affirmative: yes,
of course! Just as in the present crisis, once I had the timetable I
did come up with some very good advice (Gen 41:33–36), so too
in the future: "*I* will sustain you and your children" (Gen 50:21).
Just as Joseph dealt with Pharaoh's (and his advisors') ignorance,
with his brothers' evil thoughts and actions, it was within his

---

[10]Sarna, *Genesis,* 350, citing Lev 19:18.

power to help not only his family but also a large nation to plan for future disasters and thus help them survive. There is an important sense in which Joseph *is* God's substitute, not in the sense of subversive replacement, of taking over God's function, but of planning survival for the future. For a close reading of this passage reveals that the brothers have a second fear as well. Granted that he will not kill them outright, perhaps Joseph will simply withdraw all support from their lives in exile and they will be diminished, perhaps even to the point of extinction.

Note that this planning and survival function both avoids the usual reading: "I am not a substitute for God" and also focuses on another sense of *᾿elohim,* now highlighting the original Creator-God of Gen 1:1, the One who creates and sustains and desires life. Joseph is now explicitly placing himself *under* (the second sense of *takhath*) God's own plan. For the Judge may punish, now or in the future, or remit. But if this function is left to God, the creative task remains for Joseph, and it has not only a passive role of not doing harm but an ongoing positive role, the management of the world: "*I* will sustain you and your children." There is an abiding sense that Joseph is indeed in place of God, not as a substitute but rather as a confederate, as taking over some of the work required by the divine plan for the ongoing work of creation.

God in Human History?

In Joseph's remarkable closing speech, then, retribution is ascribed to God and sustenance to human agency. From a much larger perspective of "the survival of many people," yet a third distribution is made, another level of understanding God's interaction with humans:

> Though you intended me harm, God intended it for good, in order to bring about the present result—the survival of many people. (Gen 50:20)

In the world of the Hebrew Bible we soon become accustomed to dual levels of causation: Humans plan one thing but God plans another, thus remaining in control of history.[11] At times the master plan is, at least partially, revealed in advance—the example of the descent into Egypt comes readily to mind (Gen 15:13–14). More often, these divine plans remain opaque and certainly at variance with normal expectations. In 1 Kgs 12:15, for example, the reader finds it preposterous that Rehoboam would favor the stupid advice of the "young-whippersnapper" over the sounder proposals of seasoned experts. When he does so, it is explained that God was looking for a *sibbah,* a "cause or pretext," to carry out his designs. In such cases, are we then dealing with a variant of oracular ambiguity?

Returning to the texts already studied above, the midrash gives an astonishing reading of Judah's admission, in full court, of Tamar's innocence ("She is more righteous than I," Gen 38:26). Taking the preposition *min* no longer as a comparative "than" but rather in its more frequent meaning of provenance "from":

> A Bat Kol [heavenly voice] came forth and said these words. "*mimmeni:* from Me and My Agency have these things happened. . . . I have ordained that Kings should issue from the tribe of Judah."

This interesting midrash, through its dissociative syntax, opens the way for yet another, this one less demanding in that it does not involve a change of voice from Judah ("She was right") to the Bat Kol ("From Me"):

> She was right: [henceforth kingship will come] *from me.*

Combining the two approaches, Judah now speaks with the full force of the divine Bat Kol behind his words, making his words of acknowledgment a performative act: "It is through my declaration of repentance that I merit kingship."

This midrash affords a glimpse into the wisdom subplot connecting the Joseph story with the incident of Judah and Tamar.

---

[11]Consider for example, "Many are the cogitations in a man's heart, but the Lord's counsel, that will be carried out" (Prov 19:21) and "His [Samson's] father and mother did not realize that this was the Lord's doing" (Judg 14:4).

The *Akedat Yitzak* opens this passage or *parashah* by quoting the *Midrash Rabbah*:[12]

> Rabbi Shmuel bar Nachman opened: "'For I know the thoughts that I think towards you,' said the Lord (Jer 29:11). The tribes are occupied with the selling of Joseph, Joseph and Jacob are occupied with their afflictions, Judah is occupied with taking a wife, while God occupies Himself with creating the light of Mashiah, 'thoughts of peace and not of evil, to give you a future and a hope.'"

Now we sense yet another reason for the thrill we feel during Joseph's grand disclosure before his brothers. There is, to be sure, the sentimental, familial, and psychological relief at seeing a family reunited. There is also the ethical elevation of Joseph's forgiveness, an action precipitated by Judah's self-denial and repentance. But there is also the overarching sense that the whole thing was staged-for-good from the start, that divine providence, though hidden, is alive and well. It is Joseph himself, the man who is always speaking the name of God, who makes public disclosure of this grand latency:

> It was not you that sent me here but God. (Gen 45:8)

God is at work in history; and even when everyone goes about their own business, God is at work to advise and save, to elevate humans through repentance and prepare survival for the final in-gathering. The Tsaddik is a *knowing* participant: Noah knows the plan, builds the ark, and makes his menus; Tamar disguises herself as a whore and engenders the messianic line; Joseph can only speak and do what God reveals; and now Judah, as the midrash would have it, is privy to God's directing collusion. For, surely, Tamar has tutored Judah to restoration of all honors and privileges. This is why, when Tamar asks him to "*hakker-naʾ*," to recognize to whom these may belong, the rabbis understand this to mean also that Judah should "acknowledge his Creator."[13] This involves allowing

---

[12]The *parashah* begins in Gen 37:1, thus stressing the profound connection between Jacob's (ironic) settling down and the Judah/Tamar episode in the following chapter. See Isaac Arama (1420–1494), *Akedat Yitzak* [Commentary on the Chumash and the Five Megillot] (Pressburg: V. Kittseer, 1849; repr., Jerusalem: Yisraʾel–Ameriqah Tel Aviv, 1960), 213b, quoting *Midr. Bereshit Rabbah* 85.

[13]See Rashi on Gen 38:25.

the survival of her, her babies, and the memory of her dead husbands: in brief, creating the possibility of a future anchored in the dreams of the past, or, in Harold Fisch's fine phrase, a remembered future.[14]

Humans in God's History: Genesis 2:4 as a Narrative Hinge

From the pervasiveness of God's power just described, it seems possible to agree with the following summation:

> The central theme of Genesis is the sovereignty of Yahweh in His establishment of a nation.[15]

It seems equally possible to argue the contrary, that God's sovereignty is in high evidence only in the first creation narrative, and that everything else in Genesis depends on human initiative. Or to posit, as a compromise position: God programs the plan and humans carry it out.[16]

Despite the enormous variety of approaches to understanding the creation story in Genesis, there is consensus on the existence of two separate creation narratives: Gen 1:1–2:4a and 2:4a–25. The debate then often becomes whether these two stories represent two independent understandings or even literary traditions that have become welded together, or, as will be argued here, whether they form a single, unified, and coherent text. The debate on sources, while itself interesting, is hardly crucial, since it is quite possible that the text in its present state is coherent in its message, whether composite or not. It is this understanding of the text that I wish to pursue here: How does the Bible view the creative process as dual in nature; or, from a literary point of view, how do the

---

[14]Harold Fisch, *A Remembered Future: A Study in Literary Mythology* (Bloomington: Indiana University Press, 1984).

[15]Allen P. Ross, "Genesis," in *The Bible Knowledge Commentary* (eds. John F. Walvoord and Roy B. Zuck; 2 vols.; Dallas: Victor, 1985), 1:26.

[16]See Michael Fishbane, *Text and Texture* (New York: Schocken, 1979), 12. I said that God "programs" in the present tense so as to avoid the appearance of a strictly Deist position that argues God's total withdrawal from the world once created, thus foreclosing on the possibility of providence and the usefulness of prayer.

two creation segments form a single story? Or, mathematically speaking, do the two stories make one or do they project many more? Or both?

There is a scholarly consensus on the precise boundary separating these two narrative segments:

> Such is the story [alternatively: These are the generations] of the heaven and the earth when they were created, on the day when the Lord God made earth and heaven. (Gen 2:4)

This verse is problematic in a number of respects, though a closer look at the several textual difficulties of this crucial narrative hinge sheds light on the meaning of the two creations and their relation. First of all, this verse is stylistically clumsy in its literal repetition of the direct object as such and without the substitute pronoun. One would have expected:

> on the day when the Lord God made *them.*

Lest one think that this stylistic requirement is a modern one, consider the following examples:

> And God created *man* in His own image, in the image of God He created *him.* (Gen 1:27)

The text does not literally repeat ʾet-haʾadam, "man." Or, again:

> And God blessed the seventh *day* and sanctified *it.* (Gen 2:3)

This, rather than the clumsy "and sanctified the seventh day."

There is a second stylistic difficulty in Gen 2:4 as well. Even granted the anomaly of the literal repetition of the direct object, the repeated phrase should still have retained the established order: heaven and earth, enthroned from Gen 1:1 and repeated in the first half of this very verse! Why the reversal? I deliberately bypass the simplistic explanation of stylistic variation, which, while not impossible, is always too easy a way out and rather suspect in a text so sophisticated as the Hebrew Bible.

There is yet a third difficulty, the precise narrative function of the hinge-verse that joins the two stories, the famous Gen 2:4a:

> Such is the story of the heaven and the earth when they were created.

Does the "Such is the story" formula summarize the preceding or, rather, does it introduce what follows? Most current translations (NRSV; NJPS; Everett Fox trans.; Robert Alter trans.) follow the first view, so that the formula is seen as concluding the first narrative with a full stop:

> Such is the story of the heaven and the earth when they were created. When the Lord God made earth and heaven, ... (Gen 2:4)

Yet, in all ten of its other occurrences in Genesis, the formula refers *to what follows,* thus yielding the following translation:[17]

> Such is the story of the heaven and the earth when they were created, when the Lord God made earth and heaven. ... (Gen 2:4)

For the moment let us leave the question open in a rather bold way: not only by deferring the choice as to which translation is right but rather by allowing that the solutions are *both* convincing and thus, possibly, *both* right.[18]

> The latter translation highlights a chiasm that is already quite obvious:
>
> heaven and earth
>
> earth and heaven[19]

But what meaning, if any, is this chiasm intended to suggest? Is the rhetorical figure merely that or does it point to meanings beyond its own configuration as well? I suggest that the reversal of terms is precisely the point, that the second creation story repeats the first but "reverses" it in a significant way.[20] If such is indeed the case, then we can well understand that the direct object repetition is not stylistic clumsiness at all. It is, rather, used to draw attention to the main ideological point, namely that the second

---

[17]Sarna, *Genesis,* 16–17: "The entire verse may be understood as a unity referring to what follows." Older versions such as the Vulgate, Septuagint, and the Geneva Bible follow this approach.

[18]Such a possibility is offered in the translation of the *École Biblique de Jérusalem,* by isolating 2:4a as its own paragraph and by full stops both before and after: "Telle fut la genèse du ciel et de la terre, quand ils furent créés."

[19]This particular chiasm occurs only in Ps 148, as pointed out by Sarna, *Genesis,* 354n7.

[20]Herbert Marks, "Biblical Naming and Poetic Etymology," *JBL* 114 (1995): 25.

creation, while retaining the two elements (heaven and earth) of the first creation, also inverts them, as it were. Rhetorically, this would mean that, whereas the merisms "heaven and earth" and "earth and heaven" seem equivalent, they differ in two respects, first in the direction or order of the two elements and, secondly, in the chiasm that is emphasized from their studied juxtaposition.

Let us begin by noticing the enormous structural value in the *order of elements*[21] in the initial verse of the Bible:

> In the beginning God created *the heaven and the earth.* (Gen 1:1)

This initial structure recurs precisely at the conclusion of the first creation narrative:

> Such is the story of *the heaven and the earth.* (Gen 2:4)

Such repetition forms an *inclusio* or bracketing device which unifies and sets off all materials included therein. This self-contained text recounts in very precise terms a descending order of creation, from heaven to earth, as it were,[22] thus focusing attention on the thought that this story of creation proceeds as follows:

> Heaven → Earth.

What then is the reader to infer from a second narration, connected with and in some ways similar to the first, but now pointedly announced with the reverse formula:

> When the Lord God was making *earth and heaven* (Gen 2:4b).

Doesn't one suspect that this second version of creation is significantly different from (perhaps the opposite or the complement of) the first? For now the following formula applies:

> Earth → Heaven.

---

[21]See below, chapter 4, "Paradoxes of Liberation," for a discussion of Qoh 3:2–8.

[22]Closely attuned to the fine nuances of words, the rabbis sensed in the opening verse of Genesis the presence of *three* original elements of creation: heaven as composed of fire and water (in accord with its "etymology" *shamayim* = ʾ*esh* + *mayim*), and the earth. Since these are the three elements that structure the three days of creation (and, by parallel extension, the next three as well), and since in Gen 1:1 they occur precisely in the same order, one wonders whether the rabbis, in their midrashic etymology of *shamayim,* did not intend a literary and structural comment. See below, Conclusions, n8.

In brief, the chiasm, composed of *two* parts related by symmetrical inversion, seems to suggest that there are *two* orders of creation: the first, from Heaven to Earth and the second from Earth to Heaven.

It is also the case, however, that just as the chiasm is a single figure made up of two parts, *both* creation narratives constitute a single biblical story of creation. This organic continuity of the two creation narratives is suggested not only by their contiguity but also by the quite unusual mirror syntax through which the second creation story is presented:

> When the Lord God made earth and heaven—when no shrub of the field was yet on earth and no grasses of the field had yet sprouted, because the Lord God had not sent rain upon the earth and there was no man to till the soil, but a flow would well up from the ground and water the whole surface of the earth—the Lord God formed man from the dust of the earth. (Gen 2:4b–7 NJPS)

It is crucial to see that this syntax, highlighted by the unusually developed independent clauses and the dramatic postponement of the main clause, exactly reproduces the syntax of the start of Genesis, i.e., of the first creation narrative:

> When God began to create heaven and earth—the earth being unformed and void, with darkness over the surface of the deep and a wind from God sweeping over the water—God said, "Let there be light." (Gen 1:1–3NJPS)

What is interesting here is not only that words or even structures are parallel, but even more that these similarities make the crucial point that the two narratives are ideologically parallel or complementary, that the work of the second creation strongly resembles the work of the first, perhaps suggesting that the rule of analogy is what holds them together.

For those readers like myself who cling to the notion of a single and unified creation story in Genesis, it is not uncommon to argue that the second creation story is added to the first and thus necessary because it provides further details concerning the first creation.[23] We can now refine this approach by noticing that the chiasm allows us to see the two creation stories as comple-

---

[23]Fishbane, *Text and Texture*, 17.

mentary, as a theomorphic version of creation gives way to an anthropomorphic one.[24] For now it is not a creation from top to bottom, from heaven to earth, but rather the reverse, totally consonant with the "substitution" of the divine Creator by the human one that we saw in the Joseph story, and the definitive shift of scene from heaven to earth.

This does not mean, of course, that God vanishes from the second creation story, quite the contrary, since this second narrative also pointedly refers to the divine activity here as well:

> on the day when the Lord God created earth and heaven. (Gen 2:4b)

But now God is, as it were, in the background, much in the way that Eve acknowledges in the conception of her son:

> I have got a son with [the help of] the Lord. (Gen 4:1)

Similarly, I would argue that human beings are not absent from the first creation story either, that the first narrative's strong insistence on humanity's creation in God's image (Gen 1:26–27) must surely wish to suggest how human beings resemble God *as creative beings*. Let us now try to sort out these two complementary kinds of creativity.[25]

The point of reading Gen 2:4 as a narrative hinge can be strengthened by what may be considered more midrashic interpretations as well. Consider, for example, the phrase "when they were created" (*behibbar'am*), usually neglected by commentators because it seems uselessly repetitive. What is most curious in the written text is the diminished letter *he,* which seems intended to be both not read and read. In the first instance, the sense would be: when He created them. With the addition of the (diminished) *he,* the verb becomes passive: "when they were created," i.e., presumably by someone else other than the One just mentioned. The identity of this other figure is intimated, according to Radak

---

[24]Ibid., 11, 16.

[25]In a fascinating article Lyn M. Bechtel ("Rethinking the Interpretation of Genesis 2.4B–3.24," in *A Feminist Companion to Genesis* [ed. Athalia Brenner; Sheffield: Sheffield Academic Press, 1993], 77–117) views the content of the second phase, which we here term "from the ground up," as plotting the process of human maturation.

(1160–1235) and Ibn Ezra (1092–1167), at the end of the verse that immediately precedes:

> And God blessed the seventh day and declared it holy, because on it God ceased from all His work that He created *to do*. (Gen 2:3)

Despite the usual smooth but distorting rendering (NJPS: "all the work of creation that He had done"), the sense may also be: "all the work that He created [for others, e.g., humans] to do." The point made in both cases is that two creators are being referred to, God and also humans. Indeed, throughout the entire first creation narrative, God has been designated uniquely as *'elohim,* the universal Creator "God." At the precise point when the second narrative of creation begins, Gen 2:4, God the Creator receives a new name: Yahweh-Elohim, "Lord-God." It is upon entering their roles as creators that humans become aware that God also has a proper name: Lord (Yahweh).[26]

My suggestion, then, is that the formulaic "these are the generations" applies *both* to the preceding *and* to what follows; it both summarizes the work of God and introduces the work of humans, and no stylistic achievement could dramatize this better than to use the *same* (not even identical!) formula as a hinge between the two narratives. The double-talk or double-reading of the phrase is thus not to be explained by our exegetical failure to decide but rather by narrative and theological necessity. In rabbinic exegesis this would be an egregious instance of reading a word or expression both "above and below," of applying it to *both* the preceding *and* the following. This ambi-valent reading thus further dramatizes, on a stylistic level, the ambivalence of the previous phrase: "which He created [*for humans*] to do."

Humans now have space to realize their divine image (Gen 1:27), taking over where God leaves off and mirroring the original creation by a creation from the ground up.[27] The first one to sense the radical ideology imbedded in this metaphor was Pharaoh, as we shall now see.

---

[26]See the interesting, if somewhat idiosyncratic, discussion in John D. Caputo, *The Weakness of God* (Bloomington: Indiana University Press, 2006), 65–75.

[27]For examples of how the notion of "creation from the ground up" entered Western literature through Jewish exegesis, see Perry, *Erotic Spirituality.*

THREE

Pharaoh's Anti-Wisdom Ideology: The Semantic Puzzle of "Going Up from the Earth/Land" (Exod 1:10)

> Let the heavens shower from above and the skies
> pour down righteousness. Let the earth open that
> they may fructify salvation and, together,
> may it cause righteousness to sprout.
>
> (Isa 45:8)

God's plan for the total destruction of Sodom and Gomorrah (Gen 18:20–21) arouses an incredulous reaction from Abraham: if the righteous and wicked are treated equally, then the fundamental distinction between *tsaddiq* and *rashaᶜ* is obliterated (v. 25). While the issue is patently one of reward and punishment, from what we have already seen as a dominant ideology in the book of Genesis a further agenda is projected as well: whereas the wicked must be removed to prevent further damage, if the righteous are also removed, who will be left to carry on the work of creation? The text argues that the *tsaddiq* is certainly not like a *rashaᶜ*, and God had to discuss the matter with Abraham in particular, since to him was entrusted the method and purpose of Genesis: the program of *tsedaqah*, righteousness (Gen 15:6; 18:19). Were Lot and his family then to be considered righteous? In a compromised way, yes, for their reaction to the destruction was to rebuild, and

from the ground up, so to speak (Gen 19:30–37): "Let us maintain life," even if it be "through our father" (vv. 32, 34)!

The basic contrast between the *tsaddiq* and the *rasha*ᶜ was, as
previously noted, a favorite of wisdom writers. An interesting literary development of this distinction is seen in the contrastive
portraits of Lady Wisdom and the Foreign Woman in the book of
Proverbs (e.g., Prov 8 and 5:3–5; 6:24–35; 9:13–18). Of equal interest to wisdom writers, I think, would be the sequential contrast
between the live (as opposed to merely allegorical) characters of
Genesis and their moral opposites at the start of Exodus. Take, for
starters, the two fighting Hebrews:

> He [Moses] said to the *rasha*ᶜ: "Why do you strike your fellow?"
> (Exod 2:13)

Since Moses had no way of knowing which man was "in the
right," the question was not a judicial one, and Rashi's (1140–
1105) exegesis is to be preferred: "From the mere fact that he
raised his hand, he was to be considered a *rasha*ᶜ." Other exegetes
relate this action to the violence of the flood generation.

The major portrait of the *rasha*ᶜ is of course Pharaoh himself,
along with the Egyptians who helped carry out his program of extermination. How are we authorized to apply such a term? From
the *rasha*ᶜ himself:

> "The Lord is the *tsaddiq* and I and my people are the *resha*ᶜ*im*."
> (Exod 9:27)

If the people of the land are now included in the category of the
wicked, credit must go to the covert way in which Pharaoh sells
his ideology. It is all packaged in a fascinating metaphor of "going
up from the land," a complex statement worthy of wisdom's
riddles for its intricacy and even its prophetic, or twilight, impetus: a true inversion or caricature of a wisdom saying.

The Israelite population boom at the start of the book of Exodus marks the expansion from seventy souls to myriads, with the
following focal points:

   a) the twelve sons of the patriarch Jacob/Israel become the twelve
      tribes of Israel;

b) the individuals arising from this brotherhood are perceived as a people in Exod 1:9, the first time this expression is used, interestingly not by the Israelites but rather by Pharaoh himself; and

c) this new nation develops with such strength of numbers as to constitute a demographic explosion: "And the children of Israel were fruitful and swarmed and multiplied exceedingly; and the land was filled with them" (Exod 1:7).

All this was felt as a threat to the new leadership, so much so that Pharaoh offered the following advice to his own "people," in direct opposition to the "people" of Israel:

And he said to his people: "Behold, the people of Israel are much too numerous for us (NJPS). Come, let us deal wisely with them, lest in their multiplying there may occur a war—and they could join our enemies and fight against us—and they will go up from the land [weᶜalah min-haᵓarets]." (Exod 1:10)

The uncertainty of understanding the final expression can be gauged by such widely varying renditions as the following:

and escape from the land. (RSV)

or go up away from the land. (Everett Fox trans.)

and rise from the ground. (NJPS)

While RSV and Fox both refer to departure, each has a distinct candidate in mind. The RSV has the advantage of anticipating the language of Exod 3:8, the divine promise "to bring Israel up out of that land." In this reading Pharaoh prophesies the Exodus without even knowing it! In fact, such language was already operative in Joseph's dying words to his brothers:

God will surely take notice of you and *bring you up from this land.* . . . You shall carry up my bones from here. (Gen 50:24–25)

And when Moses does carry out these wishes, he does so by quoting the very same language (Exod 13:19).

Contextually, however, Everett Fox senses that this phrase expresses an alternative to the preceding, for if indeed Israel joins the enemies of the Egyptians, they would probably want to remain and share power rather then simply depart. For at this point in the narrative, the motivation for escape does not yet apply, the oppression to follow being the result rather than the cause of the Israelites' perceived desire to "escape from the ʾerets." Fox's version thus allows a reading popular in rabbinic exegesis, one that would require the Egyptians rather than the Israelites to "go up away from the [i.e., their] land." In Rashi's commentary, referring to rabbinic midrash:

> This is like a person who curses himself but attaches his curse to someone else. What is really meant is: "And *we* will go up from the land and they [the Israelites] will take it over."

Both the RSV and Fox proposals should be retained as possible readings of an unclear and possibly complex situation. For while the Israelites do not yet have reasons to "escape *from*" Egypt, they may indeed nurture the desire to depart *to* the land of their origins, as intimated by the verb ʿalah, "to go up" (to the land of Israel). And while Pharaoh may have no objective reasons to fear the Israelite enclave isolated in Goshen, this "new" king may indeed feel the need to consolidate his power. What better way than to mark off a group "different" from his own and thus in potential alliance with an enemy?

These proposals hardly exhaust the interpretive possibilities of the unusual expression under consideration, however, and the discussion can be expanded by considering both the broader semantics of the verb ʿalah and the identity of the ʾerets from which the rising up is to occur. In this discussion it will be crucial to bear in mind the dual purpose of the narrative voice in Exod 1:10. On the one hand, Pharaoh is speaking to his people, trying to convince them of an imminent threat posed by the Israelites. However, his metaphoric language, while strongly condemnatory of the Israelites, also encodes the Bible's opposing values, ones that are further reinforced by the dominant narrative voice.

The Semantics of ʿalah

First, let us try to sense the overtones of Pharaoh's message to his people, the echoes of "rising up" (i.e., up-rising) that he needs to convey:

Aggressive Attack

ʿalah can have the meaning "to set out on a military expedition," "to go up to battle," and can appear either with the attached preposition ʿal or without a preposition, as here.[1] The implied threat could be even more precise: "They will rise up [against us], form an uprising, from the land [of Goshen]."[2]

The Rising Plagues

For Pharaoh the Nile was identified in his dreams as the place from which cows "came up," whether for good or evil (Gen 41:2–3), and the plague of the frogs (Exod 7:28[8:3]) left little doubt about the function of the river as a place from which incursion comes: "The Nile will swarm with frogs, and they will come up." The biblical description of the locust plague uses the same verb, and while no literal rising up is implied, the preposition ʿal suggests rising up in the military sense of an invasion (Exod 10:12, 14). The parallel with the locusts in Joel captures the overtones of ambivalence of the locusts' uprising: ʿalah ʿal in Joel 1:6 portrays a population explosion of locusts, a numberless *army* that rises up over the entire land. In Joel 2 the theme returns, and in a way that retains a perfect ambiguity as to whether it is an invading army *of* locusts or an army *like* locusts.

Rising Waters

Waters are rising up from the north. They shall become a raging torrent, they shall flood the land and its inhabitants. (Jer 47:2)

Although the verb ʿalah "is not frequently employed to describe the movement of water,"[3] these rising waters, which overflow or overrun the entire region, portray an invading army and thus relate to the military use of ʿalah as "attack." The metaphor, then, echoes Pharaoh's fear of Israelite military involvement:

---

[1]See Josh 10:4; 22:12, 32; 7:3 and commentary by J. Alberto Soggin, *Joshua: A Commentary* (trans. R. A. Wilson; OTL; Philadelphia: Westminster, 1972), ad loc. Also 1 Kgs 12:24, where it is followed by the synonymous "wage battle"; 2 Sam 5:22. The aggressive sense of ʿalah is arguably present (again without the preposition) in Reuven's mounting his father's couch in Gen 49:4.

[2]For the land of Goshen, the location of the Israelite community, see Gen 47:4–6 and Ramban (1194–1270) ad loc.

[3]Baruch Levine, *Numbers 21–36: A New Translation with Introduction and Commentary* (AB 44; New York: Doubleday, 2000), 95. See, however, the examples adduced below.

Lest in their multiplying there may occur a war—and they could join our enemies and fight against us. (Exod 1:10)

Rising Winds from the Desert

And the east wind of the Lord will come, rising up from the desert. (Hos 13:15)

Instead of the hovering and protecting wind/spirit of Gen 1:2, this plundering wind rises up,[4] overflowing the desert (see below regarding the Shulamite) and destroying its victims.

Exact Parallels: Hosea 2:2[1:11]; Genesis 2:6

The only text usually cited as a possible exact parallel to our expression is a seminal passage in Hosea:[5]

And the Judahites and the Israelites will join together and appoint one head and *go up from the land* (Hos 2:2[1:11] RSV).

Despite the irresistible urge to read this as a return from foreign exile under the aegis of the restored Davidic line, as occurs later in Hos 3:5, the truth is, as Marvin A. Sweeney simply states, "no exile is mentioned here."[6] Rather than a parallel to the exodus from Egypt, then, a very different and fuller picture emerges when the passage is read from a broader context. For example, the imagery in the parallel is oriented in a different direction when read in an agricultural context. For *ʾerets* can indicate not only land (Goshen, Egypt) but also "earth, soil"; and *ʿalah* can describe not only physical removal but also all cycles of botanical growth. The term connotes sprouting:

For he sprouted before him as a tender plant. (Isa 53:2)

---

[4]This is possibly a reference to the Assyrian invasion; cf. Isa 8:7–8.

[5]Nahum M. Sarna (*Exodus: The Traditional Hebrew Text with the New JPS Translation* [Philadelphia: JPS, 1991], 5) claims that this Hebrew phrase "occurs only in Hosea 2:2." However, it also occurs in Gen 2:6 and 1 Sam 28:13; see below.

[6]Sweeney, *The Twelve Prophets,* 24.

He was creating locusts at the time that the latter growth was beginning to sprout. (Amos 7:1)

It describes budding or blossoming:

On the vine were three branches. As soon as it budded, its blossoms blossomed. (Gen 40:10)

And it speaks of growing to full maturity:

Seven ears of grain, plump and good, were growing on a single stalk. (Gen 41:5, 22)

You shall come to your grave in ripe old age, like a full sheaf of corn which matures in its season. (Job 5:26)

These examples suggest a different orientation:

But the number of the children of Israel will be like the sand of the sea, which cannot be measured or counted. . . . And the Judahites and the Israelites will join together and appoint one head and *sprout up from the earth.* For great is the day of The Lord's Planting [*yizraᶜeʾl*].[7] (Hos 2:2[1:11])

From this perspective, the theme is not redemption but rather the blessings of fruitfulness that arise from below. Just as the renewed nation is here compared not to the stars above but rather to the sand below, they will be "planted" in the land/earth/soil, whence they will burst forth in number and rise up and overflow their enemies. National and political unification on one *land* will be expressed in the fruitfulness of both the *soil* and the *people,* thus including all meanings of *ʾerets.*

This use of the metaphor of "overflow" is justified when another parallel is recalled, one never cited in this regard but that may well be the true antecedent of both Hos 2:2[1:11] and the poetic, but curiously evocative, NJPS rendition of Exod 1:10 ("rise from the ground"):

But a mist [stream (NRSV); flow (NJPS)] *went up from the earth* and watered the whole face of the ground. (Gen 2:6 RSV)

---

[7]See William Rainey Harper, *Amos and Hosea* (ICC; Edinburgh: T&T Clark, 1966), 247: "*They shall grow up from the ground,* i.e., like grain after it is sowed. *For great shall be the day of Jezreel.* Does this mean the day of sowing?"

In this first occurrence of our expression recorded in the Hebrew Bible, notions of horizontal departure and escape from a *land* are excluded and, as in Hos 2:2[1:11], are replaced by a vertical movement of rising up from below. Although we are trained by our liturgies to think of blessings as descending from heaven, these examples portray blessings that flow abundantly from below and whose source in all cases is the *'erets,* the ground or soil that will produce growth.

Rising Waters: The Meaning and Ideology of Exodus 1:10

For the proper understanding of Exod 1:10, the broader context is crucial. The entire sequence is introduced by the biblical narrative voice (and no longer Pharaoh's):

> And the children of Israel were *fruitful* and swarmed and *multiplied* exceedingly; and *the land was filled* with them. (Exod 1:7)

The first level of reference is indeed Goshen and most likely Egypt as well. But note that this language quotes that of the Bible's first commandment to humankind:

> And God blessed them, saying to them:

> "Be fruitful and multiply and fill the earth." (Gen 1:28; 9:1)

This geographical widening from the land of Goshen to Egypt to the entire earth—all indicated by the single term *'erets*—makes the theological argument that such demographic expansiveness is part of the divine blessing. How does this blessing come to be signified by the expression "to go up from the *'erets*"?

The Egyptian concerns are immediately expressed:

> Look, the Israelite people are much too numerous for us. (Exod 1:9 NRSV)

Too numerous to fight against perhaps, but only, as the text goes on to speculate, if Israelites are joined by other enemies. The more immediate concern, however, is *they are much too numerous to contain.* This connection of ideas is in fact explicitly stated in the sequel:

But the more they were oppressed, *the more they increased and spread out.* (Exod 1:12)

What then is the dual threat—expressed by the ambivalence of going up from the land—that the Israelite population explosion represents? In the first instance, the Israelites may join the enemy (Exod 1:10). But even if this is not the case, they are already bursting at the seams, so to speak. Will the Israelites then seek to escape back to Canaan? Perhaps, although the Egyptians seem incapable of imagining such a possibility. Egypt is worried that Israelites will overflow their borders and spill over *into Egypt!*

What is seen by Pharaoh as a threat both military and social ("they are not like us") is compounded, perhaps even driven, by the ideological threat of fertility, and it is on this issue that the real battle is fought and the metaphors reappraised. Thus, for example, the desert from which the militant winds of the Lord "rise up" (Hos 13:15) always recalls that desert wilderness where the generation of the exodus resided prior to their entry into the land. But through some kind of miraculous rereading it can also indicate a place of pasturage and nurture.[8] What is intriguing is that the two meanings can coalesce, that the place of wilderness can also be the place of restoration. Thus, God speaks to his bride, recalling the erotic language of Jer 2:2:

> Therefore, behold I will entice her and bring her into the wilderness and speak lovingly to her. And I will give her her vineyards from there. (Hos 2:16–17[2:14–15])

Nurture from the desert? The place of emptiness has become the place of restoration? A mysterious passage from Canticles points to the same event, using the same idiom:

> Who is this *coming up from the desert* like columns of smoke, perfumed with myrrh and frankincense? (Cant 3:6)

In this scene the Shulamite approaches the marriage canopy, overflowing the desert locus of her restoration, as a plenitude that exceeds the poverty of its origins.[9]

---

[8]Exod 3:1; 1 Sam 17:28.

[9]Yair Zakovitch (*The Song of Songs: Introduction and Commentary* [Hebrew; Jerusalem: Magnes, 1992], 79) suggests that the "columns [*TiMRot*] of

Blessings from the ʾerets Below

We must make mention of a curious interpretation of the use of ʾerets in Hosea, put forth by Francis I. Andersen and David Noel Freedman. Also concluding that current understandings of ʾerets (land, the inhabitants of the land) make little sense, they propose reading the term eschatologically as well as historically (through the exodus): "the destroyed nation will have to be brought back from *the Underworld* in order to become Yahweh's people again."[10] This reading could have been strengthened by citing yet another complete parallel available from the MT, Saul's pilgrimage to the medium at Endor to call up the spirit of Samuel:

> And the woman said to Saul: "A god did I see rising up from the ground." (1 Sam 28:13)

Although the reading "to rise up from the ground" is certainly not disallowed, *sheʾol,* the underworld, is also a common meaning of ʾerets in biblical Hebrew.[11]

The projection of such a reading into the context of Exod 1:10 is problematic, however. While it might indeed, in the mouth of Pharaoh, threaten something like "the Israelites will ever be around to haunt us," the eschatological thesis is to be rejected for the very reason that it is spoken by Pharaoh, who can surely derive no benefit from reminding his audience of Israel's potential resurrection!

A more promising suggestion for understanding blessings rising up from below is Umberto Cassuto's important comment on Gen 2:6, which also focuses not on the nature of the moisture discussed in the verse (flow, mist, etc.), but rather on its source: the primeval *tehom,* the eternal waters on which the earth itself

---

smoke may be a mist, in which case they would be consistent with Gen 2:6." He further suggests (p. 29) that these columns may also be related to the *TaMaR* or date palm, something that rises up and mushrooms. See also Crenshaw on Joel 3:3[2:30] (*Joel,* 167–68).

[10]Francis I. Andersen and David Noel Freedman, *Hosea: A New Translation with Introduction and Commentary* (AB 24; Garden City, N.Y.: Doubleday, 1980), 209.

[11]This is death, the "pit," the lower parts of the earth (Ezek 31:14), the "sheol down below" (Deut 32:22).

stands.[12] Cassuto's point is to stress an opposition: the waters arise from below rather than, as later in a post-Edenic universe, from the rains from above. Perhaps they are those very waters of Eden, "luxuriant with overflow."[13]

In sum, I have proposed that the parallel examples of *ʿalah min ha-ʾarets*—especially Gen 2:6 and Hos 2:2[1:11]—metaphorically reinforce an alternative reading of Exod 1:10, with the following focal points:

ʿalah no longer designates a horizontal movement of "escape from" but rather a vertical movement of "rise up and sprout from." This ascent, however, retains the suggestion of the holiness of "going up" to the land to carry out the divine plan of fertility.

ʾerets, in consonance with this plan, refocuses and greatly expands the source of *blessings from below* in a complex image composed of all dimensions of *ʾerets:* earth, people of the earth, ground, and even the waters of Eden. The real Israelite threat is thus not primarily military but rather agricultural and reproductive: filling the earth with people causes the ground to fructify, an action consonant with the righteousness ideology of Genesis already studied above.

Through his double-edged metaphors, Pharaoh is thus prophesying without knowing it! The Israelites will rise from out of the land and water the entire surface of the earth. From this perspective Pharaoh's superior wisdom ("let us deal wisely with them" [Exod 1:10]) has an ironic and hollow ring, the reverse of Lady Wisdom's plan for the fruitfulness of creation:

> He who finds me finds life.
> He who misses me injures himself;
> all those who hate me love death. (Prov 8:35–36; also 3:2, 18; 4:22)

---

[12]Umberto Cassuto, *Commentary on the Book of Genesis* (Hebrew; 5th ed.; Jerusalem: Magnes, 1969), 67–68.

[13]See Crenshaw, *Joel,* 15n8.

PART TWO

INTERPRETING IN THE TWILIGHT ZONE

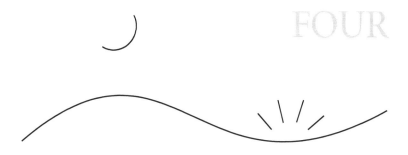

FOUR

SAMSON'S RIDDLES AND THE SIGNS OF REDEMPTION (JUDG 14)

The Godhead does not express its meaning openly
and clearly. Above all, it does not willingly mention
its name openly, and even the fact that it
is a divinity can be conjectured only
on the ground of certain signs.

(Naphtali Tur-Sinai)

A Wisdom Tale

The received text of the Samson cycle in Judg 13–16 presents a rather simple structure, all focused on his interactions with the neighboring Philistines:[1]

a) the annunciation story of Samson's birth (ch. 13)

b) episodes of his great strength (chs. 14–16)

---

[1]Robert H. O'Connell (*The Rhetoric of the Book of Judges* [Leiden: Brill, 1996], 203–29) avoids what he calls the scenic approach to analysis and focuses instead on plot development. He sees plot A, God's deliverance of Israel from the Philistines through Samson, as dominant, and identifies three subplots: the annunciation of Samson's birth; the wife from Timnah; and the Delilah episode. That is to say, this sophisticated analysis studies the sometimes complex interaction of plots but basically agrees with the overall simplicity of content.

The best known of these episodes, the concluding tale of Samson and Delilah and his heroic death, merely reworks our hero's earlier interests in Philistine women as well as a spectacular finale indicating that, indeed, he had made an at least symbolic dent in Philistine supremacy. The plot is simple in the extreme: unexpected (miraculous?) birth, barely credible military exploits, and glorious death, the whole bound together and made possible by timely invasions of God's spirit.[2] The narrative of Samson's birth ends with notation that God's spirit began to stir in the land (Judg 13:25), and its rush upon him marks both the start and the end of our episode with the lion (Judg 14:6, 19; also 15:14). The final episode, the destruction of the enemy temple, is attributed not only to the regrowth of the Nazirite Samson's hair but also—although the divine spirit is not explicitly named—to God's response to his prayer (Judg 16:28).[3]

Within this overall structure, our text presents an anomaly, the extended riddle contest in chapter 14. Extraneous to the plot, the mystery of its presence reflects the uncertainty of its meaning. Scholarly consensus seems to be settling on the term "wisdom" to characterize the episode. Marc Zvi Brettler, for example, speaks of chapters 14–15 as having "very close affinities to wisdom material and themes."[4] A central element of this argument is the wedding banquet's focus on riddles.[5] What is going on here? How do Samson's riddles have anything to do with the plot or the wisdom enterprise?[6]

---

[2]As noted above by Naphtali Tur-Sinai, ". . . a divinity can be conjectured only on the grounds of certain signs" ("The Riddle in the Bible," *HUCA* 1 [1924], 141).

[3]Thus, O'Connell (*The Rhetoric of the Book of Judges*, 296n112): "Inasmuch as Samson was more often spirit-filled than any judge, . . . it is noteworthy that . . . Samson is never explicitly said to be spirit-filled after YHWH's departure (Judg 16:20)—though one might infer that he was so empowered for his final feat of slaughter."

[4]Marc Zvi Brettler, *The Book of Judges* (New York: Routledge, 2002), 50.

[5]Eight of the seventeen occurrences of *khidah* (*hidah*) or riddle in the Hebrew Bible are to be found in this chapter.

[6]For an interesting attempt to read the entire Samson story as a riddle, see Edward L. Greenstein, "The Riddle of Samson," *Prooftexts* 1 (1981): 237–60. For the relationships between riddles and other literary genres of great interest to wisdom writers, see Hans-Peter Müller, "Der Begriff Rätsel im Alten Testament," *VT* 20 (1970): 465–89.

The social setting of the seven-day wedding celebration may indeed have a wisdom setting. *Mishteh* (Judg 14:10), a "banquet" or perhaps "symposium," refers not only to drinking but, at least here, to discourse.[7] A social setting for wisdom discourse is also evident in a number of biblical contexts, for example in Qohelet's public teaching through proverbs (Qoh 12:9–11), or in the town-hall style debate over the meaning of the proverb about "Saul among the Prophets" to be discussed below.[8] Moreover, just as the Queen of Sheba's visit focuses explicitly on solving riddles as tests of Solomon's wisdom, here too the interest is heightened by Samson's wager or riddle contest. It is not peripheral to such events that the Philistines respond to Samson's riddle with one of their own. When Samson responds with yet another it becomes a true conversation in riddles, as Alberto Soggin excellently notes.[9] To fully understand what is going on, therefore, all three stages of the conversation have to be studied in their development. Only then can we see how this wisdom conversation is in reality also a *battle* of wits, and one that conceals (as it reveals) the underlying battle of peoples and cultures.[10]

Samson's *Yeridah*

The story is one of liberation: intended by God, from Philistine dominion, and through the hand of the Judge/Savior Samson. The theological aside of Judg 14:4 sets the scene:

---

[7]"Symposium" is J. Alberto Soggin's suggestion (*Judges: A Commentary* [trans. John Bowden; OTL; Philadelphia: Westminster, 1981], 241). For the importance of such festivals of wisdom in the Middle Ages and perhaps much earlier, see T. A. Perry, *Wisdom Literature and the Structure of Proverbs* (University Park: Pennsylvania State University Press, 1993), 83–92.

[8]See chapter 5, "Saul Among the Prophets."

[9]Soggin, *Judges*, 242.

[10]Azzan Yadin ("Samson's *hidah*," *VT* 52 [2002]: 407–26) suggests an antithesis between expressing "all that was in her heart," referring to the Queen of Sheba (1 Kgs 10:3), and a formulaic exchange of riddles such as we have here. I suggest that such a formal exchange is precisely how deep secrets are both concealed, discussed, and contested. Schipper ("Narrative Obscurity," 345) refers to the "political power dynamics in this story." Steven Weitzman ("The Samson Story as Border Fiction," *BibInt* 10 [2002]: 166) also sees the riddle episode as "perceived by the narrative's author as the turning point in Israel's relation to the Philistines."

The Philistines dominated Israel at that time.

And, as according to the rabbinic adage, God prepares the cure while sending the pain:[11]

> The lad [Samson] will be God's Nazirite from the womb. And he will begin to liberate Israel from the power of the Philistines. (Judg 13:5)

How this salvation is to take place begins curiously, however, even mysteriously: the announced savior has decided—against all common sense and his parents' express wishes—to intermarry, and this with the enemy:

> Now *Samson went down* to Timnah. At Timnah he noticed a certain woman from among the daughters of the Philistines, and she was the right one in his eyes. (Judg 14:1)

Since our hero is journeying away from the Israelite domain, the vocabulary of *yeridah*,[12] "going down," is precise and appropriate (also Judg 14:5; 16:30). The verb hints at a broader argument, however, especially in its placement at the start, since it evokes the earlier incident of Judah's separation from his people:

> Now *Judah went down* from his brothers and camped near a certain Adullamite whose name was Hirah. There Judah saw the daughter of a certain Canaanite whose name was Shua, and he married and cohabited with her. (Gen 38:1–2)

In both cases a midrashic comment seems appropriate: just as Judah "went down" in his brothers' esteem,[13] so too Samson in his

---

[11]See Gen 46:28, where Jacob sends his son Judah ahead to prepare the way. According to rabbinic *drash,* his goal was to set up houses of study in order to prepare, ideologically and spiritually, for the burdens of the enslavement. See Rashi on 46:28 in *Torat Hayyim* 2, 235; also *Midr. Bereshit Rabbah* 95:3.

[12]There is a possible paronomasia or word-play on *yarad:* a) to go down (*yarad,* Judg 14:1); b) to scrape up or squeeze out the honey (*radah,* 14:9). Add to these the echo of *radad,* to conquer (in the *pi'el,* Judg 5:13, twice). These chronicle the progression of how the lowly become high, as it were: Samson's going down leads to squeezing or scraping the honey of victory. At the end, the "going down" of the family to bring him back up for burial (Judg 16:31) actually represents a glorification and reversal of his initial decline. For further examples, see Stanislav Segert, "Paronomasia in the Samson Narrative in Judges XIII–XVI," *VT* 34 (1984): 454–61.

[13]See above, chapter 1, "Judah's Sin and Levirate Marriage"; also Rashi ad loc. One aspect of Samson's "going down" has received much comment, his pu-

parents' eyes. Further, and irrespective of whether a literary influence was intended or not, both intonations of "going down" signal plots of reversal, ones in which the preparation for the salvific change of fortunes must begin with further alienations, these motivated by the hero's own unwelcome sexuality. We shall have more to say about this biblical trope of reversal later. For the moment, let us simply note that God does indeed act in strange ways!

Fantastical Events: Educating a Judge

A crucial issue of interpretation is the level of Samson's awareness of his divinely appointed political/military mission, of the stock-in-trade image of him as a model of Jewish resistance and power. At one extreme, the rabbis (*b. Sotah* 9a) see him as (almost) totally righteous from the womb, not only as a Nazirite but also as a Savior. In this view, Samson's plan is conscious and deliberate: in sync with Judg 14:4, the designated savior is to seek out a pretext for starting up with the oppressive Philistines. At the other extreme, Azzan Yadin presents the portrait of an almost collaborator:[14]

> Samson is not anti-Philistine from the outset. Quite the opposite, he is very much at home with the Philistines, is to be married to a Philistine woman according to Philistine custom, and his challenge to the Philistine wedding-guests is based on his own profound knowledge of Philistine cultural practices and literary (whether oral or written) traditions.

Yadin's focus here is on the wedding scene of chapter 14, which is centered on the famous *hidah,* "riddle":

> The *hidah* narrative bespeaks cultural coexistence, rather than political strife. In his interraction with the Philistines Samson is not a congenital enemy but . . . a betrayed lover.

What both views have in common is the theory that Samson undergoes no evolution as a character but rather stays within the

---

tative relaxation of his Nazirite vow of purity. See the discussion in O'Connell, *The Rhetoric of the Book of Judges,* 225.

[14]Yadin, "Samson's *hidah,*" 426.

boundaries given at the start. For the rabbis our hero's sexual escapades with the enemy are actually inspired by God and thus hardly reprehensible, except to the slight degree that Samson allows himself to be motivated by lust rather than grander design. For Yadin, Samson was—at the start of his public career, and quite possibly beyond it—a cultural Philistine. We should not jump to the conclusion of ongoing cultural collusion, however, noting that Samson's death also projects the image of betrayed love. For, as the story progresses, his parents' epithet of "uncircumcised" Philistines (Judg 14:3) also becomes his own (Judg 15:18). It is the riddle scene that encodes the evolution in his character and awareness of destiny, from that of an ill-fated lover to that of Judge and Savior. Thus Yadin's valuable perception is half right: "The cultural context of Judges xiv is Philistine, not Judean, and the *hidah* narrative is best understood in the context of Philistine culture."[15] Although the Philistines are indeed bound by their cultural perspectives, I shall propose that Samson's riddle performance sets him in opposition, not collusion, with them.

The narrative space between Samson's birth and adolescence is bridged by the single notation:

> The spirit of the Lord began to move him. (Judg 13:25)

We do not know whether this occurred through feats of strength, as later on, or simply through a growing spiritual awareness, as the outward signs of his Nazirite practices might suggest to others. The very first scene in his active life portrays his desire to marry. It is seldom reflected upon but crucial to notice that Samson, accompanied by his parents, made not one but *two* separate trips to Timnah for that purpose. On each occasion his arrival is delayed by a solitary event that occurs in the vineyards just outside the Philistine city. Solitary both because his parents are conveniently not present and because they are not later told what happened. During the first visit he slays a lion; during the second, he revisits the carcass and discovers bees making honey there. Yadin's description is crucial:[16]

15Ibid., 415.
16Ibid., 408.

The narrative does not inform us that Samson saw a lion, but that he slew one barehanded; not that he ate honey, but that he ate honey that was wondrously produced within a rotten carcass.

The two incidents are typically not seen as different, perhaps because they both deal with the same lion. James L. Crenshaw offers that the first incident "has no deeper meaning than that provided in Samson's later riddle," but this is saying much more than the critic projects.[17] For the victory over the lion forecasts Samson's militancy and thus may also reveal to our hero something about himself.

Building upon this discovery of truly wondrous strength, the second incident is ushered in by a significant turn of phrase:

> After a time he returned to take her, and he *turned aside to see* the carcass of the lion. And, *behold,* there was a swarm of bees and honey in the carcass of the lion. (Judg 14:8)

The same expression occurs at a critical point in Moses's life:

> He looked and, *behold,* the bush burned with fire, but the bush was not consumed. And Moses said: "I will now *turn aside to see* this great sight, why the bush is not burned." (Exod 3:2–3)

Are these "sights" also revelatory events? In both cases they certainly awaken curiosity and even astonishment ("behold!"), due to their fantastical nature.[18] Whether intended or no, the parallels point to pivotal moments in both lives, marking the emergence from private concerns to public awareness and eventually service.[19] For this is what Samson discovered in these successive incidents: in the first, a more-than-natural or indeed wondrous

---

[17]James L. Crenshaw, *Samson: A Secret Betrayed, A Vow Ignored* (Atlanta: John Knox, 1978), 84. Crenshaw also sees the need to "explain Samson's ability to overcome a lion sent by God, which would take some doing." Well, not really, if that lion was sent with the purpose of being overcome by Samson. A parallel would be the prodigious *kikayon,* sent to provide Jonah with shade but also soon to be destroyed by a worm, also sent by God (Jon 4:6).

[18]For a discussion of the concept of the fantastical, see T. A. Perry, *The Honeymoon Is Over—Jonah's Argument with God* (Peabody, Mass.: Hendrickson, 2006), 183–200. See also below, "Solving Riddles," and chapter 9, "Twilight Concepts."

[19]The verb *sur* is used to mark a turning point in one's behavior and awareness, as in Ps 34:15; 37:27: "*Turn* from evil and do good."

strength that is stronger than even the strongest of beasts; in the second, the sign[20] of yet another paradox, that from the putrefying carcass of a life-threatening enemy, life and sweetness can spring. It now remains to be seen how these disclosures—were they natural or from God?—are perceived and acted upon. The clues are in the riddles, which are mysterious by nature but lead Samson to reflect upon what may well be the Hebrew Bible's ultimate paradox.

The Riddles

Riddle 1: The Case of the Impossible Riddle

Let us briefly recap the basic data. Our hero, alone in the woods and on his way to conclude a marriage with a Philistine woman, tears apart a lion as a lion would tear apart a kid (Judg 14:6). Returning to his intended bride at a later date, he pauses to notice that bees have made honey in the lion's carcass. At the wedding banquet he coins the following riddle, which the Philistines in attendance accept the challenge to solve:

> From the eater came something to eat;
> from ʿaz ("strong/sour") came something sweet. (Judg 14:14)

Of course, since they were not present at the original event, the challengers cannot possibly come up with the answer, if that indeed exhausts the meaning of Samson's challenge. Soggin has therefore seen Samson's riddle as exemplifying an ancient literary genre, the case of the impossible riddle.[21] This is certainly true at the superficial level of knowing the empirical facts of the case, the identity of "strong" as referring to the lion slain by our hero, and "sweet" as referring to the honey of the bees that took up residence in the carcass. Since Samson was quite alone at that time and, as the text painstakingly points out, was careful not to men-

---

[20]Robert G. Boling (*Judges: Introduction, Translation, and Commentary* [AB 6A; Garden City, N.Y.: Doubleday, 1975], 230) asks whether the honey did not function for Samson as a kind of sign. See below for discussion of the nature of such revelations.

[21]Soggin, *Judges*, 243.

tion it to anyone, then at this level the riddle was really unsolvable and its author guilty of patent cheating.

Some attenuation can of course be offered for Samson's unfair contest. Yehudah Elizur makes the interesting suggestion, through a sensitive reading of vv. 11, 14, that the wedding party could easily have known the answer in all its particulars if they had observed the normal niceties of going out to greet Samson upon his arrival and thus seen the dead lion, carefully located within the precincts of Timnah itself (Judg 14:5).[22] Samson's "impossible" riddle thus seems an appropriate response to their contemptuous neglect. One might also project that Samson was already acting as God's delegate, and thus "in" on the trick on some level, and seeking not only revenge but also a pretext to initiate a war of redemption. At the very least, the riddle acted as a test, revealing both his wife's betrayal and Philistine treachery.

The reader does not know exactly what Samson revealed to his wife, this in contrast to his full disclosure to Delilah in a parallel situation (Judg 16:17–18). Did he tell her only the answers that are repeated back to him and that win the prize; or did he also include the entire personal narrative of both his encounters in the orchards of Timnah? Or, beyond that, did he also "interpret" the riddle for them as well? Since the Philistines' "solution" to the riddle—what wins them the prize of clothing—makes reference to a concrete situation, they must know of at least the second episode, the honey in the lion's carcass. There is nothing in their answer, however, that suggests knowledge either of the first episode (Samson's killing of the lion) or of his interpretation of both episodes.[23] It is thus possible that Samson told his wife only of the second episode but interpreted nothing, providing a bare minimum of information: honey from a lion.[24]

To assess my thesis of Samson's growing awareness of his stewardship as arising from and reflecting the lion and honey episodes,

---

[22]Yehudah Elizur, *Judges* (Hebrew; Jerusalem: Mossad Harav Kook, n.d.), 145.

[23]I disagree with Crenshaw (*Samson: A Secret Betrayed,* 66): "Since she [the Timnite] was able to tell the Philistines the *interpretation* [italics in text] of Samson's riddle, she sought and obtained more than the actual riddle."

[24]"Told" and "interpreted" are variant translations of the same verb *ngd*; see below.

I posit the following as Samson's interpretation of his situation, reflected in his first riddle. Samson's initial understanding of the first episode, following the programmatic announcement in Judg 13:5, is that he will have the power to carry out his plan.[25] In his reading of the Samson narratives, Steven Weitzman refers to "a topsy-turvy world in which eaters are eaten."[26] This suggests a different reading of the first part of Samson's riddle: "from the eater came something to eat," in which the verb is translated "becomes" rather than as "produces." The riddle reads:

> The eater became something to eat.

Here Samson is the eater of the eater, the lion who eats the lion.[27] That is to say, the one traditionally considered the eater or lion (Philistines) was itself lionized or "eaten" by a stronger lion (Samson), as portrayed by the graphic description of the first incident, the ripping apart of the animal. Note that this aspect is rendered by the first half of the riddle only.

The second episode—represented by the second half of the riddle—is distinct but of a piece with the first, just as the two pieces of the riddle are performed together. It projects that our hero's god-given ⁽az will produce the sweetness of victory and liberation, which will be shared with his people.[28] When the carcass is revisited sweetness is introduced, but as something produced rather than resulting from a transformation, thus remaining within the bounds of traditional readings:

> From ⁽az came something sweet. (Judg 14:14)

This literary figure is called *antanaclasis*, the use of the same word in close proximity to bear different and often contradictory

---

[25]The feeling of powerlessness at the start of a prophetic career is a familiar *topos*, modeled by Moses's hesitations in Exod 3:11–4:17.

[26]Weitzman, *The Samson Story as Border Fiction*, 170.

[27]Martin Emmrich adduces important parallels making the point that the killing of the lion is a "symbolic prelude to Samson's confrontation with the Philistines" ("The Symbolism of the Lion and the Bees: Another Ironic Twist in the Samson Cycle," *JETS* 44 [2001]: 71, 73).

[28]"God will give ⁽oz [strength] to His people" (Ps 29:11). This is the only plausible explanation of the detail of his sharing the (impure) honey with his parents. Did the detail of the honey as arising from the *dead* lion also give him a premonition of his demise, where the honey of victory comes out of his own carcass?

meanings. Thus, *yatsaʾ* means "become" in the first stich and "be produced" in the second. The effect here is to stress that each stich refers to a distinct episode. In the Philistine retort, this distinction is collapsed and *yatsaʾ* is assumed to have the same meaning in both instances.

What is the harshness that will turn to sweetness? Israel's enslavement to the Philistines. Samson, the figure for Israel, will slay the lion and the former eater will become Israel's food. That is to say, from Philistine strength comes the sweetness of liberation. Samson is the lion killer, thus the lion of the lion. And as the lion who killed the strength (Philistines), Samson is therefore entitled to eat their honey, referring either to their woman or their spoils. Samson may indeed be referring to both, but the Philistines hear only the first.

Riddle 2: Getting the Right Answer Wrong

The Philistine respondents obviously subscribe to Joseph's rule of dream exegesis, according to which 2 = 1 (Gen 41:31).[29] Thus the two parts or visions of Samson's riddle are conflated, since in their reply both "stronger" and "sweeter" refer to the second stich and no mention is made of eater/eating.

What is sweeter than honey;
what is stronger than a lion?

Contrary to Samson's opening riddle, the Philistines' rebuttal basks in the obvious, as its platitudinous style makes clear: "Sweeter than honey?" "Stronger than a lion?" Ho-hum! If the Philistine response is a riddle, it is so in a different sense. While Samson's was in reality a question that required research, the Philistine answer is actually an observation disguised as a question.[30] Their riddle is a false one in the sense that it is a question already answered. The Philistine response is also a stylistic masterpiece, of course. In keeping with its purpose as a response to a

---

[29]See above, chapter 2, "Dreams of Power, Power of Dreams."

[30]The Philistine response could have been more direct and avoided the question form entirely, something like:

There is no eater like the lion;
there is nothing sweeter than honey.

riddle, the Philistines' solution retains both an identical poetical form and, through its double question, offers the possibility of ambiguity from which an opponent may try to squirm loose. Yet the questions are in reality assertions of triumphant certitude. In fact, the doubling of a question that is not really a question further exploits the platitudes to positive advantage, as if to say: "It is all so obvious, anyone could have figured that one out!"

The Philistine interpretation retains the accepted identity of the lion. Referring to their military might and domination:

> Who is stronger than a lion, who is stronger than we are?

Further, just as Samson is aware, on his way to join with his spouse, that a lion can also yield honey,[31] the Philistines want to stress that they can produce a lovely wife for him. Note that, like Samson's, their riddle also has two parts, and the order is important.

> a) "Although we are the lion conquerors, you are yet allowed to 'eat of our honey': we are allowing this marriage."
>
> b) "We are still the stronger: Look out, buster!"

From their perspective as conquerors and from the immediate marriage context, the Philistines have thus produced "answers" (honey, lion) that also encode both an agreement and a warning. But in so doing they have missed both Samson's personal involvement in the slaying and the paradoxical interpretation (see below) that spells their demise.

Riddle 3: Plowing the Field

On the surface, Samson's retort addresses only the issue of Philistine cheating or misappropriation:

> If you had not "plowed with my heifer,"
> you would not have found out my riddle. (Judg 14:18)

Thus, Crenshaw, excellently (*Samson: A Secret Betrayed*, 113): "The Philistines' answer in question form functions rhetorically like a statement, while at the same time posing a further riddle." That is to say, the provocation of the question form allows the formal proceedings of a contest in riddles to continue.

[31]For the sexual references, see Crenshaw (*Samson: A Secret Betrayed*, 114). Crenshaw applies these metaphors to the first riddle; in fact, they are more appropriate to the second.

The virtual consensus, according to which "to plow" has sexual overtones, makes no contextual sense at all. It is admitted that "to plow a field" is widely attested as a sexual metaphor,[32] but here the wife is not a field being "plowed" but rather the heifer that is doing the plowing! Is Samson thus suggesting that the Philistines had sex with her?! And, if that were indeed the case, how does one explain his desire to take her back?[33] Samson's ensuing rampage is surely provoked by her loss. In Samson's language of accusation "to plow" (*kharash*) is echoed in the plotting (Judg 16:2). A wordplay in English may make the point, that the wife has been subjugated, she has been put under the yoke and forced to do the Philistines' work. That the wife has been forced into conspiracy is beyond doubt, but there is no hint whatever that this involved sexual appropriation as well. The issue is one of coercion.[34]

The importance of this riddle/saying is that it registers Samson's response to the second purpose of his riddle contest: a test of loyalties. For while they may have saved themselves some money, the Philistines also revealed both the woman's treachery and their own. Samson now knows two important things: that his wife has betrayed him, and that her loyalty to the Philistines is stronger than to her husband. While testing his wife's loyalty, Samson also learns just how the Philistines interpreted the puzzle of the episodes and thus whether he needs a pretext to start up with them.

Paradoxes of Liberation

One must question the usual view that Samson was guilty of cheating because his riddle was *unsolvable*.[35] The truth is that the Philistines could have come up with the answer by themselves—

---

[32]See Carole R. Fontaine, *Traditional Sayings in the Old Testament* (Sheffield: Almond, 1982), 239.

[33]Admittedly, the Levite does precisely that, he take back his concubine of Gibeᶜah (Judg 19:1–3).

[34]Again, Elizur, *Judges,* ad loc.: "This is like a crook who, instead of himself laboring and plowing, steals his neighbor's ox. And not only that: he takes a tender heifer that its masters raise tenderly and kills it through this stolen ploughing." This explanation has verisimilitude in that the Philistines show no interest elsewhere in sexual encounters but a great deal in money (14:15).

[35]Weitzman, *The Samson Story as Border Fiction,* 165n19.

and in fact most likely did—by noticing that the riddle provided
two clues for each of its components:

> an eatable that is sweet;
> an eater that is strong.

Simply looking for the extreme example in each category would
have produced the right answers of identification. But the Philistines also needed an explanation of the paradoxical relations of
causality. They needed to understand how sour can produce
sweet and an eater can produce edibles. Here the wife wheedled
the minimum necessary to win the prize; she told them the episode of the carcass producing honey. Here, to review, is my proposed reconstruction of her report to the Philistines:

> On his way to the banquet Samson noticed that honey-producing
> bees had nested in the carcass of a lion. Here then is the answer that
> will win the prize: *honey from a lion.*

In so doing she delivered to them a life *context* which, however
far-fetched, presented the paradox as possible.

A context is not an explanation, however, and certainly not an
interpretation of ambiguous signs. For Samson's riddle has a
deeper mystery, ideological rather than merely factual or contextual. Samson's riddle is a tough one because it presents paradoxical situations, ones that reverse such natural assumptions as the
following:[36]

> A generation is born, only to die.
> The sun rises, only to set. (Qoh 1:4–5)

> [There may be] a time to be born, but also a time to die.
> A time to plant, but also a time to uproot. . . .
> A time to embrace, but also a time to separate. . . .
> A time to love, but also a time to hate. (Qoh 3:2, 5b, 8a)

> We get good from God, but also bad. (Job 1:10)

---

[36]For the pessimistic interpretations of these sayings see T. A. Perry, *Dialogues with Kohelet* (University Park: Pennsylvania State University Press, 1994),
16–21.

It is the order of the elements of these sayings that seems natural from the Philistine perspective. In the dread of darkness will light ever return; in despair, can we imagine a way out? There is a natural inevitability that light will wane and vanish, that youth will yield to old age and life to death. Human existence is one of decline, from plus to minus, ineluctably.

Such natural wisdom imposes its perspectives, according to which, returning to our riddle:

> *Food produces eaters,* food is fated to be eaten (eaters do not produce food, producers do);

> *sweet things inevitably turn sour*

To project the reverse is to contradict common sense and experience, thus not even imaginable to the Philistines.

What the Philistine riddle solvers failed to imagine is the response of biblical wisdom, which loves paradoxes that precisely contradict normal assumptions and the general perspectives to which they lead. Thus, returning to Qohelet, this time in an upbeat wisdom mode:

> [There is] a time to kill but also to heal;
> A time to wreck but also to build;
> To weep but also to laugh; . . .
> To make war but also to make peace. (Qoh 3:3–4a, 8b)[37]

At a theological level such contradictions become almost outrageously paradoxical. Hannah's prayer is a good example, for can one kill before giving life? Yet, the prophet asserts:

> The Lord [first] kills and [then] brings to life;
> He [first] brings down to She'ol and [then] raises up.
> The Lord makes poor and makes rich.
> He brings low and also exalts. (1 Sam 2:6–7)

I think that strong readings are intended here, accentuating the progress from minus to plus.[38] Thus, not only "although you are poor the Lord can also make you rich," but also "the Lord makes poor *before* making rich." And when Hannah also takes note of

---

[37]See the discussion in Perry, *Dialogues with Kohelet,* 14–21, for Qohelet's balanced presentation of both sides, the natural way versus the wisdom or biblical way.

[38]However, this is not always the case; see Deut 32:39.

the reverse process, where the sated are now hungry and the mighty enfeebled (1 Sam 2:4–5), it is clearly indicated that these are no normal happenings, but are of the Lord and wisdom driven because, again, they reverse normal expectations.

Through such a wisdom prism Samson's riddle in Judg 14 is of a piece with his initial "going-down," is but a restatement of one of the deepest mysteries of Jewish history and paradoxical divine activity of reversal in the world:

> how Judah's going down (Gen 38) will be reversed;

> how Joseph's and then Israel's going down to Egypt will be reversed.[39]

From this perspective, the *natural* way of looking at things would have the paradigm of plus to minus:

> and it was day (+) and it was night (-)

Whereas the opposite, Genesis paradigm, of light from darkness and void and confusion, is a leap of faith:

> and it was evening and it was morning, the same day.

The components are the same but the direction of "normal" decline is reversed. We are tempted to suggest that, at its very inception, our Bible opens with a wisdom paradox![40]

In attempting to locate Samson's heroic exploits in an appropriate literary genre, Crenshaw has proposed the saga, which "stretches facticity to the breaking point. Saga abounds in exaggerated feats; it tends toward hyperbole, and treats the fantastic as if it were ordinary."[41] While this label may indeed characterize Samson's Paul Bunyan-like strength, it cannot accommodate other unnatural happenings such as the honey-from-the-lion event, and a broader concept is needed to describe the transitional space between the natural and the miraculous. I would say that, indeed,

---

[39]Gen 50:20; 54:5; see Gerhard von Rad, *Wisdom in Israel* (London: SCM, 1972), 200.

[40]Tur-Sinai's formulation, if applicable, is perhaps even more provocative: "day and night are the messengers which bear the word of God throughout eternity" ("The Riddle in the Bible," 148). I take this to mean that night and day, in their paradoxical combination, function as the *signs* of divinity.

[41]Crenshaw, *Samson: A Secret Betrayed,* 19.

the saga concept as presented by Crenshaw represents only the Philistine perspective in that it pulls too strongly towards facticity, viewing the miraculous as merely the extreme point of the ordinary and the ordinary as merely hyperbolic. Thus, to return to a previous example, Moses's vision at the burning bush would, from such a perspective, be translated as a "great" (*gadol*) sight appropriate to a saga, but by that same token in denial of its revelatory potential as a *wondrous* one.

In order to recover Samson's and the narrator's perspective, a different concept is needed, one that remains faithful to the particular kind of revelation that Samson is possibly undergoing. "Possibly" is the key here, for, like the reader, Samson's experiences in the orchards of Timnah occupy the twilight zone. Possibly natural, possibly miraculous: who knows where they come from or what they mean? Had he seen a fleece covered with dew, or the reverse, as requested by Gideon, his doubt would be resolved: they would constitute a *sign* sent by God. His lion and honey-bees are as perfectly natural as Gideon's fleece and dew, but were they sent to Samson by request? The text does not record that they were, but why then did he return the second time to the orchards? This sequence suggests the progressive nature of his awareness of an involvement in what our narrative projects as God's plan for Israel's liberation from Philistine domination.

Samson's riddle is insoluble less because the Philistines lack empirical information than because they have blind spots, being unable to think "out of the circle" of the "facts" of daily existence. Thus, Samson's private experiences with the lion and the honey remain extraneous to the plot, hidden not only from his parents but from his Timnite wife and the Philistine riddle-solvers as well. But they are crucial as wondrous signs that awaken Samson's awareness as a savior. What the Philistines also cannot imagine is that Samson may have plans beyond his imminent marriage, desires beyond his lust, needs to satisfy his parents and his people that lie beyond appearances to the contrary. Are these plans, desires, and needs compatible? Not for the Philistines, because they are insensitive to the national question, as their response-riddle reveals. Since they cannot think outside the present context and the status quo, their answer to the question "What is stronger than a lion (of Philistia)?" can only be "Nothing!" To the question

"What is sweeter than love/sex/marriage?" their only possible reply is again "Nothing!," since sweetness could only signify the marital pleasures granted by the Philistines. The twilight zone thus reveals the possibility of a point beyond the fixities of past ideologies and the certitudes of power.

Modes of Verbal Warfare: Debates in Proverbs, Oracular Ambiguity

The riddle scene involves an exchange of obscure sayings that seem to point to a conversation but which in fact reveal a debate and, beyond that, a full-blown battle. How this can happen through a genteel exchange of witticisms and riddle parlor games is very much the question. Our story is launched and entirely centered "at the time when the Philistines were ruling [*moshelim*] over Israel" (Judg 14:4). Noticing the frequent pairing of riddle (*hidah*) and literary comparison (*mashal*) in the Hebrew Bible, Jeremy Schipper wonders whether the remark that "the Philistines were ruling over them [*moshelim*] at that time" may not also suggest that "the Philistines were speaking in proverbs with Israel."[42] That is certainly the case at the wedding banquet, in the only verbal performance of the riddles in the Samson narratives. This is made especially evident by the double use of comparisons in the riddles, the basic meaning of *mashal*.

We have already learned that the verb *mashal* is ambivalent from the Joseph narrative, where "telling proverbs about someone" extends in a provocative way Joseph's habit of tattle-taling against his brothers. In the Joseph narrative the ambivalence stresses the rapprochement between the two activities, so that making up proverbs is seen as but an alternate form of political and/or military aggression. Schipper, while noting the possible ambivalence here, correctly refers "rule" to the "political power dynamics" underlying our story; but he sidesteps the aggressiveness of the verbal contest of "speaking in proverbs," suggesting instead a deliberate authorial ambiguity that points to the theme of the secrecy of riddles.[43] He thus prefers an ambiguity (either/or)

---

[42]Schipper, "Narrative Obscurity," 345.
[43]See above, chapter 2, "Dreams of Power, Power of Dreams."

to an ambivalence (both/and) where each term reinforces the other, thus not merely proverbs but rather aggressive ones.

These biblical situations become plausible through the findings of proverb research. We have transcriptions of card games played by women of Sephardic origin in which a full thirty percent of the discourse consists of proverb quotation, the favored incarnation of traditional wisdom. Closer to biblical situations, studies of African law cases reveal the technique of citing proverbs in an effort to defeat an opponent: each proverb provokes a proverb response from one's rival, until someone cannot find an aphoristic reply and the other party is declared the victor.[44] In a related mode, Rabelais (1494–1553; *Pantagruel,* ch. 19) narrates a "debate in signs" very much akin to the debate in proverb genre, where gestures/signs have all the opacity of riddles. Thus, to reply by quoting a relevant proverbial saying is equivalent to making an appropriate gesture, one that can cause an opponent to sweat and concede defeat. In the case of gestures, the difficulty arises from the fact that each contestant uses different cultural codes, which are opaque to the other contestant.

While skill in proverb citation thus becomes a valuable skill in verbal warfare, it is important to note its peaceful potential as well. Words are still not full-blown weapons and a courtroom is not yet a battlefield. Proper debate can thus defuse as well as further conflict, leading to solutions of accommodation.[45] That it was Samson who initially proposed the debate may thus speak to his role in accommodating his opponents (see conclusion below).

The expression "debate in proverbs" captures the latent aggression of the riddle, except that in a debate the terms are understood and winning the contest is paramount. This adequately describes the Philistine purpose, but Samson's case has another element, for his need is to uncover what the Philistines are thinking as they develop their understanding of the wider situation.[46]

---

[44]See Perry, *Wisdom Literature,* 196–97.

[45]Ibid.

[46]One thinks of Gideon's interest in overhearing his enemies talk of their dreams and their interpretations thereof as a key to assessing his chances of victory (Judg 7:15). Or of the Israelites' regard for Rahab's account of how her fellow citizens evaluate their potential invaders (Josh 2:9–11).

Here debate yields to a more powerful weapon still, oracular ambiguity, the art of putting forth Rorschach-like puzzles that provoke a response.

Different levels of "understanding" a riddle are rendered, in
our text, through the ambivalence of *ngd*. In interpreting the
riddles I posit a principle also operative in cases of oracular ambiguity, that people "read" things in terms of their own preoccupations, weaknesses, and ideologies. Here are the possibilities of *ngd*:

a) he did not *tell* or *report* to his parents what happened (Judg 14: 6, 9);

b) if you can *interpret* the riddle to me (vv. 12, 13);

c) ambiguous (vv. 14, 15, 16, 17).

When Samson addresses the Philistines, therefore, his question is
ambivalent in the grand style of oracles, having the sharpness of a
two-edged sword:

a) are you going to *tell* or *report* what you heard/extracted from my
wife? or

b) are you going to *interpret*, thinking out the solution for yourselves?

The Philistines thus have a *real* choice: no longer whether they
can steal the right piece of information, but rather which method
of solving the riddle they will choose: reporting or interpreting.

The contestants thus approach riddles from their own ideological perspectives, with thoughts that arise from their own ways
of life. While the focus is on life-context and ideology, however,
the real interest is in personal weakness. Like oracles, riddles turn
on ambiguity. They are allied to polemic and contest because
their interpreters are blinded and see only portions of the total
possible meanings, usually those that are in sync with their own
preoccupations and points of view. Thus, their answer to their
own question is itself a disclosure: as in the interpretation of
oracles, it is the questioner who is deceived. The consultation is
thus a test, not of the oracle, as thought by the consultant, but
rather of himself. Moreover, oracular consultation typically arises
in situations of life-threatening antagonism: Who will win the
upcoming battle? Will my brother try to kill me?[47] The Philistines

---

[47]See Perry, "Cain's Sin," 259–76.

cannot solve the riddle because, living by power, they understand only power, their unique source of sweetness. They are materialistic because they "know" that it is food that produces eaters,[48] rather than the reverse. As rulers (lions), they cannot imagine anything stronger than themselves.

*Mashal*s, Measure for Measure

Yadin has argued to remove the distinction between the riddle (*hidah*) and other types of wisdom "sayings," suggesting that riddles, like sayings/proverbs, rest ultimately on comparisons. We have assumed that equivalence in our remarks above.[49] Perhaps two general applications of the equivalence are now in order.

The Samson narrative can be read as a classic case of the interaction between aphorism (or riddle-*mashal*) and (hi)story. However, whereas the Saul story is a proverb in search of a narrative (as we shall see in the next chapter), here the situation is reversed. Samson is on his way to intermarry when the sign, the *mashal* situation that inspires the riddle, falls upon him like a lion, affording the possibility that his personal narrative now has a different and broader sense.

Secondly, there have been attempts, unverifiable but exciting, to see such comparisons as emblematic of broader situations. Thus, Brettler projects that the dismembered concubine of Gibeʿah (Judg 19–21) may express the dismemberment of pre-monarchical society.[50] Or, the horror of a split-baby (see below) may express Solomon's horror of a split kingdom. In our text a lion is slain, its carcass is not eaten but yields honey which feeds the killer and his parents. Is this not an inducement for *darsheni*, "midrashic interpretation" on a grand scale?

---

[48]As the sage ironically observes: "When goods increase, so too do their eaters" (Qoh 5:10).

[49]Menahem Ha-Meiri (1249–ca. 1310) stressed their similarity by the single concept of riddle-comparison (*mashal ha-hidah*), in *Perush ʿal Sefer Mishlei* [Commentary on the Book of Proverbs] (ed. Menachem Mendel Zahav; Jerusalem: Otsar ha-Poskim, 1969), 7.

[50]Brettler, *The Book of Judges*, 91.

Many have portrayed Samson as a provocateur, as on the active lookout for trouble with the Philistines in order to start a war of liberation. The opposite case is often and not unreasonably made, however, that he never acts, merely reacts, because he is vengeful rather than salvific. My final question is whether this latter reading need be viewed as negative, whether in fact his acts of aggression are to be seen as retaliatory rather than petty, even as of a piece with his amorous exploits with enemy women. The compromise position sketched above considers an evolution in Samson's character, plotting the educative steps that lead him to the position of Israelite judge and warrior.

So much for psychology and pedagogy, but there is also a principle at the base of Samson's reactions from start to finish. Robert H. O'Connell has helpfully set up the theme by showing that five of Samson's acts of aggression are retaliations against injustices.[51] Although in all cases there may indeed be a motive of revenge, Samson himself clearly propounds his operative principle:

> If this is what you have done, I will be avenged on you and then I will stop. (Judg 15:7)

To my lights, this is as good a paraphrase of the principle of Measure for Measure as can be found in the Bible.[52] In fact, this is the bedrock approach honored throughout wisdom literature and beyond; indeed, it is the usual measure through which God deals with malfeasance and has Gentile acknowledgment as well.[53] It

---

[51]O'Connell, *The Rhetoric of the Book of Judges,* 227.

[52]See O'Connell, *The Rhetoric of the Book of Judges,* 228, referring to James L. Crenshaw, "The Samson Saga: Filial Devotion or Erotic Attachment?" *ZAW* 86 (1974): 483: "So far as the plot-structure is concerned, it is the acts of injustice by the Philistines that are the main cause of the escalation of violence in the account and that justly culminate in the destruction of Gaza's temple, the Philistine rulers and their subjects."

[53]Thus, Adoni-Bezek (Judg 1:7): "Just as I have done [to others], so too has God paid me back." This example is especially appropriate, since it foreshadows Samson's principle at the very start of the book. It also serves to justify Samson as a tactician, for, spoken by the Canaanite leader, it makes clear that measure for measure is a language that the local population understands. Finally, it makes the theological point that the Israelites are seen as the instruments of God's retribution for their evil. All of these points seem to me relevant to Samson's behavior against the Philistines.

promises aggression only when provoked and, when this occurs, a limited reaction of redress. And although O'Connell does not consider Samson a deliverer, I would argue for the concept of passive deliverance, which still requires both the courage and the sense of *measured* retaliation.[54]

Samson is a realist in the sense that violence can sometimes be countered only by violence. But if he is a hero, he is also a loner, at odds with existing Israelite ambitions or lack thereof (in fact he is turned over to the enemy by Judah). And if the Philistines are not exactly good bedfellows, think about Samson's own tribe of Dan (Judg 18:27), migrating north and decimating an entire peaceful settlement. Think about Benjamin and the concubine of Gibeᶜah. Samson is an early model of peaceful coexistence, a model judge rather than a savior, midway between the massive conquests of extermination envisioned by Joshua, at one extreme, and Saul's failed attempt to be rid of the really dangerous enemy (Amalekites), at the other. Thus, he pursues not full-scale annihilation of peoples but rather coexistence, with a promise to retaliate only if the other side starts up.[55] Close to my idea is Weitzman's sociological model based on the erasure of distinctions typically made in the natural world:[56]

> The category confusion generated by Samson's behavior is mirrored by the riddle which collapses the distinct categories of nature, the eater and the eaten, the strong and the sweet, just as border-crossing collapses the boundary between Israelite and Philistine.

By contrast, the theological model offered here retains rather than collapses such distinctions but reverses them through paradox. This implies that border boundaries (that is to say, ethnic and political identities) are maintained but become permeable, no longer defined unilaterally by the side in power. They are thus always open to renegotiation and regulated by the pay-as-you-go principle of measure for measure.

---

[54]O'Connell, *The Rhetoric of the Book of Judges*, 214.

[55]The problem becomes that every act of retaliation is then seen by the other side as a fresh provocation.

[56]Weitzman, *The Samson Story as Border Fiction*, 170.

Consonant with our portrait of Samson is Francis Landy's extraordinary sketch:[57]

> Samson is a "marginal" person, caught and moving ceaselessly between two worlds, and belonging to neither. He is symbolically marked as a marginal person by his extraordinary strength, by his Nazirite status, that makes him into a wild, Dionysiac figure, a personification of intoxication who cannot drink wine, and by the social vacuum that surrounds him. But he is also that which communicates between worlds, Israelite and Philistine, and is destroyed in the process.

Samson, then, is a figural project of twilight existence, caught in its paradoxical dynamics.

---

[57]Francis Landy, "Are We in the Place of Averroes? Response to the Articles of Exum and Whedbee, Buss, Gottwald, and Good," *Semeia* 32 (1984): 131–48.

FIVE

On Proverb Formation: "Is Saul Too Among the Prophets?" (1 Sam 10:11–12; 19:24)

> This is most of all the story of a man whose life was a never-ending struggle to accommodate himself to the powerful destiny imposed upon him, a destiny he was never able to realize nor, apparently, fully to understand.
>
> (David Grossman)

The Wisdom of Many

One of the many problems facing our understanding of wisdom literature is the interpretation of individual proverbs, often its favored mode of expression. Take, for example, a perennial favorite:

A rolling stone gathers no moss.

Does this proverb speak favorably of being on the move and avoiding a "mossy" condition or not? As it happens, the answer is "yes" on one side of the English Channel and "no" on the other. Separated from its life context, however, its meaning remains cloudy or even undecipherable. The problem is compounded by the circumstance of transmission, since it is the case that thousands of proverbs have survived only in collections or lists. To remedy this situation, authors have been known to contextualize their proverb sayings: either by commentary (Benjamin Franklin), in an appended tale (see the Samson discussion above), or through a literary context (Qohelet) where a symbiotic relationship connoting meaning is established or assumed between individual proverbs and the environment of the literary work in which they occur.

A related but distinct problem of interpretation is that of provenance. It has seemed to many scholars that knowing a proverb's particular origins would contribute mightily to understanding it. Archer Taylor, the dean of proverb studies, coined what has become the most popular characterization of what a proverb is:

> The wisdom of many and the wit of one.[1]

He meant that proverbial wisdom first circulated among people until someone, a sage perhaps, gave it its striking form. Through his definition, Taylor transformed problems regarded as inherent to traditional proverbs—orality and folkloric anonymity—into a theory of origins.

I have put forward a competing formula of origins, namely that proverbs, at least those originating in the wisdom tradition, are to be seen as the opposite:

> The wisdom of one and the wit of many.[2]

My proposal was buttressed by the remarkable Story of Anchos [i.e., Ibycus] the Poet, the burden of which is precisely to provide the etiology of what must have been a current proverb, something equivalent to our "a little birdie told me." The tale recounts the murder of a famous sage, whose dying words call out to passing cranes, the sole witnesses of his death: "Be the witnesses and avengers of my blood." His words are later sarcastically quoted by his murderers, overheard, and reported, leading to their prosecution. It is only then that the wisdom dimension of the original saying is perceived, as the birds are now understood to have had a higher reference: "The Avenger is in the heavens."

---

[1]Archer Taylor, *The Proverb and an Index to the Proverb* (Hatboro, Pa.: Folklore Associates, 1931), 3.

[2]See Perry, *Wisdom Literature,* 83–103.

It still seems to me that this moving tale provides a dress rehearsal of the wisdom enterprise itself, where the kernel of wisdom arises not among the people but rather from a sage, which then goes through several adjustments or interpretations until it becomes current among the folk. The interest of this wisdom tale resides not only in its providing a context—here a literary one—for its interpretation but also in its serving as a kind of theoretical account of the evolution of the proverb's meaning, its etiology and the various stages of its interpretation.

Saul Among the Prophets

We shall now examine the well-known thrice-repeated proverb in 1 Samuel, which provides a combination of both models while addressing, in its own way, the issues of provenance and contextual interpretation. Here are the texts:

a) And they came there to Gibeah and behold a string of prophets [coming] towards him. And the spirit of God came upon him and he prophesied among them.

And it was that everyone who knew him from before—when they looked and saw him prophesying with the prophets—that folks said one to another:

> "What on earth has happened to Ben Kish!?
> *Is Saul too among the prophets?*" (1 Sam 10:10–11)

b) Now a certain man from there answered and said:

> "And who is *their* father?!"
> Thus it was that it became a proverb: "*Is Saul too among the prophets?*" (1 Sam 10:12)

c) And he went there, towards Nayot in Ramah. And the spirit of God came also upon him, and he went to and fro, prophesying, until he came to Nayot in Ramah. And he too took off his clothes and he too prophesied before Samuel, and he fell down naked all that day and all night.

> Thus it was that they said: "*Is Saul too among the prophets?*"
> (1 Sam 19:23–24)

These incidents serve the purpose of documenting Saul's development and also—since proverbs can be crucial to social relations—the all important issue of his public image. There is a second purpose as well, this one even more obvious, since the episodes are cast as etiologies, whose purpose is to explain where this old proverb came from. This saying, occurring three times in 1 Samuel, is of particular interest given our study of wisdom because it offers a unique glimpse into the origins and development of a popular proverb. The repetition of the proverb should be taken as a caution against the common-sense assumption that, within the same culture, the proverb's meaning remains stable. The upshot of its repetition, by showing hesitations at its very origin, is both to refine and multiply its interpretations.

Our narrative focuses on public evaluation of Saul's behavior. Surprised at his sudden change of personality, folks who know the family ask one another what could have happened. It seems to be the case that, at this stage in his career, Saul's only identifying marker was his familial one, and to his own mind a lowly one at that:

> Am I not a Benjaminite, of the smallest of the tribes of Israel, and my family the least of all the families of the tribe of Benjamin? (1 Sam 9:21)

Saul here only duplicates the public's own wonderment.[3] Young and handsome, he does not yet have a track record, has not yet made his personal mark on the world. Could such a modest background and credentials account for his sudden and radical transformation wrought by the prophetic spirit? At this point, however, the surprise of his observers does not yield its valence to the reader. It may in fact have been positive, in accord with the opening evaluation of Kish, Saul's father, as a man of importance, an ʾish . . . khayil (1 Sam 9:1).[4]

---

[3]And he perhaps reinforces it as well, as we learn from the experience of the spies (Num 13:33): "And just as we looked like grasshoppers to ourselves, so we must have looked to them as well."

[4]Thus Walter Brueggemann (*First and Second Samuel* [Interpretation; Louisville: John Knox, 1990], 146) describes the tone of voice of the first proverb as a question "that can be asked with expectancy, suggesting this surprising king, now strongly authorized by the spirit, will go beyond himself in obedience

Upon reflection, the public's exclamatory question could not at this initial stage have been cast in the proverb's final form, since it did not yet exist as a popular saying, nor did Saul yet have a reputation. Their surprise bordering on disbelief is thus brought into focus by the question—really an exclamation—of a "certain man," making the observation that family origins are irrelevant to the prophetic career:

> And who is *their* (i.e., the prophets') father?! (1 Sam 10:12)

The first version in circulation, therefore—really a rough draft of the completed proverb product—can only have been the following:[5]

> Is Ben Kish too among the prophets?

Since the wisdom of the many turns out to be not entirely accurate, it is corrected, anonymously but undoubtedly by some kind of sage or wise person. The collaboration proves fruitful, since the proverb's final form is said to arise from this intervention, by the wit of one. "Thus it was that [ʿal ken, the classic marker of etiologies] it became a proverb," means "it was in this way that the proverb arose":

> *Is Saul* [i.e., and *not* "Ben Kish"] *too among the prophets?*

---

to Yahweh." While possible, the point is weakened by the fact that when the proverb's question is asked the first time, no one except Saul himself knows of Samuel's decision to anoint him king.

[5]Robert Alter (*The David Story* [New York: Norton, 1999], 56) suggests that the original version is a line of parallelistic verse:

> What has befallen the son of Kish?
> Is Saul, too, among the prophets?

However, by regarding "son of Kish" and "Saul" as strictly synonymous, the remark of "a certain man" is indeed obscure. What is at stake here is, far from a pretty parallelism, an opposition that sets up the fixed version of the proverb and makes sense of the man's objection. Thus, Don Isaac Abarbanel ([1437–1508]; *Commentary on the Earlier Prophets* [Jerusalem: Torah ve-Daat, 1955], 221): "Because of this man's objection they could no longer use as a proverb: 'What has befallen the son of Kish?' and there only remained the proverb: 'Is Saul too among the prophets?'" The man's point is that since prophecy is not acquired through inheritance, it is pointless to ask who Saul's father was.

This emended version now becomes the accepted one. Its contextual meaning, here but not later in a different context, stresses that Saul is stripped of his parental and family affiliations.[6]

In contrast to the sage's intervention, however, Saul's initial diffidence was not inappropriate, since it was spoken in different circumstances and concerning an entirely different issue. For when the prophet Samuel approached him, the question was not prophecy but kingship, and here Samuel suggested a different context:

> And on whom is the entire desire of Israel? Is it not entirely on you *and your father's house?* (1 Sam 9:20)

The lines are now drawn. According to the very prophet who anoints Saul to be king, family origins *do matter,* whereas for the practice of prophecy and according to a tradition guaranteed by a proverb and not contradicted in our narrative by Samuel, family origins *do not matter.* This means that, in everybody's mind, Saul can—indeed anyone can—at least theoretically enter ecstatic states and prophesy. Did this not in fact happen even to the three groups of messengers sent by Saul to Samuel to capture David (1 Sam 19:20–21)? In the matter of kingship, however, Saul seems to have sounder intuition. This could be because the entire house of Israel may in fact not find his merits sufficient, or they may ascribe his personal failures to family unworthiness—not an uncommon confusion. It is the final reading of the proverb that will have to sort this all out.

Saul's Identity Crisis and Transformation

Samuel's disclosure of Saul's accession to kingship is carefully described:

> "You will meet a band of prophets . . . and they will prophesy. And the Lord's spirit will come upon you and you will prophesy with them, and you will be turned into another man [*weneheppakhta le'ish 'akher*]. . . ." And it was so, upon turning his back to go from

---

[6]For a similar loss of patronymic see Jonah's evolution from Jonah ben Amittai (Jon 1:1) to simply Jonah in the parallel circumstance in 3:1; see the discussion in Perry, *The Honeymoon Is Over,* 42.

Samuel, that God gave him another heart [*lev ʾakher*], and all those signs came to pass on that day. (1 Sam 10:5–6, 9)

It is worth noting several details of this scene that recall the Samson story. First, there is a one-on-one prophetic disclosure that really amounts to an annunciation of the birth of a savior. Secondly, there is a confirmation by signs. In Saul's case, there is a careful series of 3+1, of three initial signs capped by a fourth that is also wondrous but more so, an invasion by the divine spirit.[7] In Samson's case the signs are also the divine spirit, in a context of the enigmatic lion and honey-making bees. Thirdly, Saul's secrecy upon receiving the news (1 Sam 10:16; cf. Judg 14:6) points to an inner transformation, of waiting and reflecting upon events. The point of such parallels is to suggest similar experiences; like Samson, Saul is about to have his life changed by the divine spirit.

The language of Saul's transformation here is twofold. The first recalls a midrashic reading of Nineveh's *repentance* that prevents their being destroyed or *overturned,* both expressed by *hpk:* "In forty days Nineveh will be overturned." And in fact they were, but by repentance rather than a Sodom-and-Gomorrah style destruction. The Ninevites repented by both penitence and deeds; or, as Malbim (1809–1879) says of Saul (on 1 Sam 10:6), he was transformed in both body and soul. Now whereas Saul's reception of another heart may reflect inner transformation only, both dimensions are indicated by his becoming an *ʾish ʾakher,* "another man."

In all other uses in Tanak, the expression *ʾish ʾakher* refers to an actual other person.[8] For example, a woman leaves her husband for "another man," who is truly another man, not the same man who, somehow, has become "another person," through repentance or name-change perhaps. But with Saul the identity issue is pushed to its limits: How do you become another and still

---

[7]For the 3+1 disclosure series of divine revelation, see below, chapter 9, "Numerical Structures." See also Perry, *The Honeymoon Is Over,* chapter 4, "Elijah's Epiphany." In this particular series in 1 Sam 10:5, the three preparatory disclosures would be: a) the "chance" arrival of the band of prophets; b) the precise identification and enumeration of their accompanying instruments: harp, tambourine, flute, lyre; c) their state of prophetic frenzy. These will lead up to the final and culminating sign (10:6), Saul's complete transformation.

[8]Gen 29:19; Lev 27:20; Deut 24:2; 2 Sam 18:26; 1 Kgs 20:37; Jer 3:1.

remain the same person? How does Charlie become Frank and still remain Charlie? Yet, as Rimbaud said mysteriously: "Je est un autre," "I is another." Some resolve the issue by supposing that Saul adds on another heart or self, but the text does not say that. It says, rather, "different" and not "additional." A dual nature inheres in Saul; he becomes another while very much remaining himself. A crucial example of this is the low self-image with which he sets out (1 Sam 9:21) and which is confirmed by Samuel much later (1 Sam 15:17). Another solution is to stress the ʾish, which in the Hebrew Bible often refers to an important personage. Samuel would then be saying that Saul will go from a "nobody" to a real "somebody." Even his outward being will be different, in his ecstatic behaviors and perhaps even in his looks.

"Is Saul also among the prophets?" A negative reading would depend on the tone of voice: How could a lowly person like the son of Kish suddenly become a prophet? The transformation seems too radical! However, a positive valence is also possible, as the original saying is now, in its second reading, made more precise as well as more laconic, a true *mashal* that can be applied to anyone: "Is Saul too (or anyone else, for that matter) among the prophets, i.e., is not everyone eligible for prophecy?" The possibility of a universal spirit of prophecy is evoked in the case of Eldad and Medad, who went about speaking in ecstasy when Israel was in the wilderness. To Joshua's upset, Moses responded:

> Are you jealous for my sake? Would that all of the Lord's people were prophets and that the Lord would place His spirit upon them! (Num 11:29)

The prophet Joel is even more inclusive:

> I will pour out my spirit *upon all flesh,* and your sons and daughters will prophesy. . . . And also upon the servants and upon the handmaids will I pour out my spirit. (Joel 3:1–2[2:28–29])[9]

---

[9]Crenshaw's (*Joel,* 165) wish to restrict "all flesh" to the Judahites is unconvincing. The expression means "everyone" without ethnic or gender restriction. Exegetically, this is a case of a general principle (all flesh) followed by specific examples: your sons and daughters (the Judahites), and your male and female servants.

The proverb's astonishment may of course still be satirical, but it would then be directed to personal merit rather than family connections.[10]

In the final performance of the proverb in 1 Sam 19:23–24, Saul's transformation of personality is radicalized downward, as it were; Saul is seen in his entire nakedness, both literally and figuratively. That is to say, he is now fully revealed as an individual, in isolation not only from his parents but from all social identity whatever, including his kingship, as symbolized by his clothes. The easy shift from literal to figurative nakedness is demonstrated by Samuel (1 Sam 15:27), who reacts to Saul's tearing the prophet's cloak to his being "stripped" of his kingship. But some see the figurative reading as extending to the present scene as well. Isaiah da Trani (ca. 1180–1250), for example, even thinks that here *only* the figurative meaning applies, namely that Saul "was naked of his kingly attire and dressed like the other disciples."[11]

In this final stage the form of the proverb remains the same but the contextualization adds several nuances to the interpretation:

a) the unusual repetitions of *gam hemah* ("they too," three times), and *gam hu^ɔ* ("he too," four times) seem to query: "Is even Saul, the opponent of both David and prophecy itself, to be among the prophets?"

b) he is now ^c*arom,* naked as the day he was born (Job 1:21; Hos 2:5 [2:3]; Qoh 5:14), or perhaps even as naked as the original ^c*arumim* who themselves had no parents (Gen 2:25). The message is a perhaps (ironic?) confirmation of the second stage of the proverb's development, since, precisely under the influence of prophecy, Saul has recovered his original innocence.

c) he fell down in prophecy "all day and all night." Folks now wonder, again emphasizing "among the prophets," whether Saul has now permanently joined their ranks. He certainly has become more proficient, even casting off the usual decorum of his high office!

---

[10]As we saw in the case of Samson, for example, proverbs can often have a satirical purpose. See Brettler, *The Book of Judges,* 37.

[11]Isaiah da Trani, on 1 Sam 19:24 (*Commentary* [ed. A. J. Würtheimer; 3 vols.; Jerusalem: Ketav Yad va-Sefer, 1978], 38–39).

What adds importance to this final use of the proverb is that it is the nakedness *of the king* that is the focus of public attention. For since it is granted from the two previous uses of the proverb that prophets can work in the nude, the question now arises, in the form of an astonishment approaching satire, as to whether such nakedness is appropriate for a king:

> Is (king) Saul also among the prophets?!

Of course, behind the *ad hominem* argument that is of perennial interest looms the broader question of the compatibility of the offices of kingship and prophecy in the same person.

Prophecy, Kingship, and Wisdom

We have seen how the elaboration of a proverb dramatically marks both the start and close of Saul's public career. Robert Alter's literary description is of particular interest:[12]

> The conflicting valences given to the explanation of the proverbial saying add to the richness of the portrait of Saul, formally framing it at beginning and end.

Alter is here relying on J. P. Fokkelman, who contrasts Saul's first ecstatic experience ("a positive sign of election") with the second, a "negative sign of being rejected."[13] Such a view is plausible if it refers to signs of election or rejection concerning kingship, since the plot of the Saul narrative is, within the sweep of 1 Samuel, the story of the rise of Israel's first king (and not prophet). We would like to ponder, however, whether the prophetic incidents of Saul's career are intended to act as evaluations of job performance for kingship, for has this not been one of the proverb's achievements: to separate and distinguish his prophetic states from both his family background *and also his kingship?*

We should first ask whether we have got those evaluations right. Not about the kingship, to be sure, since there is widespread

---

[12]Alter, *The David Story,* 122.
[13]J. P. Fokkelman, *Narrative Art and Poetry in the Books of Samuel* (Assen: Van Gorcum), 1981–1990.

agreement that Saul's tenure was a failure, and that is not our subject here at any rate. But what of his work "among the prophets"? If the final proverb makes any point clearly, it is the incompatibility between Saul's two roles, as king and as prophet. A *mishnah* may provide a model for sorting this out. The issue is who is worthy of a crown, who deserves to be honored by others:

> Rabbi Shimeon says: "There are three crowns: the crown of Torah, and the crown of priesthood, and the crown of kingship. And the crown of a good name is above them all." (*Abot* 4:13)

A crucial distinction can be made between two kinds of crown: those that are inherited and those that depend on personal merit. In the first category are the priesthood and, beginning with David, kingship,[14] although such an expectation was already in force with Saul's son Jonathan. Curiously, prophecy is not listed as among the crowns deserving honor. Would this be because they are undeserving? Alter, citing Hos 9:7, refers to the ambivalence of prevalent attitudes concerning prophets: "they were at once viewed as vehicles of a powerful and dangerous divine spirit, and as crazies."[15] Whether dangerous or crazy, however, it would be hard to see any ambivalence here. More precisely, I think, the text argues for a suspension of judgment, since prophets—and pointedly Saul, when he is among the prophets—operate on a separate track and beyond normal social configurations.

Saul has evolved from Ben Kish to King Saul—quite a transformation!—yet remains, by proverbial definition, "among the prophets" at both ends of his career. But here too the proverb expresses the same level of surprise: How could a king also be a prophet, do kings dance around naked all day and all night? Recall Michal's shock at David's undignified behavior when he returned the holy ark to Jerusalem (2 Sam 6:16–23), dancing ecstatically and naked (vv. 16, 20). Alter pointedly observes that "the figure she sees is not 'David her husband' but

---

[14]David, as per Ps 89:37[89:36]: "His throne will be like the sun before me, it will be established forever." Moses Maimonides (ca. 1135–1204), however, ruled that any Israelite can become king ("Law of Kings," in *The Code of Maimonides: Book XIV, The Book of Judges* [trans. Abraham M. Hershman; New Haven: Yale University Press, 1949], 1:4).

[15]Alter, *The David Story*, 57.

'King David'."[16] So too does the proverb exclaim: Is such behavior appropriate for a king?!

Saul's situation in Samuel's presence anticipates David's before the ark, and the proverb-making public is shocked. Samuel, however, normally garrulous about Saul's performance, here registers not the slightest objection or surprise. On the contrary, Saul prophesied before him all day and all night! For the gift of prophecy has no relation to social identity; it operates entirely on its own track. The story, which the proverb summarizes and brings to memory, thus does not come to either glorify or belittle Saul, but rather to remove his prophetic activity entirely from public comprehension and evaluation. Just as Amos was forcefully dragged from his plowing (Amos 7:15), it was God who removed Saul from the normal course of life, not only as a king but also at another level altogether. The point of Saul's becoming another man, therefore, is that, just as God initially created him, so too only God, on each occasion through Samuel, can re-create him into a different person, whether king or prophet.

It should be carefully noted that Saul's total makeover relates only to his prophetic activities as presented, and not to his rise to kingship, which at the point of the first ecstatic episode is not a matter of public record. It could be the case that the removal of birth and inheritance from the qualifications of prophecy, as prompted by the bystander's objection ("And who is their father?" 1 Sam 10:12), can serve to authenticate Saul's accession not only to prophecy but also to kingship. Through a surprising turn, however, our text makes just the opposite point: that while qualifications for both in no way depend on parentage, there is absolutely no dependence of the one on the other. Prophecy operates on its own track. That is why Saul's prophecy performance is not discredited, since its presence depends uniquely on God's spirit.[17] Thus Saul becomes the model of the lonely man, one bereft of family and social group, a king but not among kings (neither before nor after him); a prophet but not (at least not per-

---

[16]Ibid. For a touching parallel, where the wife focuses on the national tragedy over the personal one, see Ichabod's mother in 1 Sam 4:20–22.

[17]*Pace* P. Kyle McCarter, Jr., *I Samuel: A New Translation.* (AB 8; Garden City, N.Y.: Doubleday, 1980), 330–31.

manently) among prophets. As such, evaluating him in his prophetic role is irrelevant, since prophets operate on their own track and do not fall under the judgment of outsiders. Like prophets like fools?

Conclusion

The final performance of our proverb is susceptible of two interpretations. From the point of view of Michal, Saul must observe decorum. Thus, anybody may join the prophets, but not a king. From an opposite point of view, characteristic of David with the ark, the *a fortiori* argument applies: if even the king can put aside his honor, then anyone can. The crucial difference between the two kings, however, is that David made a conscious choice, whereas Saul's prophetic states are induced from outside. His first event is explicitly announced as a sign from God; the last seems to arise from the ecstatic influence of the group of prophets.

Our story tells of Saul's evolution from a nobody to a king, rags to riches. Remarkably, these two extremities of Saul's career are both heralded by a proverb that tries to bridge the gap and evaluate the person—the person Saul and not the career—from the outside point of view of prophecy, which in the context of this book is far beyond the fray. When Saul dips into an ecstatic mode, however briefly, he escapes his social role but strengthens his total self. He is there among the prophets neither as Ben Kish nor as the king, but simply as Saul. And he is there, there among the prophets. Acting like a crazy perhaps, but who is to judge? One imagines that God had something to do with his access to those ecstatic states. Saul is a modest man, an ⸾anav. He does not know power, nor does he seem to have a taste for it. He loves music, especially to soothe melancholy, and he even loves his enemy David. Was there no better candidate for the kingship?

If the proverbs can be seen as contextualizing and plotting Saul's public career, as we have proposed here, then the dimensions of Saul's importance need to be expanded. For it now becomes not only a matter of having a king and of the implications of this radical societal transformation. Also on the table is the reexamination of prophecy's role, especially whether leadership can tolerate prophetic revelation in the same person, as was the case with Moses and some of the Judges. There is of course the temptation to give a personal interpretation, arguing that it depends entirely on the individual king and that, whereas Saul lacked the necessary personal qualifications, others would perhaps qualify. Or perhaps not. For was king Solomon also a prophet, as the exegetical tradition was vehemently to argue, or was he primarily a sage? His initiatory act of judgment, as brought down in the split-baby story (see the next chapter), will raise this issue and suggest some answers.

Our study of the formation of a proverb argues that proverbs are not timeless wisdom, but rather express opinions, evaluations, and values contextually understood and defined. From a study of their origin and evolution, it becomes possible to define who is speaking and thus to evaluate the content of their messages. In the sample provided by 1 Samuel, we have seen that the three occurrences are spoken by three different voices:

a) the family or inheritance point of view (1 Sam 10:11);

b) a sage, who wins his case concerning Saul but not concerning succession in general (1 Sam 10:12); and

c) Michal or David, depending on your reading (1 Sam 19:24).

What underlies all of these is Saul the naked individual, for Rimbaud's "I is *another*" applies here to social roles, wearing many hats, living many different lives. But that does not mean that the individual is totally accounted for by these. Saul's base identity arises when these are stripped away, when Saul, in the nakedness of his trances, recovers his original self. This self, our story argues, is beyond human judgment. Again, Grossman's characterization of Samson, asleep on Delilah's lap and about to be shorn of his strength, applies to Saul, naked like his original parents as their earthly glory is about to be stripped and their fate sealed, but in a state of ecstatic withdrawal and essential recovery:

> Samson withdraws into his childish, almost infantile self, disarmed of the violence, madness, and passion that have confounded and ruined his life. . . . Yet it is now, perhaps for the first time in his life, that he finds repose. Here, in the very heart of the cruel perfidy that

he has surely expected all along, he is finally granted perfect peace, a release from himself and the stormy drama of his life.[18]

Except that, for Saul, it is the release from the stormy drama of his social and political life that enables his return, however episodic, to his true self.

We have thus identified a biblical case where contextualization, typically absent in proverb collections, is richly provided. What is here added is not only the formation of a proverb but also its evolution: under the pressure of changing circumstances the original saying takes on different emphasis. Independent of the point of view and wisdom content of particular proverb performances, this process of evaluation is itself wisdom, indeed at the core of the wisdom enterprise. It is here pictured by "Saul among the prophets," able for brief periods to live and think outside the oppressive circle of family and politics, to try to recover a sense of being someone different, an *ʾish akher.* Was this not portrayed as a divine gift?

---

[18]Grossman, *Lion's Honey* (trans. Stuart Schoffman; Edinburgh: Canongate, 2006), 5. Just as in the epigraph for this chapter, Grossman (*Lion's Honey,* 1–2) applies these words to Samson; I find them equally appropriate to Saul.

SIX

SOLOMON THE WISE AND THE SPLIT-BABY STORY (1 KGS 3:16–29)

When a case is too baffling for you to decide . . .

(Deut 17:8)

Talent may frolic and juggle; genius realizes and adds.

(Emerson, "The Poet")

ממוות יצא חיים ומשניים חצי[1]

Two women come before a judge with identical claims on a new-born, and the absence of evidence is so total that a verdict seems impossible. The judge therefore orders that the infant be cut up and equal portions be distributed to each of the claimants. One woman accepts the ruling, the other renounces her claim on the child. The judge awards the infant to the latter, and we are invited to admire the judge's wisdom.

Two ways of reading emerge from the text itself. Some readers, yielding to an unmistakable hagiographic tease in surrounding texts (1 Kgs 2:12; 3:28), simply pause to admire Solomon's

---

[1] The riddle, a local production, reads as follows: "From death came forth life, and from two a half."

wisdom, said to be beyond compare. Others, while probably in agreement, sense a pedagogical imperative and try to fathom and evaluate that wisdom. In this second approach, it matters not only *that* Solomon was wise but especially *how* he was wise and, by an extension that must be explored, how he *became* wise. For, as Meir Sternberg warns, "unless the reader undergoes the drama of knowledge himself, the whole tale will have been told in vain."[2] This study argues the latter way of reading—without denying the former—with the important difference that the human wisdom embodied in this story may belong to the "real" mother rather than to Solomon himself.

The (Absolute Lack of) Evidence (1 Kgs 3:16–23)

The tale has two distinct phases: the trial itself (1 Kgs 3:16–23) and the judgment (vv. 24–27). The first is normally a precondition of the second, since verdicts are based on evidence. Except that, here, each phase is hermetically sealed, and failure to distinguish this rupture has led to considerable confusion.

The entire case, with the single exception of v. 26—a narrator's intervention which proves nothing (see below)—is spoken by the two female disputants before the Judge/King Solomon. The plaintiff (A) claims that the defendant (B) stole her newborn during the night and substituted her own dead infant. The defendant retorts that the truth is exactly the opposite: the live infant is hers and the dead one belongs to the other mother. There are no witnesses and no circumstantial clues that would advantage one claim over the other. For example, it is a given that the live child has no physical or biological characteristics such as birthmarks or look-alike features favoring one mother over the other. As to the dead infant, he is out of the picture, perhaps already buried, but by which "mother" seems not to be an issue. If he just died and is

---

[2]Meir Sternberg, *The Poetics of Biblical Narrative* (Bloomington: Indiana University Press, 1985), 166. See also Lasine's important analysis as to whether Solomon's wisdom is essentially divine, on the one hand, or whether it can be "emulated by ordinary human beings" (Stuart Lasine, "The Riddle of Solomon's Judgment and the Riddle of Human Nature in the Hebrew Bible," *JSOT* 45 [1989]: 75–76).

still available for examination, it must be assumed either that the two infants bear no resemblance to either mother or that they both look alike (could they both have had the same father?).[3] Solomon's summation in v. 23—a mere verbatim repetition of the counterclaims—brings glaring focus on the absence of any evidence whatever, and we are left with a single baby and two women who both claim to be its biological mother. In Sternberg's words, "that is what the evidence boils down to: the one prostitute's words against the other's."[4]

Such a situation has not deterred critics from speculation or even manufacture of evidence, and sophisticated discussions have focused not only on the precise evidence for Solomon's wise verdict but also on who has privileged access to this knowledge. Here are the candidates:

The Women

Since, at the evidentiary phase, guilt and innocence cannot be established from outside sources, critics have sought psychological motive from the characters' style of presentation. Now, there does exist a clear difference between the two women in the manner or length of each presentation: the first woman is long-winded, the

---

[3]This would extend the argument, ultimately derived from folklore, that both women are widows of the same man (see Carol Fontaine, "The Bearing of Wisdom on the Shape of 2 Samuel 11–12 and 1 Kings 3," *JSOT* 34 [1986]: 76). Yehudah Keil (*Commentary on the Book of Kings* [Hebrew; Jerusalem: Mossad Harav Kook, 1989], 59 n. 72) cites the interpretation of Rabbi Judah the Hasid, according to which both women were the widows of a very wealthy man, thus compounding the maternity controversy with the issue of inheritance. In this latter case, Solomon's verdict gains in at least poetic verisimilitude, since—again, in the absence of decisive evidence—any financial assets could be "split." It would seem that such a situation would require the rabbinic alternative of seeing the women as innkeepers, since their status as prostitutes would presumably remove the issues of paternity and accompanying inheritance.

[4]Sternberg, *The Poetics of Biblical Narrative*, 168. Don Isaac Abarbanel (1437–1508) had come to the same conclusion: "The king said: 'Of what use are all the words that you said, since you have not produced witnesses for them? Therefore nothing remains in all of this except your claim that the live child is yours and the dead one hers, whereas the other woman claims that the live one is hers and the dead one yours. Moreover, all other claims fall flat, for there is no convincing evidence whatsoever in favor of one over the other: both are equal before the law'" (*Commentary on the Earlier Prophets,* 482).

other is taciturn. What can be inferred from this difference is anything but clear, however. Even Gary Rendsburg, who rejects out of hand this kind of "evidence," allows an exception here:

> If there is anything in the first woman's words in vv. 17–21 that suggests that she is lying, it is not the story itself that she relates, but rather the repetition of the word *we-hinneh*, "and behold", in v. 21.[5]

May it not rather suggest that she is nervous? Rendsburg's only supporting parallel for such a flimsy theory is the Amalekite's explanation of Saul's death in 1 Sam 1:6, where it is not at all clear that he is indeed lying. And in the supporting text referenced, Adele Berlin admits (as would Rendsburg, see below), that these may not be the Amalekite's own words but rather "words put into his mouth" by the narrator, thus not words of actual testimony but rather authorial projections.[6]

Critics' arguments are usually first advanced on psychological grounds, then on what is claimed to be "usually the case in biblical style."[7] Thus, Stuart Lasine makes a case for "the true witness of strong emotion."[8] Surprisingly, even Sternberg falls for this one: "The extreme responses provoked are as good as a confession."[9] In fact, however, the judgment "will depend in no way upon the women's exposé of the case in vv. 17–22."[10] There is even a possibility, rarely discussed except tangentially, that neither woman is lying because they too are not sure of the evidence.[11] Thus, the issue of detecting false testimony raised by Lasine may not even be an issue.[12]

---

[5]Gary A. Rendsburg, "The Guilty Party in 1 Kings III 16–28," *VT* 48 (1998): 535n8.

[6]Adele Berlin, *Poetics and Interpretation of Biblical Narrative* (Winona Lake, Ind.: Eisenbrauns, 1994), 81.

[7]Jean-Noël Aletti, "Le Jugement de Salomon 1 R 3, 16–28," in *Toute la Sagesse du monde: Hommage à Maurice Gilbert, S.J.* (ed. François Mies; Namur: Lessius, 1999), 321.

[8]Lasine, "The Riddle of Solomon's Judgment," 61, 69–72.

[9]Sternberg, *The Poetics of Biblical Narrative,* 169.

[10]Aletti, "Le jugement de Salomon," 317.

[11]Contra Lasine ("The Riddle of Solomon's Judgment," 64), who claims that "it is clear that both women know who is who." For a discussion of mirror twinning, see below, "Who's Who?"

[12]See Lasine, "The Riddle of Solomon's Judgment," 72.

Solomon

The leading candidate for access to the knowledge necessary to decide the case is of course Solomon himself, who, it is claimed, is able to filter the inconsistencies in the guilty woman's testimony and has heightened powers of perception. The problem with all such approaches is the absence of any convincing textual basis. Casting for straws, it is claimed that "thus they spoke" (1 Kgs 3:22) refers not to the preceding testimony (or lack thereof) but rather Solomon's further probing interrogation. In the absence of a transcript, however, we must conclude that, even if such further inquiry did occur, it had no profit and the conclusion remains the same.

Literary Style

Rendsburg agrees on the absence of information but counters by shifting the burden to "biblical narrative style," which, it is claimed, never gives such information explicitly but rather through clues to the reader such as repetitions or elaborate structures like sustained chiasmus. Simply put and as Lasine demonstrates, however, such patterning "does not constitute evidence."[13] Thus, the non-existent internal evidence available to Solomon (and to the reader) is bypassed in favor of external features of the story, which here is "the manner in which the author narrates the story."[14] Assuming that the author and narrator are one and the same—though it really makes no difference—this approach privileges a source external to the legal case itself, so that we have to put the same question to the author/narrator that we put to Solomon and to ourselves as readers: How did you come to the guilty verdict? For, ultimately, the question is not how one reads the text but how one thinks through the issues, not what clues the narrator's prejudice is sending forth but rather what is their basis. We are of course interested in what the author/narrator thinks but are in no ways bound by it, for then we would be allowing the narrator to

---

[13]Ibid., 80n9.
[14]Rendsburg, "The Guilty Party," 536.

out-Solomonize Solomon, something that Rendsburg would be loath to do.[15]

The Narrator/Author

Closely related but distinct is the author's status as a source of evidence. It might seem that the entire question of authority is obviated by a clear indication from the narrator, the one according to which the entire proceedings are traditionally interpreted:

> *Then spoke the woman whose child was the living one to the king, for her love was enkindled towards her son,* and she said, "O my lord, give her the living child but do not slay it." (1 Kgs 3:26)

In fact, however, the narrator's explanation (in italics) is only a hypothesis and smacks of being ex post facto: since Solomon-The-Wise judges her to be the biological mother. . . . But it is precisely Solomon's wisdom that we are trying to fathom! And if even he is unsure of the evidence, then how are *we*, including the narrator, to know the woman's motivations?

Lasine's appeal to the narrator's "rhetoric and authority" naively assumes that the one follows from the other.[16] Similarly, Ellen van Wolde claims that in biblical Hebrew the particle *ki* sometimes departs from its causal meaning to characterize embedded discourse, which here would be the projection of the character's emotion or perspective into the narrator's. Fine, but we are still left only with the narrator's point of view, not any transcendent authority per se; and this is now fused with the perspective of *one* of the women—and we do not know which!—who may be lying.[17] Such stylistic/linguistic criteria cannot possibly solve the

---

[15]Ibid., 535. To cite but one further example, Lasine's ("The Riddle of Solomon's Judgment," 68) search for "reliable literary clues as to the true mother's identity" is flawed from the start because reliable clues can only come from real life. Van Wolde's methodology, based on linguistic markings in the text, is unfortunately subject to the same limitations (Ellen van Wolde, "Who Guides Whom? Embeddedness and Perspective in Biblical Hebrew and 1 Kings 3:16–28," *JBL* 114 [1995]: 623–42).

[16]Lasine, "The Riddle of Solomon's Judgment," 71.

[17]Thus, *ki,* it is claimed, is a "unique intermediate form" that can "bridge the gap between direct representation [the character's direct speech] and narrator's text" (van Wolde, "Who Guides Whom?," 636).

court case in which "both the king and the reader are faced with an insoluble problem and do not have the means to come to a well-founded opinion."[18] For, again, how can the author/narrator have such information? What all this really boils down to is that through the mixed or embedded style "the reader is drawn into this intense feeling" of the presumed mother, and this is but a re-working of the fallacy of the "witness of strong emotion" rejected above.[19]

God / Bat Kol

The desperation of all such authorial *deus ex machina* approaches is most evident in the midrashic theory of a voice from offstage—off the stage of real life—claiming that the verdict "she is the mother" is spoken not by Solomon but rather by a *bat qol* (in English, Bat Kol) or prophetic voice from heaven.[20] It is quite likely, however, that the heavenly voice merely confirms the absolute dearth of evidence: the judgment has to be portrayed as delivered from heaven because nobody, not even Solomon, has a clue. This approach is also risky because, if taken literally, the wisdom for the decision is moved upstairs and Solomon loses most of his credit. Finally, whether we are talking about a Bat Kol or divine influence, to understand its true function we must still examine "the mediation of purely human factors."[21]

The Reader?

Rendsburg's distinction between the king and the reader, both of whom admittedly have the same information, is but a variant of the all-knowing-author fallacy mentioned above in the

---

[18]Van Wolde, "Who Guides Whom?," 631.

[19]Ibid., 638. Again, van Wolde (639n34) argues tendentiously that "the narrator himself/herself has already identified the mother of the living child." Indeed!

[20]Sources cited on page 2 in W. A. M. Beuken, "No Wise King Without a Wise Woman (1 Kings iii 16–28)" in *New Avenues in the Study of the Old Testament* (ed. A. S. van der Woude; OtSt 25; Leiden: Brill, 1989), 1–10.

[21]Moshe Weinfeld, *Deuteronomy and the Deuteronomistic School* (Oxford: Clarendon, 1972), 258–59; cited in Lasine, "The Riddle of Solomon's Judgment," 73.

sections on Bat Kol and Liberary Style, and Jean-Noël Aletti's analysis is to be preferred: "The reader is placed in a position analogous to the king's, who . . . is placed before an insoluble problem."[22]

In sum, the purpose of the narrative is to subject all of these points of view to analysis in order to question their validity, thus moving to the perception that the crucial point is not the wisdom of the narrator, the biblical style, the women, or even Solomon, but rather wisdom itself. I propose that this wisdom tale is a laboratory example of a case in which the rigorous pursuit of evidence yields nothing, so that the absence of evidence, as established in the evidentiary hearing, is a given that in a court of law must of course be demonstrated. What a challenge to the judge's and the reader's wisdom! And, of course, this lack of evidence does not run counter to the tale's propagandistic purpose but rather enhances it, since Solomon's fame increases in direct proportion to the difficulties involved. But if his ability is to be explained as intuition or skill in questioning witnesses, he may qualify as a good judge but one hardly worth a trip from the Queen of Sheba.[23]

Who's Who? (1 Kgs 3:24–27)

The second or judgmental phase of the trial is attached to the preceding by v. 23:

> Then said the king: "This one says 'The live one is my son and the dead one is yours,' and the other one says 'Not at all: your son is the dead one and the live one is my son.'"

This verse has a *dual* function. On the one hand, through its mere repetition of the testimony and in the same chiastic form, the women's specular discourse is doubly so, thus stressing that

---

[22]Rendsburg, "The Guilty Party," 535 and n5. Aletti, "Le jugement de Salomon," 322.

[23]To be "beyond compare," the Judge/King has to be like Houdini, going under for the third time and with no visible avenues of escape until the fantastic occurs: superior trickery, acumen, wisdom, or even the "voice of God" itself. For the literary notion of the fantastic, see Perry, *The Honeymoom Is Over*, 183–200.

"there is no more information to be expected from them, that they can only go on repeating themselves indefinitely, thus emphasizing that words simply refer to other words without our ever being able to determine whether they refer to reality."[24] But v. 23 also has a forward motion, that of jump-starting the failed action through means other than direct evidence.

Current discussions have agreed to call the two women at the evidentiary hearing (A) and (B) and to award the verdict usually to (A) but occasionally to (B). Yet, when we turn to the judgment phase itself, we lose further contact with (A) and (B) as distinct identities. This is because, added to the lack of evidence and the mirror twinning of the two women, the blurring of identities now becomes systematic, so that we ask at every turn: Who is speaking, to whom does this refer, to (A) or to (B)?[25] And, as Mordechai Cogan observes, "We are not told whether she ["and she said"] is the complainant or the respondent," i.e., whether "she" is (A) or (B).[26]

Cogan's observation can be applied even more broadly. The usual approach is to assign the speakers as follows:

(A) says: "Give her the live child."

(B) says: "Cut him up!"

But why would (A) ask that the child be *given* to (B), since the latter is already in possession of the child? The sequel reinforces the ambivalence:

But the [one] woman . . . said to the king: . . . "Please, my lord, give her the live child, but by no [i.e., any] means don't kill him." And the other one was saying: "Neither I nor you shall have him! Cut him!" The king replied: "Give *her* the live infant and by no [i.e., any] means don't kill him. She is the mother." (1 Kgs 3:26–27, Cogan trans.)[27]

---

[24]Lasine ("The Riddle of Solomon's Judgment," 64) claims that "in the judgment story, it is clear that both women know who is who." On the contrary, no one really knows—certainly not the narrator, who does everything to withhold such information—and that may include even the women.

[25]See Aletti, "Le jugement de Salomon," 314–15.

[26]Mordechai Cogan, *1 Kings: A New Translation with Introduction and Commentary* (AB 10; New York: Doubleday, 2001), 195.

[27]Ibid., 193.

To avoid the distasteful possibility that the king is referring to the second woman—and, do not forget, we still are not sure whether she is (A) or (B)—some have imagined that here the king actually pointed his finger at the first woman, although there is no textual basis for such a claim. A stronger point (Sternberg) would be that the king is referring to the first woman because he quotes her exact words. It seems more likely, however, that the order to "Give *her* the live infant" would refer to the immediate antecedent, the woman just mentioned ("Cut him up!"), rather than, as always supposed, the first woman.

Such an unpopular possibility could be explained in several ways:

a) her call to "cut him up" is a sarcastic provocation, pronounced fast[28] upon the king's announcement and intended to show Solomon just how absurd he is being. Thus, Solomon: "Cut him up!"

The [second] woman: "'Cut him up!!!' Kill a living, innocent child?! What kind of justice is that!?"

b) Freud: "If one woman's child is dead, the other shall not have a live one either. The bereaved woman is recognized by this wish."[29]

c) "If I can't have my own child, I certainly will not abandon him to this abusive child-snatcher! Go ahead and cut him up!"[30]

In fact, such arguments are all of the same cloth as the narrator's own: mere psychological speculations that again highlight the absolute dearth of hard evidence. Again in Sternberg's words, "the defendant's strongest point is that she has no story to tell: she did nothing, saw nothing, suffered no loss, and would not care to advance any theories about the death of another's child."[31] And if, as we think, even the women themselves are not sure, then the element of motivation is removed and such speculation becomes not only irrelevant but impossible.

---

[28]See below, "Interruptions."

[29]Sigmund Freud, quoted in Lasine, "The Riddle of Solomon's Judgment," 71.

[30]See George E. Mendenhall, quoted in van Wolde, "Who Guides Whom?" 639n34.

[31]Sternberg, *The Poetics of Biblical Narrative,* 168.

In sum, the lack of evidence leads to a situation in which *one of the women* is awarded the infant, but we do not know—*nor are we supposed to*—whether it is (A) or (B)! The whole matter of (A) versus (B) thus becomes irrelevant, and we now move to a new confrontation:

> (X) "Give her the child!"

> (Y) "Neither I nor you shall have him."

And, since we have passed beyond the biological criterion, we must now ask what Solomon can possibly mean in deciding that "*she* is the mother"?

Interruptions

The plot outlined in the evidentiary phase (1 Kgs 3:16–24) is now stalled and can be jump-started, so to speak, only by disregarding it altogether, since the verdict will now be based entirely on the spoken reactions of the two litigants as presented in v. 26:

> (X) said to the king: "Please, my lord, give her the live child; don't kill him by any means."

> And this one (Y) was saying: "Neither I nor you shall have him: Cut him up!"

Before analyzing the content of the responses, it is important to notice several legal problems with the verdict itself. First of all, since plaintiff (X) renounces her claim ("give it to her"), then there is no longer a case and the proceedings should come to an end at that point. Secondly, according to the argument that "possession is nine tenths of the law," the burden of proof falls squarely on the one who would take from the possessor. In the absence of any evidence or proof, the verdict is bypassed altogether and matters must stand where they are.[32]

These issues come into sharper focus if we take another look at the usual translations of 1 Kgs 3:26–27. All agree that, in the

---

[32]As per the well-known Talmudic principle, "The burden of proof is upon the one who wishes to take from another." The problem was quoted in Abarbanel, *Commentary on the Earlier Prophets,* 482.

heat of the debate, there is some interruption going on. The accepted impression is that the testimony is sequential, thus that (X) spoke first and was interrupted by (Y). However, such a view disregards the verb tenses, which are past (*waw*-conversive) in the first instance, and participle in the second. A more accurate translation would therefore go as follows:

> (X) said [*wato'mer*] to the king: "Please, my lord, give her the live child; don't kill him by any means," *while* (Y) was saying [*'omeret*]: "Neither I nor you shall have him: Cut him up!"

Thus, it was "while the other one was saying 'Cut him up'" that the *first* woman interrupted her.[33] The temporal sequence, as presented before the judge, is thus the opposite of the syntactical one:

> While (Y) was saying: "Neither I nor you shall have him: Cut him up," (X) [interrupted and] said to the king: "Please, my lord, give her the live child; by no means don't kill him."

Thus, both difficulties fall since it is now the case that *both* women give up their claim of possession: the current possessor who could retain the infant, and the one who brings the claim in the first place. This is why a verdict must be rendered, because otherwise the infant is ownerless and, in the absence of someone to raise him the king's verdict "Cut him up" seems to be the only resolution.

Rendsburg cleverly, perhaps overly so, establishes the identity of woman (A) with (Y) and (B) with (X) on the basis of the repetition of the conjunction *waw* (in *wezo't 'omeret*) "*and* this one said," arguing that since the speaker in the first occurrence is (A) in 1 Kgs 3:22a, then she must also be the reference in Solomon's (perhaps overly clever) repetition in v. 23, as well as in the narrator's repetition in v. 26.[34] But, surely, some kind of connective is

---

[33]See also 1 Kgs 3:19: "And she arose [*wataqom*] at midnight and took [*watiqqakh*] my son from beside me while your handmaid was sleeping [*yeshenah*]." The identical examples in 1 Kgs 3:22, 23 further emphasize the *mêlée* that must have occurred. Gesenius (116o) cites Gen 19:1: "And two angels came [*wayyavo'u*] to Sodom at evening, while Lot was sitting [*yoshev*] at the gate." Thus, when one woman states that "the child shall be neither yours nor mine, *cut*," van Wolde's surprise ("Who Guides Whom?" 639) is thus unfounded: "this is an odd reaction, since the first woman (the real mother) has just yielded her child."

[34]Rendsburg, "The Guilty Party," 536.

required to join and separate the references to the two women; and, as argued above, the *waw* connective, attached in all three cases to the participle, has the meaning of "while," thus serving to further blur the identities of the two women rather than set them clearly against one another. Thus, Rendsburg's conclusion is doubly suspect: "The author invited the reader to interact with the text in a very active way. Solomon needed to solve the text in his way, alongside which the reader is able to solve the case in another way."[35] However, we are never told *how* the case was solved. It is merely asserted that indeed Solomon had his own way, whatever that was, and the narrator simply echoed his own prejudice through stylistic niceties.

On the Education of Princes: Solomon's Genius, Mother's Instinct, and God's Wisdom

To adjust our admiration of Solomon to its proper dimensions, we would like to ask whether his verdict was based primarily on intuition (Gerhard von Rad), "juridical cunning" (Walter Brueggemann), "pure folkloristic genius" (Burke O. Long), or whether other more tangible factors were involved.[36] Of course, the king has no intention whatever to kill the infant—does any reader surmise that he does?[37]—and if the Gordian knot is to be cut, at least it will not be with a real sword. Further, the scales of justice being so equally balanced, to what purpose is the often accompanying "sword" of further precision?[38]

There is a minimalist escape, one bound to leave the admiration school dissatisfied but not inappropriate to the current impasse. Supreme Court Justice Louis Brandeis believed that a verdict is just because it is a verdict, that the good of justice is not

---

[35]Ibid., 539.

[36]Von Rad, *Wisdom in Israel*, 297. Brueggemann, *First and Second Samuel*, 118. Burke O. Long, *I Kings, with an Introduction to Historical Literature* (FOTL 9; Grand Rapids: Eerdmans, 1984), 68.

[37]Cogan (*I Kings*, 197) apparently does: "Had one of the women not acted upon her motherly feelings and saved the king from carrying out his threat, a wholly other conclusion might be imagined." See below, "Renouncement."

[38]Abraham J. Heschel, *The Prophets* (New York: JPS, 1955), 212.

that it is just but rather that it is the law. Even a wrong (and who knows such a thing?) decision promotes social stability.[39] Or, as Lasine puts it: "Because people must continually make determinate decisions . . . on the basis of indeterminate data, they must . . . act as though their decisions *were* solutions."[40]

Another level of wisdom is revealed in Solomon's analysis of the women's responses. Practically speaking, a crude calculus would award the infant to (X). For, from a purely factual point of view, if woman (Y)'s solution is adopted, then there will be no mother at all since the second infant will also be dead. The award of the infant to (X), therefore, is based on the survival of a residual concept of "mother." According to this, since Solomon's judgment that *she is the mother* does not refer to historical or biological evidence (since such knowledge is denied), another sense of "mother" (e.g., Judg 5:7) must emerge. Since only (X)'s solution allows for the very possibility of there being a mother to the child, reasons Solomon, she *will be considered* the "mother"; it is she who is worthy of being called such.

With this kind of thinking we now pass from the question of *who* the "real" mother is to the more crucial one (not necessarily for justice but for pedagogy and ideology) of *what* a real mother is. Since the biological facts of the case are quite out of reach, William Beuken's observation that "motherhood and life bear witness to one another" has to be taken in a different sense entirely.[41] For if "this sentence corroborates only the outcome of the struggle between life and death, which is already decided in favour of life," then the true sentence is rendered by the woman who chooses life, to be merely acknowledged and corroborated by the judge. Thus, "she is the mother" becomes: The Mother is this one because she responds like one.

As we consider the actual ideology of the women's responses, two criteria now seem decisive: preserving life and renouncement. Each deserves comment.

---

[39]In his dissenting opinion, Louis D. Brandeis wrote, "It is usually more important that a rule of law be settled than that it be settled right" (Louis D. Brandeis, *Di Santo v. Pennsylvania,* 273 U.S. 34, 42 [1927]). I thank Yale Law School Librarian Fred Shapiro for the exact reference.

[40]Lasine, "The Riddle of Solomon's Judgment," 63.

[41]Beuken, "No Wise King," 6.

Preserving Life

The status of the live child is in double jeopardy. First of all, the harlots have the status of *ʾalmanah,* "widows," being without husbands. Secondly, the child has the status of *yathom,* "orphan," since he has been renounced by both mothers. Solomon now adds to the moral of the David story of the wise woman from Tekoa (2 Sam 14:1–24), which is also a case story of two sons, one of whom is killed by the other and is now subject to blood retribution by the redeemer of blood.[42] The case is argued on two grounds: that the mother will be left with neither protector nor heir to her dead husband (2 Sam 14:7). Here neither factor applies,[43] so that Solomon's only reason is the *life* of the child.

Of course, as has already been pointed out, *both* women, acting like twins, renounce possession of the child. But they do so in radically different ways. The one renounces possession in favor of life; the other does the opposite, rejecting life itself. We thus finally we have a clear difference between the two women: (X) chooses the infant's life and (Y) refuses it.

Let us say then that, just as each individual *ʾadam* represents all of humanity, all mothers are imaged in Eve (Gen 3:20), *ʾem kol-khay:* each woman/mother is a mother of *all* and every living creature. For this to happen, at its most basic level numbers are crucial, since "from nothing comes nothing" (*King Lear*), whereas from one person may issue an entire world, as the midrash puts it. Thus, not only "the one who advocates life is mother," as Beuken puts it.[44] Rather, "mother" is one who advocates life. Or, with K. A. Deurloo: "To bear a son and to preserve his life is the out-

---

[42]Beuken, "No Wise King," 9; also, but in a different sense, K. A. Deurloo, "The King's Wisdom in Judgment: Narration as Example," in *New Avenues in the Study of the Old Testament* (ed. A. S. van der Woude; OtSt 25; Leiden: Brill, 1989), 11–21.

[43]Unless the midrashic reading has currency. The woman who cries out: "In no wise kill him" (*hamet ʾal temituhu*), where *hamet* is traditionally read as adding emphasis ("in no wise"). If read as a noun, however, we would have another reading altogether: "And do not kill *the dead person.*" And who would that be, especially if he is *already* dead?! The dead husband/father, who now would be left without an heir to perpetuate his name, thus twice dead.

[44]Beuken, "No Wise King," 7.

standing image of the future."[45] Solomon, in his wisdom and in the absence of evidence, adjusts the formula to present circumstances: to preserve a life is equivalent to bearing a life. We thus return to the original sense of Tsaddik that characterized Noah and other heroes of Genesis, where preservation of life actualizes the wisdom of the Creator-God.[46]

An Ethics of Renunciation

In the reactions of the two women, there is a second element, intimately bound up with the first, and that is the notion, intrinsic to the biblical idea of parenting, that renouncement of one's child is prerequisite to its possession. The prototype is undoubtedly the binding of Isaac, where the youth is spared *because* the father gave him up to death:

> Because you have done this and have not withheld your son, your only one, I will surely bless you and make your offspring numerous as the stars of the heavens and as the sands upon the seashore. (Gen 22:16–17)

From this paradigm one might conclude that it is the second woman ("cut him up"), the one who accepts Solomon's harsh verdict, who deserves the child! Solomon's point, however, is a renewal of the lesson of Gen 22: that the injunction to give up one's child is not to be honored through homicide such as literal child sacrifice, that dedication to some other divine purpose (here, life itself) is an acceptable substitute.

It is of course possible—who can be sure?—that Solomon did have evidence that would establish the biological mother as the one who declared: "Split the baby." What then? Would this be a case of allowing scientific evidence to be overridden by ideology, a subject very much à la mode today? Or, as seems more likely: since this biological mother ("split the baby") has already agreed to the baby's death, she had also agreed *not* to keep the baby. Her

---

[45]Deurloo, "The King's Wisdom," 20.
[46]For God's wisdom see Beuken, "No Wise King," 2. Preserving life is tied to God's character and command, e.g., "And you shall choose life" (Deut 30:19) and "For in You the orphan finds mercy" (Hos 14:4 [14:3]).

philosophy would then be like the Moloch practice of child sacrifice (Lev 20:2–5; 2 Kgs 23:10), but even at a lower degree, since her motivation would not be a religious sacrifice but merely one of jealous revenge: "If I can't have it, then nobody can."

Renunciation is certainly the moral of Hannah's negotiations about her childlessness (1 Sam 1:11). Hannah's story is a riddle: the cost of "having" a child is "not having" a child?! Rather, Hannah can have her child only after she expresses her agreement, in the form of a vow, to give him up. In so doing she becomes the true "mother" of Samuel and to the whole world he worked to preserve. Here the sacrifice points to public service, which, as is well known, is itself a form of sacrifice bordering on self-mutilation. Retrospectively, this throws light on the paradox of the binding of Isaac: a parent is one who can give up a child! Thus, "she is the mother" means "she is deserving to be the mother."[47]

The dramatic moment of "Cut the baby up!" has a parallel in Judah's violence, also in a courtroom scene at which he presides: "Let her be burned!" How sensible (and easy) to make a difficult problem go away by resorting to *les grands moyens* ("great means")! In both cases, however, the women's renouncement inspires its equal, arousing a sensitivity to issues greater than the judges' justice. It might be said, paradoxically, that Solomon and Judah were wise precisely in letting their own rightness be subject to the wisdom incarnated in Tamar and the "real" mother. Such dramatic reversals characterize not only the men of our stories, however, for both women embody the paradox of a prostitute turned mother. I just love this Bible!

---

[47]This reading finds parallel support in the further training in renunciation that Solomon received in this very chapter of 1 Kings at Gibeon. There blessings, in the form of riches and honor, are granted as a gift to one who renounces their pursuit by looking beyond them and to the public good. The moral, again: give up honor and riches and thus you will deserve them (and perhaps even get them).

SEVEN

WISDOM'S CALL TO HUMANS: PSALM 1 AS A DIALOGIC PROLOGUE

> O Lord, open my lips, and my mouth
> will declare Your praise.
>
> (Ps 51:17[51:15])

The Problem: Psalm 1 as an Introduction to the Psalter

The question to be dealt with here is the message of Ps 1.[1] The answer far exceeds the textual boundaries of this psalm, in view of its present literary and spiritual function as an introduction to the entire book of Psalms.[2] For how are we to understand the selection of this psalm, which seems purely declaratory and expositional, as an appropriate introduction to a collection of petitions and songs of thanksgiving? Again, if, according to a solid and to my mind correct scholarly consensus, this text is to be numbered among the "wisdom" psalms, then its introductory function is seriously eclipsed, since fewer than one-tenth of the succeeding

---

[1]The text of Ps 1 appears at the end of this chapter, translated so as to reflect the nuances and changes proposed below.

[2]"As the opening psalm in the collection, Psalm 1 sets the tone for what follows, and suggests that the Psalter should be read in the light of the Torah as a source of wisdom" (John J. Collins, *Jewish Wisdom in the Hellenistic Age* [Louisville: Westminster John Knox Press, 1997], 16 and the works cited there).

psalms are so classified by modern scholarship. How, in short, does Ps 1 fulfill its awesome role as an approach to our Book of Prayer? Through what themes and focus does it orient our attentive devotion?

Nahum M. Sarna has proposed four reasons for the selection of Ps 1 as an introductory text:[3]

a) the centrality of Torah (v. 2);

b) the importance of study as a religious act (again v. 2);

c) the existence of a divinely ordained universal moral order;

d) the "power of the individual to transform society" (relying on the grammatical singular of the "Happy one" [v. 1], as opposed to the plural "wicked" vv. 4–6).

Despite the clear danger of anachronism (since Torah study in Ps 1 may not already possess the character and centrality it later acquired in rabbinic Judaism), Sarna finds the theme of the centrality of Torah to be Ps 1's "first and foremost" qualification as an introductory text, and, following Abraham Heschel's terminology, he justifies this criterion as follows:

> The Torah and the Psalms are, in a very real sense, complementary. The former, revelation, is anthropotropic; it represents the divine outreach to humankind. The latter, worship, is theotropic; it epitomizes the human striving for contact with God.[4]

Sarna seems to be suggesting that, since Toranic revelation (in the rest of Scripture) and prayer (in the book of Psalms) are complementary, a kind of bridge is needed, and the introductory psalm performs this transition by explicitly mentioning Torah before the actual performance of prayers.

My purpose here is to suggest a deeper understanding of Sarna's concept of Ps 1 that he himself did not spell out but that is implicit. My thesis is that Ps 1 argues the *complementary* nature of prayer and study as presented by another of Heschel's concepts: God in search of man. For even when we reach up in prayer, there

---

[3]Nahum M. Sarna, *Songs of the Heart: An Introduction to the Book of Psalms* (New York: Schocken, 1993), 27–29.

[4]Ibid., 27.

is an awareness that prayer already requires the reciprocity of dialogue and *mutual* striving: "O Lord, *open my lips,* and my mouth will declare Your praise" (Ps 51:17[51:15]).

Psalm 1 as a Wisdom Psalm

There is impressive consensus on naming our text a wisdom psalm, and this tendency is by no means a purely modern one.[5] Already Menahem Ha-Meiri (1249–ca. 1310) intoned the theme as follows:

> The intention of this song is to praise the excellence of wisdom, which is the goal of human perfection, for it is fitting that all human actions be geared to this noble goal.[6]

One can object that the word "wisdom" does not occur in Ps 1, but Ha-Meiri may be thinking of Prov 1–9, where the identification between wisdom and Torah is explicit. In chapter 3 in particular the themes of Torah (v. 1) and wisdom [*khokmah*] (v. 13) are brought to bear in v. 18 on the opening verse of Ps 1: "She is a tree of life to those who grasp her, and whoever holds on to her is happy (*me'ushar*)," parallel to the *'ashre* formulaic opening of Ps 1.

Modern research has greatly expanded the canon of wisdom literature to include, beyond the traditional Job, Qohelet, and Proverbs, such texts as Esther, Ruth, Canticles, the Joseph narrative, and occasional "wisdom" psalms.[7] What it means to be a wisdom psalm or text can of course vary, depending on one's critical tendency, but the following characteristics seem well established.

---

[5]For a dissenting view see Avi Hurvitz, "Wisdom Vocabulary in the Hebrew Psalter: A Contribution to the Study of 'Wisdom Psalms'," *VT* 38 (1988): 41–51; also *Wisdom Language in Biblical Psalmody* (Hebrew; Jerusalem: Magnes, 1991). It must be noted that Hurvitz does not absolutely deny admission of Ps 1 to the corpus of wisdom psalms; he excludes it because, due to its brevity, it does not stand the test of his methodology, narrowly focused on the accumulation of wisdom terminology.

[6]Ha-Meiri, *Perush 'al Sefer Tehilim,* 11.

[7]See Roland E. Murphy, *Wisdom Literature* (FOTL 13; Grand Rapids: Eerdmans, 1981); also *The Tree of Life: An Exploration of Biblical Wisdom Literature* (New York: Doubleday, 1990), 103.

I list them here in what appears to me to be their order of increasing relevance to Ps 1:

a) a non-cultic approach to spirituality

b) origin among the sages

c) a pedagogical and didactic function

d) an admonitory style

e) the ʾ*ashrei* formula ("Blessed is the one who")

f) the theme of fear of the Lord (= observance of Torah)

g) the contrastive description of the *tsaddiq* and *rashaᶜ*, the "righteous" and the "wicked"

h) the theme of reward and punishment

i) God's (apparent) absence or mitigated presence

j) God or Wisdom's outreach to the Righteous

As a prelude to the study of these last four wisdom themes in connection with Ps 1, let us briefly review the poem's thematic structure.

The Structure of Righteous / Wicked in Psalm 1

A single reading or recitation of Ps 1 gives the impression of a highly structured presentation of the materials (three sections of two verses each), most notably the central opposition between the wicked and the righteous. The exact nature of this structure is, however, a matter for debate. Sensing the presence of such an overriding structure, for example, Leo G. Perdue perceives vv. 1 and 3, on the one hand, and vv. 4–5 on the other (v. 2 is excised as a "later insertion") as antithetical and thus parallel to the concluding v. 6, and defines the construction as a "chiastic antithetical saying."[8] Beyond the problem of the excision, however, the parallel does not work because what Perdue defined as the first two strophes are not chiastic.

---

[8]Leo G. Perdue, *Wisdom and Cult* (SBLDS 30; Missoula: Scholars Press, 1977), 271.

By retaining the MT, however, a more convincing chiasmus is clear:

A   v. 1: the wicked

    B   v. 2: the righteous

    B′   v. 3: the righteous (compared and successful)

A′   vv. 4–5: the wicked (compared and condemned)

This ABB′A′ chiasm would then be concluded by the B′A′ figure in the final verse, explicitly naming once again the righteous and the wicked. There are, to be sure, two difficulties with this analysis as well, one a structural imbalance and the other a conceptual incongruity. As for the first, the grouping of vv. 4 and 5 is threatened by the strong disruption of "therefore" (*ᶜal ken*) at the start of v. 5. Secondly, on the basis of this structure we are asked to conclude ("therefore," v. 5) that the wicked will perish "because" (*ki,* v. 4b) they are like chaff, a weighty conclusion to be based on a simple comparison or metaphor.

The truth is that the present verse division suggests a different chiasm, itself perfectly balanced in terms of the number of subdivisions of the individual verses:

v. 1: the wicked   1a–d

    v. 2: the righteous   2a–b

    v. 3: the righteous   3a–d

v. 4: the wicked   4a–b

The psalm's conclusion is therefore not simply the final verse but rather the final two verses, which again chiastically recapitulate the central dichotomy of the righteous and wicked, placed at or near the end of each segment:

v. 5   wicked / righteous

v. 6   righteous / wicked

The structural unity of the two final verses, it seems to me, gives a theologically more plausible explanation of the destruction of the wicked announced in v. 5: because the Lord "knows," watches humans and ensures justice.

It should be carefully noted that this restructuring and interpretation rest on an important grammatical point which apparently only Rashi (1140–1105) emphasized. First, commenting on ᶜal ken ("therefore," v. 5), Rashi proposes: "This is to be attached to what follows." And, more explicitly on v. 6:

> Since He knows the way of the righteous . . . and the way of the wicked is hateful in His eyes, . . . therefore the wicked will have no salvation on the day of judgment.

Indeed, grammatically speaking, ᶜal ken draws an inference from evidence presented by a clause introduced by ki, and this causative particle may follow rather than precede the conclusion.[9]

The Theme of Reward and Punishment

Let us recapitulate our last point by proposing, consistent with Rashi's reading, a new translation of the final and concluding chiasm:

> This is why the wicked will not survive judgment
> Nor sinners in the assembly of the righteous:
> Because the Lord cherishes the way of the righteous,
> But the way of the wicked will perish. (Ps 1:5–6)

The careful language of this formulation of reward and punishment will give some guidance on the interesting question concerning the source of justice, whether it comes directly from God or whether it simply flows from the "order" of the universe. This theme of justice, common to the entire Hebrew Bible, has a particular twist in wisdom texts. Especially in the form of the retribution meted out to the wicked, it is viewed as a fact of life, as a perfectly natural, predictable, almost fatalistic structure of reality.

---

[9]Cf. Gen 11:9; 20:6; 21:31; 32:33; Num 21:27–28; 2 Sam 7:22; Isa 9:16; 16:9; Jer 5:6; 20:11; Jon 4:2; Hab 1:4, 16; Zech 10:2; Job 6:3–4. For elaboration see T. A. Perry, "The Coordination of ky / 'l kn in Cant. i 1–3 and Related Texts," VT 54 (2005): 533–35.

There is never a doubt that such a state of things derives from God, of course, but the stress is on the pre-existent universal moral mechanism rather than on providence and God's explicit imposition of justice. By contrast, in many passages in the Torah punishment is directly meted out by God. Psalm 1 replies that both are operative, but with distinct roles: it is the Lord Himself that rewards or cares for the righteous, whereas the wicked, being left to their own devices, self-destruct or perish from their own movement and without any outside intervention. Thus, in close parallel:

> Oh that a full measure of evil might come upon the wicked,
> And that Thou wouldst establish the righteous. (Ps 7:10 [7:9], Soncino trans.)[10]

> For evil doers will be cut off; but those that wait upon the Lord will inherit the land. (Ps 37:9)

> For the arms of the wicked will be broken; but the Lord upholds the righteous. (Ps 37:17)

> Evil will kill the wicked. . . .
> The Lord redeems the soul of His servants. (Ps 34:22–23[34:21–22])

> The nations drown in the pit which they made;
> In the net that they hid their own foot is caught. (Ps 9:16[9:15])

It seems to me that this latter characteristic of our text, the (apparent) absence or at least mitigated presence of God, contributes to its membership in the wisdom canon.[11]

---

[10]*Soncino Books of the Bible: The Psalms* (trans. A. Cohen; London: Soncino, 1945), 16.

[11]See also 1 Sam 2:30: "Those that honor me I shall honor; but those who despise me will be lightly esteemed"; 2:9: "He will keep the feet of His pious ones, but the wicked will be silent in darkness." Yehudah Keil, on 1 Sam 2:9 (*1 Samuel* [Hebrew; Jerusalem: Mossad Harav Kook, 1981], 18), sees an intermediate stage in such passages, in which God is also the subject of the wicked's destruction but the Holy Name is not explicitly named, thus not associated with them: "The Lord watches over His beloved ones, but the wicked He will destroy" (Ps 145:20). Citing *Midr. Bereshit Rabbah* 3:8 ("God associates His name with good and not with evil"), Keil derives this stylistic and ideological tendency from Gen 1:5: "And God called the light day, and the darkness He called night."

God's Absence / Presence

While God's verbal or grammatical absence[12] can be found throughout the Hebrew Bible, this is more the case in biblical wisdom texts.[13] The extreme example is the book of Esther, where the name of God does not occur even once; but one thinks also of the book of Ruth and of the Eliezer episode in Gen 24. Of course, in Ps 1 God's name does occur in two important verses (vv. 2, 6), but before examining these let us consider how biblical authors and their readers were accustomed to "read in" God's name.

Psalm 1:3 provides us with evidence of this technique, where the righteous person is compared to a tree planted by streams of water,

> which brings forth its fruit in its season . . .
> and all that *it* produces prospers.

Nahum M. Sarna rightly points out an ambiguity here, since the subject could as well be the righteous person:[14]

> who brings forth *his* fruit in its season . . .
> and all that *he* does prospers.

One could go even farther, however, since there is yet another ambiguity in the verse. In a remarkable linguistic parallel it is said of Joseph in Potiphar's household:

> And his master saw that the Lord was with him *and all that he does the Lord causes to prosper.* (Gen 39:3)

This parallel passage also reminds us of the two meanings of the verb *tslkh:* on the one hand, "to prosper, succeed" (Gen 39:2); on the other and consonant with the causative sense of the *hip'il* form: "to cause to succeed or prosper." Anyone familiar with the Joseph text, especially in an oral culture, would quite automati-

---

[12]For a recent discussion see Amelia Devin Freedman, *God as an Absent Character in Biblical Hebrew Narrative: A Literary-Historical Study* (New York: Lang, 2005).

[13]See Perry, *Dialogues with Kohelet,* 83, 97, 102, 104, 140.

[14]Sarna, *Songs of the Heart,* 43.

cally read our passage like the Genesis one, supplying the unwritten subject and, along with it, the causative sense of the verb:

who brings forth his fruit in its season . . .
and all that he does the Lord causes to prosper. (Ps 1:3)

Or, reading backwards, one might alternatively "read into" the first part of the verse as follows:

[the Lord, mentioned in the previous verse] who brings forth its / His fruit in its / His season . . .

Psalm 1:6

To introduce God as an active participant in this otherwise "wisdom" psalm is not that far-fetched, since the text goes on to conclude in Ps 1:6, rather surprisingly and boldly, that

For the Lord knows the way of the righteous,
But the way of the wicked will perish.

The surprise here is that, unless v. 3 is read as I have just proposed, this concluding verse is the first time in the poem that God is seen as playing an active role. Crucial to our understanding here is the precise nature of God's activity. Scholars have rightly insisted on the rich and expanded sense of "knowing" implied in the biblical Hebrew *yada^c*, closer here to the French *connaître* than *savoir,* which also suggests "emotional ties, empathy, intimacy, sexual experience, mutuality, . . . protection and care."[15]

There does seem to be a softening of "knowledge" here, however, where the context of the term indicates somewhat of a withdrawal from the frontal knowing of another being suggested in Adam's knowledge of Eve or Hosea's "and you shall know the Lord" (Hos 2:22[2:20]):

For the Lord knows *the way* of the righteous.

The addition does not minimize the intimacy, however, quite the contrary. The Hosea passage itself is but a clear echo of God's first great love in the Bible:

---

[15]Ibid., 47.

For I have known/loved him, . . . that he may keep *the way of the Lord* to do what is just and right. (Gen 18:19)

And I will betroth you with mercy and justice. (Hos 4:21)

Just as the Lord has a *way* of *tsedeq* and *mishpat,* so too do the righteous have a way of *tsedaqah* and *mishpat.*

One might further refine this by also reflecting upon the two contrasted "ways" of this verse. Consider what seems to me an apposite parallel, also from a wisdom text:

Three things are too wondrous for me,
four I cannot fathom:
The way of an eagle in the sky,
the way of a serpent upon a rock;
the way of a ship upon the seas;
and the way of a man with a young woman.
Such too is the way of an adulteress:
she eats and wipes her mouth and declares:
"I have done no wrong." (Prov 30:18–20)[16]

The "way" of an adulteress is both her behavior and her inscrutable manner of thinking, and to these meanings the example of "a man with a young woman" adds what is called in English "a way with women," a kind of personal manner and appeal. Transposed to our text, the suggestion would be that the righteous "have a way with God," a level of intimacy and mutual appeal, almost of seduction. Also noteworthy in this parallel passage is the juxtaposition of two opposing "ways," both enigmatic.

Psalm 1:2

There is a second explicit mention of God's name in our Psalm:

Rather in the Torah of the Lord is his delight,
and on His Torah he meditates day and night. (Ps 1:2)

---

[16]Indeed, *b. Qidd.* 2b extends the erotic connotations of "ways" to include cohabitation. See chapter 9 for further elaboration.

Unless one be overly committed to the principle of "synonymous parallelism," there are good reasons for seeing the second part of the verse as an expansion of the first rather than its mere "artistic" repetition—after all, the three propositions of v. 1 show a progression of thought rather than a simple list of variations. Let Rashi's homiletic gloss summarize the matter: "At first it is referred to as God's Torah, but then [because of laborious acquisition] it is called *his own* Torah." Ha-Meiri approves of what he calls a rabbinic "*drash*" and justifies it as follows:[17]

> If the word "and on his Torah" [*ubetorato*] refers to God, then the text would have to state: "and in His law" [*ubedato*], as is the custom in repeating a subject with different words [i.e., synonymous parallelism].

According to this, the verbal repetition excludes the thought repetition and requires different meanings. Thus,

> Rather in the Torah of the Lord is his delight,
> and on *his* [not His] Torah he meditates day and night. (Ps 1:2)

In terms of the theme described above of God's active "personal" involvement in the life of the righteous, one could go on to propose yet a further way of reading this ambivalent verse:

> Rather, in the Torah of the Lord is his delight,
> and on his Torah *He* meditates day and night. (Ps 1:2)

This establishes a chiastic arrangement of the grammatical subjects and objects:

> God's Torah / human's delight;
> human's Torah / God's meditative delight.

Such ambiguities are of course not limited to Ps 1. In Ps 37 the same level of divine/human ambivalence is exploited (and, interestingly, with an echo of the same verb *khepets,* "to take delight"):

> It is of the Lord that a man's steps are established,
> and in his way He takes delight.
> OR: and in His way he takes delight. (Ps 37:23)

---

[17]See *b. ʿAbod. Zar.* 19a.

Each is grammatically possible, but it seems that here too the ambiguity permits (requires?) not an either/or decision but rather that *both* be read.

But is it reasonable that the Lord should be meditatively involved in humanity's acquired teaching, even in the Torah of the righteous? The end of this very Psalm gives the requisite parallel:

> [The reason is that] the Lord knows, has regard for, the way of the righteous.

As we extend ourselves to the Beloved, the Beloved extends himself to us; or, according to the thought of Ps 51:17[51:15], our prayer already contains an awareness of God's active participation, even initiation.

We can now add a further reason as to why this Psalm was chosen to introduce the Psalter, for in addition to important themes of the wisdom canon there is the notion that the Lord cares for us and has high regard for our Torah (learning and involvement) and righteous ways. The very subtlety of its presentation—as a remote midrashic possibility in v. 2, as a linguistic reminiscence in v. 3, and finally as a strong and positive assertion in the concluding verse—underscores God's involvement in human affairs, as at first barely perceptible and ambivalent, then, gradually, as fully declared.

In Proverbs 1:20 and again 8:1 Wisdom's active search of humans is boldly proclaimed: "Wisdom cries aloud in the street." If Ps 1 is to remain in the wisdom canon, then we must note that Lady Wisdom's outreach, as it were, is to be identified as God's own. With this explicit analysis of God's love as the *reason* for being happy, Ps 1 has achieved its wisdom purpose as the introduction to the Psalter.

Here, in conclusion, are new proposals for the translation of Ps 1, as suggested by the previous discussion:

> [1]Happy is the one
> who walks not in the counsel of the wicked,
> or stands on the way of sinners,
> or sits in the seat of scoffers.
> [2]But in the Torah of the Lord is his delight,
> / and in *His* Torah *he* meditates day and night.
> / and in *his* Torah *He* meditates day and night.

³He is like a tree planted by streams of water,
who yields *its/his* fruit in *its* season,
and its leaf does not wither,
and all that he does *prospers / He causes to prosper.*
⁴Not so the wicked,
rather they are like chaff that a wind blows away.
⁵This is why the wicked will not survive judgment,
Nor sinners in the assembly of the righteous:
⁶Because the Lord cherishes the way of the righteous,
but the way of the wicked will perish. (Ps 1:1–6)

This expanded reciprocity of verses 2–3 can be extended to Ps 37:23:

It is of the Lord that a man's steps are established,
/ and in His way he takes delight.
/ and in his way He takes delight.

The interpretive mistake would be, in such a situation of perfect ambivalence, to choose one alternative over the other, since both are intended.

PART THREE

THE REBIRTH OF VULNERABILITY AND WONDER

EIGHT

Planning the Twilight Years: Qohelet's Advice on Aging and Death (Qoh 12:1–8)

Even those who live many years
should rejoice in them all.

(Qoh 11:8)

Better the day of death than the day of one's birth;
better the end of a thing than its beginning.

(Qoh 7:1, 8)

It is better to go to a house of
mourning than to a party.

(Qoh 7:2; cf. v. 4)

Logically you cannot have an end without a beginning, but we somehow imagine or hope that there can be a beginning to life without an end. In fact, both are logically related and according to the nature of things: each beginning must have an end. Why then is the end of a thing better than its beginning (Qoh 7:8)? One reason is because this idea dispels one of our pet fantasies, reminding us, as Graham Ogden put it, that "death and life are intertwined, and mutually defining."[1] The point of the present inquiry is to ask how "the living must, if they are to be accounted wise, devote their minds to discovering what death means,"[2] or, perhaps more poetically, whether Qohelet's lesson of wisdom is "joy in the face of death."[3]

In its grand concluding chapter, the book of Qohelet momentarily changes its literary form, shifting from collections of pithy proverbs to a sophisticated and integrated narrative that has been called an allegory on old age, an elegy on dying, a vivid poetic description, a *memento mori*, to name only a few.[4] This difficult passage—Michael V. Fox has judged it to be "the most difficult passage in a difficult book"[5]—has generated much discussion, notably of its theme, its literary form and, most crucially, its interpretation. Fox, at one extreme, finds only a "succession of images of distortion and despair: trembling, writhing, cessation of activity, darkening, shutting, silence, bowing, fear," while Harold Fisch judges that "never was there a gentler poem on the approach of death."[6]

Here is the text:

> [1]Remember your creator in the days of your youth, before those days of trouble come, and the years draw near when you will say, "I have no pleasure in them"; [2]before the sun and the light and the moon and the stars are darkened and the clouds return with the rain. [3]In the day when the guards of the house tremble, and the strong men are bent, and the women who grind cease working because they are

---

[1]Graham Ogden, *Qoheleth* (Readings: A New Biblical Commentary; Sheffield: JSOT Press, 1987), 100. See also Qoh 4:2; 6:3.

[2]Ogden, *Qoheleth,* 100.

[3]Norbert Lohfink, *Qoheleth: A Continental Commentary* (Minneapolis: Fortress, 2003), 93.

[4]For the perennial favorite "allegory on old age" see, for example, Robert Gordis, *Koheleth: The Man and His World: A Study of Ecclesiastes* (New York: Schocken, 1968), 197. For the "elegy on dying" see Harold Fisch, *Poetry with a Purpose* (Bloomington: Indiana University Press, 1990), 177. For "a vivid poetic description" see Thomas Krüger, *Qoheleth* (Minneapolis: Fortress, 2004), 195. For the phrase *memento mori* see Michael V. Fox, *A Time to Tear Down and a Time to Build Up: A Rereading of Ecclesiastes* (Grand Rapids: Eerdmans, 1999), 319.

[5]Michael V. Fox, *Qohelet and His Contradictions* (Sheffield: Almond, 1989), 281.

[6]Ibid., 289; Fisch, *Poetry with a Purpose,* 177.

few, and those who look through the windows see dimly; [4]when the doors on the street are shut, and the sound of the grinding is low; and one rises up at the sound of a bird, and all the daughters of song are brought low; [5]when one is afraid of heights, and terrors are in the road; the almond tree blossoms, the grasshopper drags itself along and desire fails; because all must go to their eternal home, and the mourners will go about the streets; [6]before the silver cord is snapped, and the golden bowl is broken, and the pitcher is broken at the fountain, and the wheel broken at the cistern, [7]and the dust returns to the earth as it was, and the breath returns to God who gave it. [8]Vanity of vanities, says the Teacher; all is vanity. (Qoh 12:1–8, NRSV)

Literary Method (Allegory, Symbolism, *Pshat*) and Theme

The allegorical reading of this passage has held sway for centuries, to varying degrees, and is still a favorite. The most thoroughgoing is perhaps the rabbinic reading, where all details from Qoh 12:2–6 are assigned meanings with reference to the body of a dying person. Such is the way of allegorical interpretation, long ago defined as *alieniloquium,* saying one thing in terms of another. Thus, when the author of *Pilgrim's Progress* speaks of climbing a steep and rocky mountain, we understand the landscape to be the Mount of Virtue and climbing to be the difficulty of becoming virtuous. Of course, clear meanings are most easily conveyed when the "answers" are given; they become more challenging when they are not and typically generate multiple readings. At the start of Dante's *Inferno,* for example, the identity of the leopard (of lust? pleasure?) has generated much discussion. The *Romance of the Rose* has inspired—if that is the right word—two different readings within the same text. Yet in all cases it is clear that these are mere figures of speech, that Dante did not meet up with a flesh-and-blood leopard in real life. And as for the famous French text, well, a rose is not really a rose, is in fact not a rose at all.

In the so-called allegory in Qohelet, however, most of the details seem quite realistic, descriptive of scenes from everyday life (or, as some would have it, death). And while die-hard allegorists would still cling to assigning meanings to the details of Qoh 12:6, even here authors such as Henry James, followed by Fisch, have basked in its literal reference. Their reading of v. 6 sees the message that even art is ephemeral, provocatively adding that, in this magnificent work of art, the only allegory we are given is at best "an allegory of art."[7]

It seems to me that, while allegory will continue to entice readers, the literalist option may be ripe for renewed elaboration.[8] Let us then propose that, instead of reading as if one thing is said and another thing meant, we consider the model of saying something and really meaning it. This would displace the literary or stylistic guessing game by a method that looks intently at the plain meaning (the surface *pshat*) rather than beyond it. André Neher states this requirement nicely, asking that we "grant the text its integral literalism," a move that would impair neither the complexity nor the literary interest of what is being said, as we shall see.[9] It is true that whereas allegory is a matter of contrived referentiality, a literary device highly conscious of its own artifice, *pshat* is often colored by the notion of *pashtut,* a concern for surface or "simple" reality—as if there were any other kind. Verisimilitude, however, literally means a show of what is truly there. Thus, a symbolic reading could easily be the *pshat,* which means its most likely reading in the given context.[10] The focus on the literal level may not be seen as a limitation, quite the contrary. For while it is true that a text never entirely leaves its *pshat* or literal meaning, it can range far abroad while clinging to this basis. The basic rule of the interpretative act must be to abandon the usual distinctions between outer and inner, higher and lower, surface and hidden layers, since the surface literary landscape itself has many highs and lows, thank you very much.

As for the theme of Qoh 12:1–8, the ongoing favorites are aging, dying, and death. Whereas a strong majority of critics—

---

[7]Fisch, *Poetry with a Purpose,* 178.

[8]See, for example, Krüger's (*Qoheleth,* 199) open and balanced approach: "The diversity of detail in the proposed interpretations already shows the questionable nature of a thoroughly allegorical interpretation of 12:2–7."

[9]"Si on concède au texte son intégrale littéralité," André Neher, *Notes sur Qohélét* (Paris: Éditions de Minuit, 1951), 100. Maurice Blanchot's (*Écriture du désastre* [Paris: Gallimard, 1980]) insistence on the *dehors* may be taken in this extended sense: not only what lies outside (the system) but also the surface (as opposed to the inner sense dear to allegorists). By some kind of coincidence of opposites, it is the surface (of the text) that will best uncover or reveal its freedom beyond the system (the totality).

[10]Fox (*A Time to Tear Down,* 333) has argued for a broader palette by including symbolism, which he correctly sees as an extension of the literal.

myself included—understand the theme in reference mainly to the individual human being, other intriguing possibilities have been suggested: an advancing storm, the fall of night, and the ruin of a wealthy estate.[11] Rather than providing further alternates, however, I think all of these can be related to the general theme of change or transience, incorporated in Qohelet's key concept of *hebel*, "vanity," since they represent eventualities which the youth addressee must be prepared to confront as his life moves through personal development and changing circumstances. It should also be noted, as it seldom is, that changed circumstances may have little to do with death or aging. The young, for example, may develop cancer or undergo a paralyzing accident. And while it is the case that the most universal and inevitable instance is individual death, when the human being "goes to his eternal home" (Qoh 12:5) accompanied by mourners, the overall focus of Qohelet is less on either death or dying than on how a person, already at an early age, can be prepared for these eventualities.

By maintaining the text's focus on the young addressee, we can more easily sort out and orient the more peripheral themes just mentioned.[12] For example, Qoh 12:2–4 can plausibly be applied to the fall of a house or city, and v. 2 has strong echoes of the prophetic theme of a universal end of the world. Yet, such extended possibilities become funneled by their clear final application to the funeral of an individual human in vv. 5 and 7. We can thus read these other interpretative possibilities as points of comparison. To take one example, the demise of a person can be compared to the very undoing of creation itself, much like the moral undoing of Jerusalem can be described as a *tohu*, "formlessness," a reversion to the universal state of things preceding its creation.[13] The extraordinary power of such comparisons, based on a much

---

[11]For example, some details seem more appropriate to more general cataclysms such as drought, etc. For a sampling of these theses in the previous generation of scholarship, see Gordis, *Koheleth: The Man and His World*, 338–39.

[12]Krüger's (*Qoheleth*, 202) outline is crucial here.

[13]"And the earth was *tohu* . . ." (Gen 1:2). It must be said that such images do not require pessimistic interpretation. Thus, for example, while the disappearance of light in Qoh 12:2 can indeed signify universal catastrophe, it can also symbolize the alternatives of glorious restoration and apocalyptic promise, as in Isa 60:19–20; Ps 139:11–12.

broadened context and making it possible to scan a range of cosmological, anthropological, and theological contexts, is the principle of analogy, the notion that creation is structured on levels of reality that mirror one another and can be so understood.[14] Such understandings are in fact so embedded in our ordinary language as to appear simply descriptive rather than metaphorical extensions. Thus, one's youth can quite naturally be described as the "morning" of one's life:

> For youth and the morning twilight are fleeting. (Qoh 11:9)

Although the philosophical implications of our theme may be postponed until we have worked through (not around) its concrete and complex literalness, by way of anticipation we shall try to focus on death and dying in the following way. In a humanity that is both physical and metaphysical, what happens when the two are separated and "go their own way," as in death? Our literalist method requires, rather than blithe dismissal, full focus on decline and loss. But does this require, for all that, pretending that contrary evidence does not also exist? Indeed, in a universe of stunning regularity that is taken by some as depressing (e.g., Qoh 1:9), will the sun not rise again tomorrow? Or, as the mourners go about their business (v. 5), does not the almond tree also blossom (v. 4)? There is a second, overriding theme that informs the wider text, in fact the entire book: nature, its cycles and seasonableness, based on the biblical ideology of creation, its undoing, and its renewal.

As for interpretation, the usual pessimistic one is often thought to be mitigated by the epicurean thesis of carpe diem. Thus, Fox's summary of Qoh 12:1–8: "Enjoy life before you grow old and die," thus limiting enjoyment to the earlier years.[15] How this can accommodate Qohelet's more global advice is problematic, however:

---

[14]See, for example, Michel Foucault, *Les mots et les choses* (Paris: Gallimard, 1966), 36–38.

[15]Fox, *A Time to Tear Down*, 333. His full statement, referring to our poem, is as follows: "Actually, we do know what it [the book of Qoheleth] means: enjoy life before you grow old and die." In my view this statement is problematic on several counts. Agreed: enjoy life, but *all* of life, as per Qoh 11:8, since growing old also has its joys. Is old age not a "season" as much as youth? And is old age only about death, about which we have neither knowledge nor experience? As Epicurus put it (quoted in Levinas, *Dieu, la mort et le temps,* 28): "If you are there, death is not there; if death is there, you are not there."

Even those who live many years should rejoice in them all. (Qoh 11:8)

This pointedly refers to the elderly, to those typically thought to be the subject of our passage. Qohelet says that they too should rejoice?! What then if "life" presents them with "vexation" and "unpleasantness"?! The imperative is resolute: "enjoy them *all!*" Then, too, there are dissonant details that further question, if not entirely derail, the gloom-sayers: the sound of a bird, the blossoming almond tree, the sexuality and fertility of nature. . . .

These positive meanings come into clearer focus when the broader frames of our passage are considered. Recent critical discussion of Qoh 12:2–7, moving beyond the view of a self-contained artistic achievement, is now willing to consider its centrality to the summary of the entire book.[16] For, strictly speaking, the allegorical thesis can be applied, at its widest parameters, only to vv. 2–7. It is widely held, however, that vv. 1 and 8 must be brought into the discussion. Fisch has observed, for example, that the subject is "death as a warning, an incentive to effort. The meaning of the ending is contained not only in the great elegy itself but in the verses that frame it, verses that urge the remembering and doing and bearing witness *while there is yet time.*"[17] While Fisch's remarks about effort are especially appropriate to the activism of Qoh 11:1–6, the remainder of chapter 11 foregrounds a second major theme as well, also incumbent on the young man or *bakhur* (11:9) being addressed in this entire section (11:1–12:8), namely the importance of enjoyment:[18]

⁷The light is sweet, and it is good for the eyes to enjoy the sun.

---

[16]Krüger, *Qoheleth,* 191, sees 11:1–12:7 as "the closing summary of the 'teachings' of the book of Qoheleth and its consequences for the life one leads." Choon-Leong Seow, *Ecclesiastes: A New Translation with Introduction and Commentary* (AB 18C; New York: Doubleday, 1997), 346, views 11:7–12:8 as the book's conclusion. Closest to the point of view expressed here is Roland Murphy's (*Ecclesiastes* [WBC 23A; Waco, 1992], 111) view of Qoh 11:7–12:8 as "Instructions concerning Youth and Old Age," except that I take youth and old age as also extending beyond their literal meaning. See below, the discussion on *puer-senex.*

[17]Fisch, *Poetry with a Purpose,* 177. See also Perry, *Dialogues with Kohelet* on 7:2, 10.

[18]In agreement with Krüger (*Qoheleth,* 191), who views this closing section (11:1–12:8) as the concluding summary of Qohelet's teachings. I differ only by including 12:8 as part of this summarizing section; see below.

[8]Even if a person lives for many years, he should rejoice in them all, while being constantly mindful (*weyizkor*) of the days of darkness, for they will be many: all that dies is *hebel*.

[9]Young man, enjoy your adolescence,[19] and let your heart cheer you in the days of your youth. And follow the intuitions of your heart and what is before your eyes, and know that [if you do not, or in any case] God will bring you to judgment.

[10]Remove anger from your heart and suffering from your flesh, for adolescence and the dawn [of life][20] are transient.

[1]And remember your Creator in the days of your youth!
(Qoh 11:7–12:1)

This grand summary, in its upward, optimistic swing, actually begins in Qoh 9:1 and includes all of chapter 9, which is interrupted by a miscellany of proverbs in chapter 10, before resuming in 11:1. The wider context of this previous passage is valuable in saying what this constant mindfulness or "remembering" implies: not an esthetic withdrawal from a fleeting world but rather a full, confident immersion and enjoyment. Further, since it specifies what youthful immersion in life entails, it serves as the best commentary on the enjoyment that is to be put aside, or rather transformed, in aging and death. Within these broader parameters, the interlude of Qoh 12:2–7 can now be seen as a projected and necessary leave-taking from the desires and pleasures (*khepets*) of one form of life, since *these* particular pleasures and interests will no longer be present or appropriate. But, for all that, does that mean that the *bakhur* will then be "dead"? To the "normal" workaday world, perhaps.

---

[19]Joseph was called a *yeled*, "child," at age seventeen (Gen 37:30). Alternatively, childhood may be literally intended. Addressed here to a young man, the reference would then be either a fond memory of a carefree childhood or an invitation to parents to strive for this ideal in their parenting.

[20]For "dawn" meaning "dawn of life" see Seow, *Ecclesiastes,* 346; Fox, *A Time to Tear Down,* 319. The *hapax, shakharut,* seems based on *shakhar,* which can mean either "dawn" or "black," presumably the stage of life when the youth's hair is not yet gray. This would of course not cover those whose hair is blond or red to begin with. Although both refer to the period of youth, dawn seems preferable because it relates to the basic unit of measuring human life: the day. The youth is reminded that days have evening as well as morning twilights.

If then, as many think, the theme here is indeed dying and death, it is so at a remove, since we are not spectators to a real demise but to an imagined or projected one. That is to say, the authorial voice is not describing an actual death but rather a virtual one, one that may (or may not) apply. Fox's assertion that all of this is necessarily gruesome in the extreme thus remains a possibility, but only that. Rather than a description of what Qohelet thinks death is really like, it projects how gruesome death could be if the youth remained without development and maturity. That is to say, its perspective is decidedly pedagogical: just imagine what it *could* be like! A parallel case would be the observation that "it is better to go to a house of mourning than to a party" (Qoh 7:2). This is not advice as to how one should set out to enjoy a fine evening but rather an observation on the possible benefits of what, on the surface and beforehand, can be unpleasant and not fun at all. There is also the suggestion that, at some important level and in retrospect—one does not normally pursue unpleasantness for its own sake—a greater benefit can accrue and lies concealed.

A Literal Reading of Qohelet 12:1–8

Before jumping off the edge of the real world into either some allegorical never-never land or depths of degradation, therefore, let us attempt as literal and neutral an understanding as possible, taking care not to intrude or project personal or cultural attitudes towards death. This passage should be thought of as poetic in the sense that its images have been selected to depict, to the youthful addressee, the broadest possible range of references. In this brief commentary, I shall highlight possibilities of literalist interpretation that tend to be dismissed by univocal readings.

[1]So, remember your Creator in the days of your strength: Before those "bad days" come, and years arrive when you will say: "I have no interest in them. . . ."

[2]Before the darkening of the sun and the light and the moon and the stars, and the clouds return after the rain.

[3]In the day when the watchmen of the house tremble, and men of strength and influence have been corrupted; and the grinding women cease their work—indeed, they are become few—and the women watching at the windows grow gloomy;

[4]And the doors to the street are shut. And, at the lowering of the sound of the mill, one will rise up at the sound of a bird (and all the singing women are silenced:

[5]they are afraid of a Higher One, and there are dangers along the way); And the almond tree will blossom, and the locust shall fatten itself [on it] until its desire fails;[21] Indeed [before] the human being goes to his eternal home and the mourners go about in the streets.
. . .

[6]Before the thread of silver is snapped and the pot of gold broken, and the pitcher smashed at the fountain, and the wheel broken at the cistern;

[7]and the dust returns to the earth as it was, and the spirit returns to God who gave it. . . .

[8]"A transient transience," said the Qohelet. "All is transience." (Qoh 12:1–8)

12:1 *So*   Although this section is sequential with important themes in the preceding chapter, the *waw* connective is often ignored, creating the (false) impression of an independent and self-contained unit.[22]

remember your Creator   While it is true that the word "Creator," *bor'eka,* occurs only here in this work, the only divine name used in this entire book is *'elohim,* the name of the Creator-God in the very first verse of the Bible: *'elohim bara'.* This name concludes Qohelet's poem, and his book (12:7), in a final act of creation which is the creation's in-gathering. This is the Creator-God who, in the context of death of Qoh 12:7, is evoked as the same god who "gives" life (Job 1:21). It is not the case that God's creative activity is limited to Qoh 12:1, since, as Thomas Krüger points out,

---

[21]*until its desire fails;* alternatively, "and the caperberry bursts open," or "buds again" (JPS).

[22]As, for example, NRSV, Seow, Murphy.

this verse "recalls the whole breadth of 'theological' statements in the preceding context."[23]

remember your Creator   The One who equipped you for this life and the resources necessary to figure it out for yourself and live it in a dignified way, as a grownup.

your strength (bekhuroteka)   This takes up the "young man" theme of Qoh 11:9: "Rejoice, young man (*bakhur*), while you are young," allowing a closer identification of the addressee. The person addressed is no longer the general receptor of advice of Qoh 11:1, 6; nor is he the "my son" of Qoh 12:12 and especially Proverbs, with its tenderness and pedagogical urgency. Rather, it as quite likely, as Fox asserts, that this refers to a young man at the age of military service and thus in his physical prime.[24] This is the time when, in full strength, he "goes out" into the world. For the military theme see also v. 3, the "women at the window."

"bad days"   "Bad days" does not present either the author's or Qohelet's view but is rather a projection of what the youth may come to "say," i.e., "think." The expression is thus a quotation, not to be considered as "days of misery" (Norman Whybray) in themselves, but rather as days in the addressee's future that, from his present perspective, he does not believe he will enjoy:[25] "I have no pleasure in them."

days and years   It is the way people talk even today: "I am having a bad day," or "we had a bad year." For those who hold to simple synonymy for stylistic variety, there is no puzzle about the occurrence of "days" and "years" in this verse (also Qoh 11:8). Alternatively, "day" often has a more individual reference ("I am having a bad day"), whereas "years" can have a more general (e.g., agricultural) application. Both are in fact required if together they reference the solar cycles (daily and annual), thus introducing the

---

[23]Krüger, *Qoheleth*, 198, citing Qoh 6:2; 7:29; 5:17–18; 8:15; 9:9; among others.

[24]Fox, *A Time to Tear Down*, 318, citing 1 Kgs 12:21; 2 Chr 25:5.

[25]Norman Whybray, *Ecclesiastes* (NCB; Grand Rapids: Eerdmans, 1989), 163. This perspective can be either literally young or "young"; see below, *puer-senex*.

solar theme in the very next verse, which it joins to the light theme as well ("the light is sweet," Qoh 11:7). Pedagogically, the youth is re-minded that life is apportioned or "given" out in days and years.

interest   The popular reading of *khepets* as "pleasure" certainly captures one of the intended meanings here, but it also side-steps more active wisdom possibilities, as we shall see. Also, the text does not say that he will be miserable, rather that he will have no pleasure or, better, interest in those years. Absence of pleasure is not equivalent to misery. It may even be a prelude or precondition to joy. A Buddhist prayer refers to such a state: "Please send me a difficulty that will enable me to climb to the next level."

The pedagogical move here, by presenting the world from the perspective of the youth's *khepets,* is to expand the notion so that at *all* times and stages of life new possibilities can be gathered under the same term, his "interests," broadly speaking. Thus, in youth "pleasure" may include a broad range of exploits: sexual, military, commercial, and business interests.[26] The wisdom suggestion will be that, once these age-appropriate pleasures are removed or outgrown, as one day they will be, other kinds of age-appropriate *khepets* will replace them.

12:2 *Sun, light, moon, and stars*[27]   Qoh 12:2 describes the sequential parallel diminution and withdrawal of light. First the day: the sun, then its twilight or residual light after sunset;[28] then the night: the moon and, even when the moon is not visible, the stars.

---

[26]For sexual pleasures, see commentary on Qoh 12:3. For military themes see commentary on Qoh 12:1, 3, "your strength." For commercial interests see Isa 58:3: "Behold, in the day of fasting you pursue your business (*khepets*)."

[27]There may be an elegant literary reference here to Joseph's dream of future power, as symbolized by these three sources of light (and in the same order) doing obeisance to him (Gen 37:9). The meaning would be that for the *bakhur* such dreams of ascendancy and power are no longer possible.

[28]This reading makes a distinction between the sun and its light, as in Gen 44:3: "And when the morning was light," i.e., before the sun's actual rise. So too the evening twilight refers to the remaining light after sunset and before the appearance of the stars, which are parallel to the light of day in that their light covers the entire night, as the sun's light covers the entire day.

Alternatively, first the sun—no, its light—is darkened, then also (the light of) moon and stars. What has then happened to the sun/moon/stars themselves? Apparently, they strive to return to their place, whence they will shine again, as per Qoh 1:5.

Some see this combination of sun and light as a literary figure called hendiadys, "the light of the sun." This seems too restrictive, however. In Qoh 11:6 light itself was described as sweet (Dante's "*dolce lume*"), with the sun's light as the prime source of such pleasures, but surely not the sole one. The point would be the gradual dimming either of life forces or of visual pleasures, and although literal blindness and glaucoma are not excluded, such a condition would severely limit the range of the symbol. More likely is the transition from visual pleasures to auditory sensitivities, most notably *the sound of a bird* in v. 4.

the clouds return after the rain.   The clouds return after the rain? Normally it is the sun that returns, after the clouds have emptied! Such a situation contradicts normal expectations. A previous passage provides a likely situation:

> When the clouds are heavy they pour rain upon the earth. . . .
> whoever looks at the clouds will not reap. (Qoh 11:3, 4)

As opposed to the youthful perspective that will take a chance and reap, this more sedately-minded person looks for clouds, expects them, has lost interest in doing battle with the elements. From the perspective of an aging person, a first level of withdrawal is from daily living and activity (the sun), which is the main source of light, so much so that sunlight is viewed as life itself. Next comes the moon, the main source of nightly light, and then the final withdrawal of light, the distant light of the stars, a literal dis-aster.

The focus here is on the clouds: it is the clouds that occlude the light on all levels because of the threat of perpetual rain. We are here definitely in the winter or rainy season in the Middle East. Homiletically and symbolically, this is often seen as vision that "grows blurry from tears" (Fox), but it could also suggest tears as a gift expressing vulnerability. Further, just as perpetual clouds occlude the light, constant tears close the eyes to visual enjoyments, and the focus then shifts to sounds.

Thus far the waning of light has been understood in consonance with the daily cycle of day and night, thus an appropriate
parallel to the youth's natural progression towards old age. However, in the event of an *un*natural occurrence such as an accident
or disease, then the unlikely advent of perpetual clouds would
achieve an analogous effect. For this figure to work, one does not
need to assume an endless season of clouds, since human life is
here figured as a single day.

12:3–5a This section describes a general shutdown of typical pas-
times, with an interesting focus on women; or, rather, a focus on
female activities as perceived and perhaps filtered by male preoccupations. Thus, watchmen, whose prime moral quality should
be courage, are brought to trembling, while the moral guarantors
of the city—the men of influence—have lost their credibility.
Women who eagerly anticipate the victorious return of their
studly heroes (another level of security and defense), begin to
grasp the truth. The women singers no longer excite pleasure. The
grinding of mills and whorehouses (both sexual and food) are on
reduced or declining activity.[29]

12:3 *the women at the window grow gloomy*   The most memorable
illustration of this theme is Sisera's mother, as she impatiently
awaits the return of her son from battle with booty and captive
women (Judg 5:28). Qohelet's warning to the youth is that there
will come a time when one's military and sexual strengths and interests will fail, and the public will cease to admire him.

12:4 *the doors to the street are shut.*   This sentence summarizes
and closes the house scene begun at the start of v. 3. This detail
signifies the end of active life, as one no longer goes out either for
business or social activities. Closing the doors, withdrawal from
the windows, signifies a gradual retirement from public to private
life, from activity to either passivity or patience, or, as I think, to
heightened awareness and contemplation.

at the lowering of the sound of the mill   The image of the mill is
again used, as in the previous verse. The focus shifts from the

---

[29]For the sexual sense of "grinding" see Job 31:10, where the second part
of the verse leaves little doubt. See Rashi ad loc.

house, to which one who is aging is progressively consigned, to a change also in such a person's perception, and at two levels. First there is a transition from ocular (see v. 3) to auditory sensations, then a refinement of focus: as the "sound" of grinding ceases (industrial sounds, perhaps also based on a diminished need for food), the aging man becomes aware of another "sound," and this renders him indifferent to the singing ladies. This shift, from the artistic to the natural, is pursued in the natural images of the next verse.

one will rise up at the sound of a bird The return of the third person seems curious here, since the first line of reference is to the "you" being addressed at the start. In fact, this subtle touch generalizes the *bakhur* addressee to signify "everyman," as the reference to "the human being" makes clear in the very next verse.

rise up In 2 Kgs 13:21 this verb (*qum*) indicates both rising from the dead and standing, the latter notion explicitly specified by the addition "on his feet." In Isa 26:14 the meaning is also to "rise from the dead." Out of the growing silence (absence of noise) about him, the aging man is awakened, brought back to life, as it were.

the sound of a bird . . . [30]

are silenced Alternatively, "are no longer esteemed," i.e., by him; they are no longer of interest, as was also the case for Barzillai (see below). The relationship with the sound of a bird is ambiguous: either his interest in natural things—the startling intuition of higher things triggered by the sound of the bird—now trumps his former love of artistic delights; or his natural decline of interest in the latter now allows him to hear different sounds.

12:5 *They* It is likely that the plural subject (the singing women) is continued here.

---

[30]See the interpretation below, "Twilight Images of Dissonance." Alternatively, the bird theme has a proximate antecedent in Qoh 10:20, where it is a figure of retribution ("a little birdie told me"). In this scene of universal decline or dis-aster (see below), what rises up is the voice of conscience, the suspicion that the individual may have something to do with the disaster upon everyone. See Perry, *Dialogues with Kohelet,* 167.

A Higher One   This is a parenthetical explanation of why the songstresses are silenced. They too are "putting their house in order," so to speak, and now—perhaps because of the withdrawal of their patron—have a heightened awareness of the "Higher One" (see Qoh 5:7 and Ps 113:5).

dangers along the way   Such women as wander about on the highways have more proximate dangers to worry about (Cant 3:3; 5:7; Ruth 2).

the almond tree will blossom   The almond tree is the first tree to blossom in the land of Israel, signaling that spring is just around the corner.

locust, caperberry   Although the precise meaning of this verse is contested, the general meaning is apparent: the cyclical fertility of nature. *The human being, ha-ʾadam,* generically speaking, is "everyman."

eternal home   Unless the statement is ironical, "going home" is hardly depressing, and the coupling with "eternal" could be taken as a hint of life after death. So also, by the way, the reference to the perpetual return of the lights in Qoh 12:2, recalling the sun's daily desire to shine again (1:5).

12:6 thread . . . wheel   What is first noteworthy about this verse is that all four broken or destroyed items—thread, bowl, pitcher, wheel—are human artifacts, here distributed in two distinct categories. In the first are those prime biblical symbols of wealth—silver and gold—which had been put to practical and possibly artistic use: a thread for ornament, a bowl for drinking. In the second instance, human invention had facilitated the recovery and transport of a crucial support of all life: water. When these artifacts are removed and their human purpose eliminated, the elements simply fall to the ground, so to speak, returning to their basic element or original place, just as, at the dissolution of the *human* being, the dust returns to the earth "as it was" (v. 7).

silver, gold   Wealth and its symbols do not matter. Even things made of these precious metals will break. This is a poignant review of Qohelet's ambitious project of accumulation ("I also collected silver and gold for myself," [2:8]), now judged by a repentant narrator to be sinful (2:26). For the view of King Qohelet's autobiographical narrative as also confessional, see my forthcoming *Joyous Vanity: Qohelet's Guide to Living Well*.

12:7 *the dust returns / and the spirit returns*   Just as there are two twilights, so too are there two kinds of death. The more familiar is that of common humanity, when the body declines and falls away from the soul. The second, the philosopher's death, is when the soul withdraws from the body.[31] The death described in Qohelet seems closer to the first, if we are to credit the order of events as presented: first the dust turns away and only then the spirit.

upon the earth   Unless this ʿ*al* is a variant of ʾ*el*, which is always possible, then the reference is not to burial, a return to or *into* the earth, but rather one's continuance "upon" the earth, in one's seed and the good deeds that one has planted (to continue the image). At any rate, this verse describes the final dissolution of the human being's earthly life, following upon his or her progressive withdrawal from the life-involvements presented in the previous verses.

12:8 *"A transient transience"*   See also Qoh 11:10. The usual translation "Vanity of vanities" makes little sense here, for if there is no meaning or value to anything, what motivation does a person have to sow or harvest or seize the day? What is hard to imagine, especially during the strength of youth, is that it will all end, that in fact that is how it was all set up from the start. "You can't take it with you" thus applies not only post-mortem but throughout one's entire life.

But if transience is itself transient . . .

Life's Integration: Seasonableness and *Puer-Senex*

The question is one of an integration of human existence wherein the start and end points—birth and death, the two ultimate and definitional twilight moments—are both good in their

---

[31]See Perry, *Erotic Spirituality*, 40–43.

time (Qoh 3:2, 11). As Montaigne reminds us, death is a part of life.[32] From Qohelet's wisdom perspective, two movements can be distinguished: seasonableness, which is diachronic, and the ideal of *puer-senex,* which is synchronic.[33] The first has a literal application, whereas the second easily fuses with the symbolic. How so?

We can now go beyond earlier binaries or oppositions such as "better anger than laughter" (Qoh 7:3), since the "better than" formula preserves the value of each component.[34] So too the opposition youth/old age does not implicitly disadvantage one over the other. No, argues Qohelet, both youth and old age are good and must be experienced as such and at their proper time or season. Thus, the Epicurean thesis must be adjusted and expanded: adjusted because of motivation, as one must enjoy one's active, physical strength not only because it will end but because it is age-appropriate;[35] expanded because this motivation allows and even requires us to find other, more age-appropriate pleasures and interests at other seasons in life.

The concept of age-appropriate pleasures and interests applies at two levels.[36] For the individual: "When I was a child, I spoke like a child, I thought like a child, I reasoned like a child; when I became an adult, I put an end to childish ways" (1 Cor 13:11). Possible reasons for putting them aside? "I no longer have pleasure or interest in them," I am no longer in that place. For example, as a child I enjoyed playing with dolls and toy trucks. As Qohelet repeats, there is a time for this and a time for that, stay on board and hold on! At another level, the age-appropriate concept also applies to things themselves, as the ambivalence of *khepets* suggests:

---

[32]"You do not die of being sick, you die of being alive." Michel de Montaigne, *The Complete Essays of Montaigne* (trans. Donald Frame; Stanford, Calif.: Stanford University Press, 1976), 836.

[33]"Seasonableness" is Fisch's expression, *Poetry with a Purpose,* 178.

[34]The "better than" formula, in order to have its wisdom effect, requires contextualization. Thus, "better anger [which leads to wisdom] than laughter [which leads to folly]." In themselves, neither laughter nor anger have intrinsic priority one over the other. See Perry, *Wisdom Literature,* 30, 95.

[35]And also because, theologically speaking, it is a gift of God.

[36]*khepets* can mean "interest, desire," as we saw in the commentary to Qoh 12:1.

There is a season for all desires / things. (Qoh 3:1)

For example, one might hope that God would give creatures food in *their* time, at the moment of their need (Ps 104:21). There is an additional requirement, however:

He gives them food in *its* time. (Ps 145:15; also 104:27)

To yield its nourishment and taste, food needs its own time to ripen.

Age-appropriateness is an important aspect of *hebel,* of the transience of every *khepets,* every thing and every desire. Just as nature has its own cycles, the human world also changes, as do my body and perspectives. What happens when these enter into conflict; when, for example, I need my food before it is ready, or old age "jumps upon me" before I am prepared for it? One wisdom favorite is that, when things change, then perhaps I need to change perspectives and attitudes in order to accommodate them:

If it is not what I wish, may I wish what it is.[37]

This stoical principle found a central place in rabbinic ethics:

Who is rich? One who is content with what one has. (*m. Abot* 4:1)

Qohelet in fact views the contentment principle as central to human happiness.[38]

Seasonableness does have its limitations, however, namely in the oppositions that acquire integration only sequentially and as part of a comprehensive synthesis. Thus, if one loves life, then death will seem problematic; but if, like Job, one longs for death, then the problem is life itself. And when seasonableness does come to accept old age and death, then the synthesizing perspective often amounts to rejection of the earlier "season" or phase, when one comes to regret the "folly" of one's youth. One of Qohelet's enduring glories is to reject such *ex post facto* repentance, his main reason being that *not* enjoying one's youth at its

---

[37]"Si no es lo que quiero, quiera yo lo que es." See T. A. Perry, *The Moral Proverbs of Santob de Carrión: Jewish Wisdom in Christian Spain* (Princeton: Princeton University Press, 1987), 19.

[38]See Perry, *Dialogues with Kohelet,* 31, 39.

appropriate time can breed its own type of regret. It is apparently better to have something concrete to be sorry for than an empty regret over *not* having lived one's life, consistent with Montaigne's principle that "since there is a risk of making a mistake, let us risk it rather in pursuit of pleasure."[39]

There is a long European tradition of the human ideal of *puer-senex,* of a *puer* or "youth" who already has the wisdom of a *senex* or "aged person."[40] Biblical examples might include Samuel, who is suddenly catapulted into the prophetic condition while still a *na^{c}ar,* or "lad" (1 Sam 2:27–4:1). Or the child Jesus, teaching venerable sages even before his bar mitzvah age (Luke 2:41–52). The paucity of such examples in the wisdom literature may possibly be ascribed to the fact that wisdom was felt to depend on experience, which in turn depends on age. Thus, Qohelet's wisdom book is written from the perspective of one who has done it all in the past: "I *was* king." His wisdom book is presented as the acquired and remembered wisdom of an older person.[41]

There is, however, a concept of a remembered future, a fruitful notion for the experience of prophecy but also useful in a pedagogical wisdom context as well.[42] A *puer*—the typical addressee— is asked and encouraged to focus on the future consequences of his actions. In Qoh 12:1–8, which begins with the advice to "*remember* your Creator," the *puer* is fast-forwarded to the status of a *senex,* to a situation so changed as to constitute the exact reverse or underside of his present one. Will this be seen only as a contradiction, so that his only appropriate response will be the popular Epicurean one, to enjoy his youthful strength while there is still time? Or is there embedded in the projected *senex* also a wisdom that will enable him not only to cope but, indeed, to thrive both in

---

[39]Montaigne, *The Complete Essays of Montaigne,* 832.

[40]For the notion of *puer-senex* see Ernst Robert Curtius, *European Literature in the Latin Middle Ages* (New York: Harper, 1953), 98–101. The obverse, what we would call a *senex-puer,* one who does not "act his age," could be exemplified by the popular medieval image of Socrates playing with infants and their baubles.

[41]"Who is old? One who has acquired wisdom." This saying is based on the rabbinic analysis of the word *zaqen,* an "aged person," as *zeh she-qanah khokmah,* one who has acquired wisdom. Cf. Wisdom of Solomon 4:9: "Old age is not honored for length of time, or measured by number of years; but understanding is grey hair. . . ."

[42]Fisch, *A Remembered Future.*

the present and the future as well? Note that only this latter possibility gives grounding to the Epicurean thesis itself. For do not even youths need wisdom to enjoy life, and does not the *absence* of youthful vigor—as now imagined by the fictive *senex*—add a strong, even necessary impetus to that enjoyment? As Montaigne observed, we tend to "enjoy" health in its absence, only when we are sick!

Reclaiming the unity of one's life and identity thus involves, in the first instance, the judgment, the assertion, that "this too is good," that both youth and old age must be balanced and integrated. And while this seems especially the case in one's literal old age, here in Qoh 12 it is urged already in one's youth, when one is advised to imagine the later season. It proclaims loudly: do not think that I am requiring you to renounce your youth, G-d forbid!

Twilight Images of Dissonance: The Sound of a Bird

> There were empty parts of the day, . . . no traffic in the streets, no audible human voices, now and then no sound at all. In this hushed world, a bumblebee was a physical presence, the sound of a cicada could dominate an August afternoon. (Paul Theroux)[43]

> I rejoice that there are owls. Let them do the idiotic and maniacal hooting for men. It is a sound admirably suited to swamps and twilight woods which no day illustrates, suggesting a vast and undeveloped nature which men have not recognized. They represent the stark twilight and unsatisfied thoughts which all have. (Thoreau, *Walden*, "Sounds")

> The doors on the street are shut,
> and the sound of the grinding is low,
> and one rises up at the sound of a bird,
> and all songs fade away. (Qoh 12:4)

I am well aware that some may take Henry David Thoreau's tranquil reveries at Walden as little more than, well, surrealistic

---

[43]Paul Theroux, "America the Overfull," *New York Times* Op-Ed, Sunday Dec. 31, 2006.

dabbling: the allusion to the wild and usually unacknowledged hootings that all men have; the twilight dusk not softly graded but stark with its own kind of sharp ambivalences and modes of pre-cognition, neither the hoped-for clarity of knowledge nor the secure dumbness of night. Ho hum. . . . But ho hum, too, the fashionable dismissal of such dissonance, based on a positivistic propensity to always seek noon at the twilight hour (to adapt a French idiom to my own purposes). For, warns Qohelet, there will come a time when the heavenly lights will dim (read: the clarities and certitudes of youth) and returning clouds will foster a pervasive penumbra wherein life will be experienced (synchronically) at all times as a twilight mixture that (dia-chronically) can turn either towards restored light or total dark-ness. The challenge, offers our text, is to explore the positive valences of the latter, for did the Creator-God not also "create darkness" (Isa 45:7)?

And did He not also create quiet? For Theroux's "hushed world" is an environment fit for reverie and somnolence and heightened attention to nature's rhythms and silences. And the Sabbath. And if death is now in the offing, then the real Sabbath, already tasted in the first.

What symbol could convey this twilight situation better than the bird (Qoh 12:4), Noah's scout for restoral, the harbinger first of ongoing shutdown and then, on the second try, of life's return; the creature that traverses the space between heaven and earth, belonging to both? Its surprising appearance in Qohelet does seem dissonant to a number of critics, but not at all, I would ven-ture, to the *senex-puer* himself, now withdrawn from the turbu-lence of what we are pleased to call "normal" life.

So too with the almond tree and the locust (Qoh 12:5). Now that the sound of the bird has rekindled interest in the broader picture, other associated natural forces are also noticed. Some have argued that these disruptive images point to a contradiction between eternal nature and frail humanity. Diethelm Michel, for example, speaks of "images of nature full of vitality in antithesis to the frail old man."[44] To be sure, there is the sense that, when so-

---

[44]Quoted in Krüger, *Qoheleth,* 199.

cial interests fall away, nature recovers its dominion, but it is not necessary to view this as an antithesis since, like old age, frailty may also have a positive valence.[45]

The perspective proposed in our text is that of an old (I would say mature) person, one who has grown up to reality and has made a realistic assessment of its losses but also its compensatory gains. Thus, as the sound of grinding is lowered and all songs (culture, social hilarity, banquets [Qoh 7:2]) fade away, one "rises up" to another kind of music. The sense of enclosure, perhaps solitary, is colored by a seclusion, a withdrawal from normal social intercourse, as signaled both by the shutting of the doors to the outside and by the lowering and perhaps even removal of those sounds that betoken human activity, whether useful (grinding) or pleasurable (songs). But such removal also signals, rather than a deadening of sensations, a heightened focus on other and perhaps higher (more permanent and radical) things. And, behold, amidst the lowering there is a rising up, as normal sounds of activity and purpose recede and sounds not usually heard now reveal their presence. Natural sounds become acutely perceived, as one is reminded of a sound from heaven, so to speak, which normally would seem to be nothing but a bird but which, by his reaction or responsiveness, reminds one of Thoreau:

> A slight sound at evening lifts me up by the ears, and makes life seem inexpressibly serene and grand. It may be in Uranus, or it may be in the shutter.[46]

The expansion—rather than the deadening—of consciousness here is hinted not only by the "rising up" but even more by the unexpected grammatical switch from the addressee "you" to the third person "he." The author now refers to "one, everyone," an impersonal that is perhaps super-personal, that sensitivity dormant in every person, a capability of "rising up" in such focused

---

[45]See below, Conclusion 2, on Vulnerability.

[46]Quoted from Thoreau's *Journals* by W. S. Merwin in his introduction to *Walden*, by Henry David Thoreau (*Walden, or Life in the Woods; and "On the Duty of Civil Disobedience"* [introd. W. S. Mervin with an afterward by Perry Miller; rev. and updated bibliography; New York: New American Library, 1999]), xiii.

conditions of solitude, when the daily "grind" is not heard because it is no longer interesting.[47]

Conclusions

Conclusion 1: Time and Eternity

Rather than the literariness of this beautiful passage in Qohelet, we have chosen to focus on its literalness. This requires a manner of reading not texts but reality, an attention less to comparisons to other texts that may clarify the present one than to moments of reality—here a sound at evening twilight, for Marcel Proust the taste of a madeleine biscuit—that reach far beyond themselves, yielding a sense of an underlying coherence of distant times and realities. The method is not one of esthetic contrivance but of a quality of awareness, an attentiveness and experience of perception that uplifts the spirit.

The philosophical dimension of this theme is movingly evoked by André Neher's comment on Qoh 3:11:

il y a une éternité (עוֹלָם) que le coeur de chaque homme rencontre, mais qu'il ne peut rencontrer que dans *son* temps (עִתּוֹ).[48]

If I understand correctly, this remark argues that individual death—and aging is a form of dying—is that time (*ʿet*) each day when a human being has the intuition of *ʿolam*, of eternity:

He has placed the *ʿolam* into their hearts. (Qoh 3:11)

This intuition of eternity[49] becomes concretized and finalized at the event of one's final death, when the individual, advancing to

---

[47]Thoreau (ibid., 108), referring to a substratum of human consciousness shared by all: "no more I than it is you." All other references to persons other than the addressee who are experiencing death are given in the plural (v. 5: they fear). NRSV appropriately translates both (3d person singular and plural) by "one."

[48]Neher, *Notes sur Qohélét*, 100–101: "There is an eternity that the heart of each person encounters but which he can encounter only in *his* own time."

[49]This does not argue that *ʿolam* literally means eternity in the Hebrew Bible, since the verse goes on to suggest a vast time extension (the entire extent of God's creation from start to finish!) that is still limited by a possible before and after beyond human comprehension. The argument, rather, is that the

the "house of his ʿolam," realizes the final shape and depth of her true personality:

"Tel qu'en lui-même enfin l'éternité le change,"

as Stéphane Mallarmé eulogized Edgar Allan Poe.[50] This theme is the one of human death, the place where or when physics and metaphysics seem to split (Qoh 12:7) but where in fact they finally unite, or at least become sequential, members of the same system.

Such "moments privilégiés" may or may not occur to everyone; Proust thought them controlled or at least provoked by involuntary memory. More general perhaps is the regular and universal experience of time that results from the daily and life-long appreciation of seasonableness itself. According to Emmanuel Levinas:

> Time is not a limitation on being but rather its relation to infinity. Death is not annihilation but rather a necessary question so that this relation with infinity or time can be actualized.[51]

In Qoh 3:11, ʿolam can mean either eternity or world. But Levinas sees these as continuous, sees time in our world as a figure of eternity.

Just as youth was a gift of your Creator, God's gifts can be duplicated and recovered at a deeper level, through one's own efforts as a self-creator. Neher raises the question and wisely leaves it as only a possibility:

> Perhaps [God's] works [12:14] include the *gift* which God has made to humans, and also the transfiguration that human time and existence will have imprinted upon this gift. Perhaps the works of human beings are themselves also capable of being eternal ("éternizable").[52]

---

mere imagining of that huge block of time still gives the feeling or intimation of eternity, all the more so because of its suggestion of a point out of the box and from which the created world is conceptualized, as suggested by the title of Emmanuel Levinas's magnum opus, *Totality and Infinity* (trans. Alfonso Lingis; Pittsburgh: Duquesne University Press, 1969). See my forthcoming *Joyous Vanity: Qohelet's Guide to Living Well.*

[50]"Such as finally into himself eternity changes him."

[51]Levinas, *Dieu, la mort et le temps*, 28.

[52]Neher, *Notes sur Qohélét*, 109.

Conclusion 2: The Rebirth of Vulnerability

A youth is asked to think about future, less fortunate days, ones he will be less interested in. The conclusion usually drawn is a hedonistic one of carpe diem. This is true but only part of the story, and not even the better part. Think of the two-pronged advice of the following:

> It is better to go to a house of mourning than a banquet.

This advice could be directed not only to one already at a wake and wondering what she is doing there or how nice it would be to be at a banquet. It also tells a person attending a banquet: do not get *too* carried away by frivolity, mix some sobriety into your joyfulness. Here, too, the youth is urged to incorporate displeasure and to balance opposing moods.

Why this should be the case is a bit more complex. The bottom line is that the lesson learned from images of dying and death is one of vulnerability.[53] This would certainly temper the feelings of power typical of youth. Should it dampen them altogether? No, enjoy! But the lesson of vulnerability has a flip side, an intrinsic value of its own. A condition that may come upon you against your will to pleasure, as may occur in older age, may also be accepted at any age for the insight or awareness that it brings, the level of consciousness that leads to deeper sensitivities. When the "doors are closed to the outside," when one has turned from the normal activities of the world, when commercial activities have been put aside, either slowed down or suspended altogether, when bodily needs such as feeding and sexuality are less of a preoccupation, when one no longer expects the women waiting at

---

[53]For the notion of vulnerability recall the fragility of Elijah's "still small voice" (1 Kgs 19:12); the frail "vanity" of Abel (Hebrew *hebel*, "vanity"; Gen 4:1–16), whose gift was acceptable to God; the delicate nature of a winged creature that effortlessly glides on air. It is not argued here that victimhood is to be ardently desired, certainly not before the fact and not after either. There is, of course, a merit in the stoical position (see above) of accepting the inevitable. The concept here, rather, is what Blanchot, referring to the project of writing, has called the transmutation of passivity into patience, an alert and calm but also combative waiting to see what will be: "ce combat (de l'écriture) est débat pour la patience. . . . La passivité passe en patience, enjeu qui sombre" (Maurice Blanchot, *L'Écriture du désastre*, 78).

the window after a battle: then the strength and focus of one's desires yield to a more general and diffuse awareness of nature's recurrent and pervasive fertility (the swarms of locusts, the blooming tree that signals springtime, or simple beauty, or God's diligent concern, or all of these together—my door or Uranus, in Thoreau's phrase). When I am freed to imagine that all the *hebel* of this life can be loosened and dissolved, that part of me will return to the Creator, perhaps to try again, and part to the *ʾerets,* signifying both the eternal material from which all future creations will rise, and also—through my good deeds and my children—to the human family, the earth of Qoh 1:4 that shall endure forever . . .

So too in a house of mourning, where I momentarily close the door to life as usual and reconnect both with my deeper purposes and my solidarity with the suffering of the human family, all of whom "go to the same place" (Qoh 3:20).[54] Where my normal powers yield to a vulnerability, so that even my speech is replaced by an awkward silence as I sit not knowing what to say. And where my simple dumb sitting is also a glorious expression of friendship and community. Then all the rest can only appear as a vanity of vanities. *N'est-ce pas?*

Indeed, in our usual reflections on Qoh 12 an important detail is often overlooked: the mourners who go about the street, who still tread the earth but wander about. Together in their purpose, however, they carry out the duties of charity to the highest degree, since there is no reward for their actions other than the actions themselves. This is the highest show of their dignity: You have now forgotten them, and yet they still attend to your needs. . . . The presence of mourners, of course, constitutes an oxymoron; for, even as the doors to the public are shut and social contacts cease, the mourners come forward to assert that even in death "life is with people," that the demise of the individual is still, and egregiously so, a social event.

---

[54]Krüger (*Qohelet,* 167) delicately explains the important distinctions: "vv. 9:1–6 relativizes the distinctions between different people in life through the juxtaposition of the living and the dead: in view of death, which strikes all people in the same way, distinctions between the wise and the fools, the righteous and the wicked, and so forth, are invalidated. This does not mean that they lose any significance for the limited realm of life, but they are not to be overvalued."

Returning to the central notion of wisdom as a pedagogy, I know of no better summary of Qohelet's concluding "elegy" than that of Lyn Bechtel, who relates human life to the first myth in the garden, signifying a project to grow up and see exactly what the experiment of living involves:

> Eating of the Tree of Mature Knowledge means learning to discern and accept both poles of the essential binary forces of life, which allows them to relate to life and, most of all, to God on a mature level. As long as commentators perpetuate the idea that limitation, pain, and death are punishments imposed on creation for human sin (an extremely egocentric presumption), human beings will neither accept life as God created it nor accept the Creator.[55]

To this list of commentators, whose ancestors are Job's three theologian friends, there is another group (let us call them egofugal), those who gather around Qohelet, seeing limitation and pain and death but missing their opportunity for growth; stressing the negatives but not their call to character formation; complaining about human passivity and the overworked "vanity" theme but missing the contentment in vulnerability patiently endured; lamenting the transience of all things but overlooking their beauty. As the conclusion to the book of Jonah argues, the Eternal God is Himself in love with the works of time.[56]

Conclusion 3: Final Advice: Enjoy Life, Prepare for Its Departure!

Our poem addresses a youth about to step out into the active life, a world of commerce and war and the like. What might have been a direct narrative, however, falls victim to a pedagogical trick that evokes these upcoming middle years by their absence, by what they will look like when one day all of this is left behind! What a pedagogical scheme: the aching anticipation of "real life" short-circuited by its demise! For the delicate, itemized leave-taking from one's active life is here projected at the very entrance of that life itself.

---

[55]Bechtel, "Rethinking the Interpretation of Genesis 2.4B–3.24," 109.
[56]For God's esthetics of transience, see Perry, *The Honeymoon Is Over*, 159–63.

But preparation for old age, one would hope, exceeds the needs of estate planning and the selection of a burial plot. Youth had its strengths and virtues to meet personal, family, and social interests: bravery, enterprise, fertility, etc. Other and more dormant strengths are in reserve, however, and may be activated when these fail. They include a faith in the future, but with the lessons acquired during youth and from real experience and mature reckoning.

Because human life is transient—although it may not yet have occurred to you:

1) enjoy youth while you have it;

2) be prepared so that you may enjoy old age as well.

While enjoyment of one's youth may seems obvious, one wonders why Qohelet takes the trouble to stress the point. We need to be reminded that the advisor's perspective here is that of an older person, whether the regretful narrator or the *bakhur*, now himself aged. And, as we all recall, adolescence no less than old age has its own anxieties and perplexities. The suggestion is that both require a level of wisdom in order for enjoyment to occur. In brief, the synchronic principle of *puer-senex* is an enjoyment obligation that works in both directions; for while the *senex* needs to incorporate "youthfulness," the *puer* must "remember the future" and that strength, too, will pass. Bottom line: enjoyment is a life-long affair, but its forms change. The limitation of youth is that it does not have enough wisdom to enjoy its vigor. The shortcoming of age is that is does not maintain enough "youth" to enjoy its wisdom.

A second principle is compensatory: what is lost is replaced by something also beautiful.[57] For does not the song of a bird equal or even surpass the pleasurable sounds of singing women and men? This is the diachronic principle of seasonableness. Underlying

---

[57]John D. Caputo speaks of a "provocative and uplifting weakness of God" that "obeys the law of reversals in virtue of which whatever is first is last, whatever is out is in, whatever is lost is saved, where even death has a certain power over the living, all of which confounds the dynamics of strong forces" (*The Weakness of God,* 14–15). Compensatory replacement may not be at the same miraculous level as divine reversals, but I would like to suggest that it is in the same ballpark.

both is an ethical principle to which Qohelet gives a theological formulation. Krüger puts it succinctly:

> The proper attitude towards life grows out of the fact that one receives and accepts "good" as a "gift" and "bad" as the "judgment" of God (cf. 7:14).[58]

This would seem to me an acceptable *pshat* reading of that otherwise impossible concept that the Creator-God also "makes peace and *creates evil*" (Isa 45:7). Exactly like the "evil" of "those bad days" in Qoh 12:1, it is quotational, referring to those actions of God (divine judgments, sickness, etc.) that humans at some point in their lives would call "bad." In their liturgy the rabbis refused this possibly misleading formulation (even though it was scriptural!) and revised it in a way that speaks volumes about Qohelet's central concept: "He makes peace and creates everything (*hakkol*)."

David and Barzillai the Gileadite (2 Sam 19)

A biblical passage frequently cited in connection with our passage is the incident of David and Barzillai the Gileadite in 2 Sam 19. When the disgraced and pursued king was forced to leave the country, the wealthy Barzillai, at great personal risk of retaliation from David's son Absalom, provided food for David and his retinue. Now that David is returning to Jerusalem in triumph, he extends to Barzillai the offer of maintenance and full honors at the royal court for the rest of his days. Barzillai's investment—if that is the right word—in David's future has paid off, and in some proportion to the gravity of the risk. And even if his support of David was motivated by pure love and rightness, the reward is still perfectly commensurate and appropriate: to spend the rest of his natural days in the royal presence, indeed at the king's very table. Barzillai, however, declines the offer:

> How long have I to live that I should go up with the king to Jerusalem? I am this day eighty years old. Can I [still] discern between

---

[58]Krüger, *Qoheleth*, 198.

good and evil? Can your servant taste what I eat or what I drink? Can I still listen to the voices of singing men and women? (2 Sam 19:35–36[19:34–35])

One does not refuse the king except for the very best of reasons, and Barzillai's central premise—old age—must seem surprising if not suspicious to the younger king, still on the rise and eager to regain power and all its prerogatives. For, as regards Barzillai's first point, is one ever in the position to suspend one's moral judgment, the discernment between good and evil? Further, even if normal foods "all taste the same," could not the king's own table provide the exception? And as for entertainment . . . In brief, the debate is as much about David as about his servant, for is not the king in precisely the same position as Qohelet's young addressee or even of a younger Qohelet himself, now asked to imagine the unimaginable, a life without such power and pleasures? It is thus only Barzillai's final point that clinches the argument and gains his dispensation: his desire to "die in my own city" and be buried with his parents (2 Sam 19:38[19:37]): doing what is seasonable and socially appropriate—attending to his death, projected as close at hand, in his own family environment.

What wins the argument with King David may not at all accord with Barzillai's deeper motivation, however. For while the argument of cessation of enjoyment and power politics can be pulled in the direction of decrepitude, it also responds quite well to the pull of personal inclination and choice; and what is often taken as his involuntary withdrawal may instead express the sense of empowerment that this withdrawal connotes. For Barzillai may well have his own agenda, not wishing to be dragged around, no longer interested in flattery and the blandishments of worldly power: finally his own person in his own place. Is not Barzillai's lordly contentment with where he is perfectly expressed by the Shunamite: "Among my own people do I dwell" (2 Kgs 4:13)?

Such an interpretative possibility is only that, of course, and the catalogue of Barzillai's arguments needs not be taken globally. That is why Qoh 12 paints with such a wide canvas, so as to include as many "everyman" situations as possible. In David's own case, when the lusty king does reach old age, his sexual interests do seem quite diminished (1 Kgs 1:1–4), but his ability to judge between right and wrong is still available (1 Kgs 1:29–30). For the author of Qoh 3:1–11, who affirms that all things are good in their time—that there is indeed a time to die and that the wise should take this to heart—the usual assumptions concerning aging and death must be expanded to broader perspectives. For Barzillai has also reached an outlook—an age and condition in life—in which the defects of the "usual" arrangements have come to seem both obvious and oppressively vacuous.

Is not the *bakhur* addressee of Qoh 12 a composite portrait of David and Barzillai, of the *puer* setting out and the *senex* settling down?

NINE

WISDOM BEGINS IN WONDER: THE RIDDLE OF PROVERBS 30:18–20

> [We thank You] for the miracles that are with us
> every day, and for the wonders [*nifla'ot*] and the
> goodnesses that are with us at all times.
> (Jewish Daily Liturgy, Morning Blessings)

> Blessed are you, Lord our God, king of the universe,
> who stretches the earth upon the waters.
> (Jewish Daily Liturgy, "Modim" Prayer)

Twilight Concepts: The Fantastical or Wondrous

The theme of things that exceed human understanding plays an important role in the thinking of the sages. Whether in Job's conclusion or Qohelet's resignation, the Creator-God is said to have placed limits, beyond which it is impossible to know anything and hazardous to attempt. What moves this boundary into the twilight zone is its alliance with a theme less well understood: the phenomenon of the wondrous (*pele'*). Job puts this connection succinctly:

> I have spoken what I did not understand; things too wonderful [*nifla'ot*] for me, which I did not understand. (*lo' 'eda'*; Job 42:3)

Between clearly miraculous events such as the sun and moon standing still (Josh 10:13–14) and purely natural phenomena lies a zone of doubt that can lean in either direction. When, for example, Moses stood at the burning bush and wondered at this "great" or strange vision (Exod 3:3), he was not referring to size— the bush was probably quite small—but to a level of reality and perception that I have elsewhere termed the "fantastical."[1] This literary concept refers to a twilight area of hesitation such that, if one decides in favor of either a supernatural interpretation or a natural one (a popular example would be Jonah's "whale" that swallows him alive for three days), then doubt yields to certitude and the fantastical vanishes. In Moses's case, the phenomenon of a bush that burns but is not consumed leans towards a *super*-natural interpretation, which is soon confirmed by the divine voice. At first blush and until that point, however, the event, occurring in the natural world but with an unusual and unexplainable twist, excites a question but remains within the realm of the unusual or strange or "fantastical."

If the burning bush example illustrates a twilight zone of doubt leaning towards the supernatural, there is also, occupying the same zone but looking in the opposite or natural direction, another category of events and phenomena that retain normal appearances while still exciting a sense of puzzled admiration and surprise such that one is inclined to exclaim: "These I do not understand!" Their paradigm is provided in the numerical saying from the book of Proverbs that we shall examine here:

> Three things are too *wondrous* (*nifleʾu*) for me, four which *I do not understand* (*yedaʿetim*):
> The way of the eagle in the air;
> The way of a snake upon a rock;
> The way of a ship on the open sea;
> And the way of a man with a young woman. (Prov 30:18–19)

The secular use of "wonder" in this passage comes itself as a surprise, since in the Hebrew Bible the semantics of *peleʾ* are often weighted in favor of clear and explicit divine intervention. Thus,

---

[1]See Perry, *The Honeymoon Is Over*, 183–200; also 191, where the translation "strange" is explained.

the nominal form *pele$^{\circ}$*, referring to God's direct miracles at the Red Sea, are related to God's holiness (Exod 15:11).[2] There is also occasional attenuation, where the stress is on things too great for me to understand, but not necessarily miraculous.[3] When combined with the nominal *nifla$^{\circ}$ot*, a subtle but important distinction of levels seems to be implied in such texts as the following:

> The children of Efraim . . . forgot His works and the wonders (*nifla$^{\circ}$ot*) which He had shown them. Miraculous things (*pele$^{\circ}$*) did He do in the sight of their fathers. . . . He divided the sea, . . . and made the waters to stand like a heap. (Ps 78:9–13)

The suggestion seems to be that, whereas the older generation had witnessed clear miracles, a later one (the children of Ephraim) saw only "wonders" and were unconvinced.

When a text ascribes "wonders" to God alone, the suspicion arises that such happenings might plausibly be attributed to other causes—indeed, the adjective "great" may have been appended to further minimalize such suspicion:

> To Him who alone does great wonders (*nifla$^{\circ}$ot gedolot*) . . . ;
> to Him who stretches the earth upon the waters. (Ps 136:4, 6)

In daily reckonings one does not pause to shudder about such contrivances, surely not ascribe them to God. Except for catastrophes such as a tsunami, we go about our business and regard the present arrangement as merely natural. Upon reflection, however, perhaps provoked by the rising water levels due to global warming, a twitch of admiration bordering on wonder

---

[2]See also Ps 77:15, and the preceding verse: "Your way, God, is in holiness." The verbal forms of *pele$^{\circ}$* are more nuanced. One meaning is to "set aside for holy purposes," usually in the form of a vow (Lev 22:21; 27:2; Num 6:2; 15:3, 8), thus a human movement towards the Holy rather than the other way around, as in miracles. In Lam 1:9 as well, it is best rendered as "astonishingly," to what seems out of the ordinary but not necessarily miraculous.

[3]See Deut 30:11, where it is aligned with "great things" (*gedolot*), i.e., too high above or distant from my comprehension. Such things may be either beyond my reach (Deut 30:11) or too baffling to decide (Deut 17:8), and the reason may be due either to human inability or incompetence, or to their very nature. The vocabulary of the fantastical or strange includes *gadol*, large or strange, *pele$^{\circ}$*, wonder, and skeptical formulas such as *mi yimtsah* ("who can discover?") and *mi yodea^{c}* ("who knows?").

may well become our response to the religious imagination's account as to how threatening aspects of our world have been managed until now.[4]

Consistent with these latter examples, the wondrous in Prov 30:18 has been seen as a promise of clear understanding that would replace wonder with one of its two opposites. Thus, at one extreme, Norman Whybray: "It is no doubt to be inferred that all these things are part of the mysterious action of God."[5] His "no doubt" of course maintains it, in a text where no mention is made of God or the miraculous. At the other extreme I list the reactions of not a few of my students, who ask with (literal) incredulity, and anticipating the adulteress's response in Prov 30:20: "What is so wondrous about all that, it is all perfectly natural!?" It is at either of these extremes of certitude that the category of the wondrous vanishes, since its nature is precisely to maintain the extremes as possibilities. This, once again, is the point of the distinction between the miraculous and the natural: precisely like the category of the fantastical, the liminal category of the wondrous occupies the midpoint. It cannot be rationally explained and thus provokes hesitation and surprise over mystery that is here termed wonder. It seems to me that the wisdom writers, with patience, intellectual honesty, and open mindedness, held to this middle ground.

Numerical Structures

The casting of our theme in the well-known incremental numerical structure of 3+1 is itself congenial to the thematics of wonderment.[6] Typically, four items are given, all similar in some aspect. The fourth, however, teases the definitional limits so as to

---

[4]If our wicked failure to manage global warming leads to catastrophic results, an opposite kind of "wonder" is here predicted, the pattern for which is outlined in the last verse of our saying (Prov 30:20). For discussion, see below, "Wonder in Reverse."

[5]Whybray, *Proverbs*, 416. See below, Conclusion.

[6]Numerical sayings "never press their lesson, but leave it to the reader to ponder and tease it out" (Kenneth T. Aitken, *Proverbs: The Daily Study Bible* [Philadelphia: Westminster, 1986], quoted in Bruce K. Waltke, *The Book of Proverbs: Chapters 15–31* [Grand Rapids: Eerdmans, 2005], 488). See also Perry, *The Honeymoon Is Over*, 66–70.

suggest a possible step beyond, like the exception that proves (i.e., tests) the general rule of the other three. Given the qualitative difference between the three and the culminating fourth, the process of reading is first to ponder what the first three items have in common. Only then will the surprise of the climactic fourth yield its full impact. In this case it will not provide any conclusion or "answer" but rather, true to the topic of the saying, ratchet the wonderment to another level altogether. This is of course consistent with the progression in Prov 30 from the mute creatures of the first three (eagle, snake, ship) to the human.[7]

Interesting proposals have been adduced to explain why these three examples (and all the more so the fourth) were chosen to illustrate wonder. Many have observed that all three (four) revolve around the concept of *derek* ("road"), which often suggests *movement,* since one "goes" along a path or way. This has been taken quite literally, as in the central declaration of Jewish faith specifying what you do when you "walk on the road (*derek*)" (Deut 6:7; 11:9). And, still literally and also congenial to halakic adaptation, the concept of a road is one that has clear limits:

> Let me pass through your land. I will go only on the [well-defined] highway, not turning to the right or the left. (Deut 2:27)

Derek is also one of the key concepts of wisdom, as we shall see.

All sorts of wonders can be attached to this notion, beginning, I suppose, with Zeno's paradox showing the impossibility of explaining how you get from one point to another and therefore how movement is even possible. The usual focus, however, is the notion of both path and trace, the points that both precede and follow motion, those within which motion occurs and which in fact allow its measurement (a motion which, again according to Zeno, does not actually exist). Since in all three cases (eagle,

---

[7]To make the progression perfect one would imagine an inversion in the order of the first three, such as: ship, bird, snake. To retain the given order and also the theory of strict dramatic progression would seem to require an animated ship! To be sure, such connotations do apply to Jonah's ship, if only metaphorically, in that it does have bowels or a belly ("innards"). More likely is the fact that, whereas the first two are natural creatures, the ship is human-made, thus serving as a transition to the fourth item, the human couple (see Waltke, *Proverbs: Chapters 15–31,* 490).

snake, ship) there is no discernable road being followed, nor does their passing by leave any trace, we come away with very tidy paradoxes indeed: a path that is pathless and an immeasurable (and therefore non-existent) progression.

At a strictly literal level these suggestions can be easily dismissed. As for the absence of both well-defined road and trace, the explanation lies not with the eagle, snake, or ship but rather with the medium upon or in which they move: air, stone, and water, and this hardly provokes any kind of significant wonder, as these are the kind of elements they are. These literal suggestions do create a supportive poetic atmosphere for the real point, however, about which we shall have more to say later. For these three cases exemplify a motion which, as it were, escapes the Zeno paradox. Here the absence of road and trace instances the absence of points of departure and destination. And since the motion cannot be measured or plotted, does it actually exist? Indeed, these creatures do not seem to be "going" anywhere! We have thus moved from a concept of movement as an infinity of disconnected points to one having no points at all: pure movement, free, effortless, unattached, a motionless glide across open space (air, stone/earth, water). We are left with the impression of motion for its own sake, as it were: a paradox of motionless movement. In our text, motion, while implied, is further denied by the stasis of these cameo scenes. For there is no movement *through* the air or sea, only *in* or *upon* them. The elements are thus not mere conveyances, delays between two points, but rather partners, as it were. The final blow to the "movement" (on a path or road) argument emerges from its inability to reveal anything wondrous about the remaining fourth example—the man with a woman—beyond the silly or prurient.[8]

This still leaves ample room for different kinds of reflection on the relationship between the creatures (bird, snake, ship) and their environmental medium of support and interaction: air, stone,

---

[8]Thus, Waltke (*Proverbs: Chapters 15–31*, 491) discovers or perhaps uncovers a "rocking motion" among all four. The focus on movement also sponsors a wildly fanciful hypothesis of environmental love-making between ship and sea, snake and rock, and bird and air, whose ways are all "undulating," presumably like those of the adulteress as well (ibid., 490–91).

sea. As for the creatures, while Roland E. Murphy correctly points out that "it is not the eagle, serpent, ship, or man that is the real target," these cannot be dismissed without noting their importance or, almost literally, their weight and gravitational pressure.[9] For the eagle, as Bruce K. Waltke insists, is "one of Palestine's heaviest birds," with "the largest wing-span of any bird."[10] As for the ship, it is presumably a heavy one, of the type that sails the open sea. These factors may also apply to the rock, not an ordinary stone but rather a mountainous crag, one that normal beasts (cows but even goats) would not attempt. And the man? Not a normal *ʾadam* or "man," and not an *ʾish* or "important person" either, but a *geber,* related to a *gibbor,* a "strong and virile man." When these "heavy" creatures interact with environments unlikely to support their weight or nature (snakes are slippery and would thus be expected to slip off a rock), the effect is to ratchet up the wondrous impression a notch or two.

If we turn from the creatures to their supportive elements, there seems to be evidence of a kind of budding scientific interest.[11] Attempting an underlying model for the given data (heaven, rock, sea, woman), Menahem Ha-Meiri (1249–ca. 1310) also suggested the notion of trace, focusing less on motion (as we saw above) than on the wondrous nature of elements that are perfectly transient in that they leave no memory of whatever passes over or through them.[12] The weakness of this model is in the interpretation of the fourth member, which requires the supposition that the woman has already experienced intercourse and as a result, on subsequent mating after her hymen is broken, would reveal no trace of sexual activity (much like the adulteress who immediately enters the scene). It is more likely, however, that the woman in question here is meant to provide a contrast to the adulteress in

---

[9]Roland E. Murphy, *Proverbs* (WBC 22; Nashville: Thomas Nelson, 1998), 235.

[10]Waltke, *Proverbs: Chapters 15–31,* 491.

[11]See Wolfgang M. Roth, *Numerical Sayings in the Old Testament* (VTSup 13; Leiden: Brill, 1965). Roth argues that such classification was an attempt to understand the world.

[12]Menahem Ha-Meiri, *Perush ʿal Sefer Mishlei* [Commentary on the Book of Proverbs] (ed. Menachem Mendel Zahav; Jerusalem: Otsar ha-Poskim, 1969), 285.

this respect also, namely that she was previously a virgin and thus would certainly show signs of first intercourse.

It may have been dissatisfaction with this first theory that led Ha-Meiri to a more "scientific" and comprehensive model.[13] Science as traditionally conceived provides an attractive alternate model here, the ʾarbaʿ yesodot of Aristotelian physics, the four foundational elements of creation: fire, earth, water, and air, already rehearsed in Prov 30:4.[14] Thus, Ha-Meiri interprets as follows:

    (eagle) : heaven = fire
    (snake) : rock = earth
    (ship) : sea = water
    (man) : woman = air

While the second and third correlations do not require much explanation, the first and fourth are unclear. Thus, the eagle is likened to fire because "its movement is light and upward and higher than the others," perhaps referring to the position of the sun. As for the likeness of the man to wind, "the wind or airy element (ruakh) is a figure for [sexual] desire [taʾavah], that is to say, it is the element in which the man moves."[15]

It is easy to grasp how the incremental 3+1 structure was deemed suited to this kind of scientific meditation on creation. It also, I think, offered a theory of an integrated universe. In other words, whereas the final purpose of our riddle is to gain insight into gender and moral relationships, the marshalling forth of parallels or analogies from the physical and animal world was intended to suggest both the interrelatedness of all of creation and thus also the importance of more elemental forms in the understanding of the human world. According to this method, there is

---

[13]Waltke has detected here a reference to the entire cosmos, either through the merism of the sky above and the sea below, or in the "cosmic dimensions of sky, rock/land, and sea (see Genesis 1)" (Proverbs: Chapters 15–31, 490).

[14]For a sense of the importance of this concept in the Bible see Qohelet 1:4–7, modeled on Gen 1:2. See also the study by T. A. Perry, "A Poetics of Absence: The Structure and Meaning of Chaos in Genesis 1:2," JSOT 58 (1993): 3–11.

[15]Menahem Ha-Meiri, Perush ʿal Sefer Mishlei, 286.

no antithesis between the human and the so-called lower orders of creation, only levels that mirror one another, as it were. The process of reading and reflection thus requires careful attention to the first three levels before considering the fourth. Alternatively to Ha-Meiri's reading, I would propose the following as more likely:

(eagle) : heaven : air
(snake) : rock : earth
(ship) : sea : water

The riddle or puzzle, of course, would be (in the first instance) to identify the presence of the traditional quadripartite structure of elements and to supply the missing fourth. Thus,

(man) : woman : fire

The "scientific" discovery or solution of the riddle, thereupon, would be to grasp how the fiery (rather than the airy, as per Ha-Meiri) female element interacts with the male, as well as vice-versa. This question would then lead back to further pondering the three interactions that lead up to the fourth.

And, as it happens, the interpretation of the woman as the fiery element is attested in the Bible. Think of the aged King David, getting along in years and "cold":

> Let there be sought for my lord the king a young virgin, and let her stand before the king and be his attendant.[16] And let her lie in your bosom, that my lord the king may become warm. (1 Kgs 1:2)

This may, of course, be a purely medical prescription, bringing warmth to a cold body. But this does not accord with the traditional behavior of the lusty king towards women, nor would this require that she be such as to win a beauty contest. If it is only literally a problem of heat, get the patient some hot water bottles!

Proverbs 6:27–28 tells of all the ills that may befall the adulterer, which here means the man who has intercourse with a married woman:

---

[16]There is an exegetical tradition (Rashi, Rashbam [ca. 1085–ca. 1158]) of relating this *hapax, sokenet*, to Qoh 10:9: "He who cuts down trees will be warmed (*yissaken*) with them."

Can a man take fire[17] into his bosom and his clothes not get burned? Can one walk on hot coals and his feet not get scorched? *So too* he who goes in to his neighbor's wife: whoever touches her will not go unpunished. (Prov 6:27–28)

The commentary within the text focuses on jealousy, apparently offered as a note on the heat metaphor: "For jealousy is the rage (*khamat*) of man (*geber*)" (Prov 6:34), literally the "heat" of the virile man, referring to the wounded husband, who will not delay his revenge.[18] More plausible would be the understanding of Ben Sira:

Her lovers she burns with fire. (Ben Sira 9:8)

If we are talking about the fires of the male's desire, we would rather expect the text to say: "Her lovers burn with fire." Or, again: commenting on Prov 6:27–28, Michael V. Fox cites Job 31:12 to show that "adultery is playing with fire." However, a perfectly plausible alternate reading gives a more blunt reason:

She *is* fire. (Job 31:12)[19]

Contextually, our saying is the second in a series of numerical structures ascribed to a sage called Alukah, which may also mean "leach." The first goes as follows:

Alukah has two daughters named Hab Hab (i.e., "Give Give"). They say:

---

[17]Murphy (*Proverbs*, 39) senses a word-play on *ʾish* ("man") and *ʾesh* ("fire"), due to their proximity, which he relates to the man's passion. Murphy's question points in another direction, however: "What does the youth expect if he plays with fire?" This suggests that the "fire" with which he plays is the *woman* rather than the resulting passion in him. This would also give a closer pun: *ʾesh* ("fire") and *ʾeshet* ("woman"), as in *ʾeshet ʾish* (v. 25), a married woman (literally, "the woman of a man"), or *ʾeshet raʿ*, an evil woman (v. 24).

[18]Commenting on Job 31:12, Marvin Pope (*Job: Introduction, Translation, and Notes* [AB 15; 3d ed.; Garden City, N.Y.: Doubleday, 1973], 232) sees the same text as referring to the *judicial* penalty for adultery, which was burning. See, for example, Gen 38:24–25 for the punishment that Judah sought to inflict upon Tamar. Such too was the punishment for the daughter of a Cohen guilty of adultery (Lev 21:9).

[19]The feminine *hiʾ* is regularly taken here as referring either to a general antecedent "it" or to the idea of sin, thus "this"; it could also take the woman in v. 9 as the true antecedent.

Three things are never satisfied,
four never say "enough!":

> Sheol,
> a barren woman,
> the earth never sated with water,
> and fire which never says "enough!" (Prov 30:15–16)

The fourth does not seem to deserve its exalted position, since it shows less a culmination than simply provides yet another similar example of insatiability. It takes on much greater importance, however, as laying the groundwork to the next saying. For now we can read the insatiable fire as a feminine force, what one would expect from the *daughters* of Alukah.

Wonder in Reverse: The Adulteress

While our examples of things wondrous tend to focus on the cognitive—things beyond understanding—there is also interest in their moral import. And although the stress is often on the wondrous nature of the divine, wonder can have a negative valence as well:

> Lord, my heart is not haughty, nor are my eyes: I have not walked in things too great or wondrous (*nifla'ot*) for me. But I have stilled and quieted my soul. (Ps 131:1–2)

Here wonder promotes not attraction but rather repulsion. So too, in its analysis of the mechanics of wonder, our text examines the case of the adulterous woman, what might be termed wonder in reverse.

The case is appended to the usual 3+1 saying, thus doubling the incremental fourth, here by the comparison ("so too"):

> Three things are too wondrous for me, four which I do not understand:
>
> The way of the eagle in the air;
> The way of a snake upon a rock;
> The way of a ship on the open sea;
> And the way of a man with a young woman.

So too the way of [a man with][20] *an adulterous woman: she eats and wipes her mouth and says, "I have done nothing wrong!"* (Prov 30:18–20)

Murphy has the merit of sensing one of the most interesting themes of our numerical saying: "this openness to wonder and the contemplation of one of the deepest mysteries in human relationships is not to be forgotten."[21] However, on the basis of the same formalistic criteria he goes on to exclude the subsequent reference to the adulterous woman: "it is not a harmonious sequence to vv. 18–19. It goes beyond the numerical saying which closed with the fourth item of v. 19d. Moreover, it betrays no wonder, which was a key to the previous verses."[22]

I think, on the contrary, that the surprise is every bit as strong here as before, in the case of kosher sex. First of all, one wonders why it is necessary to change perspective in evaluating the two actions, the way of a man with a woman and the way of a man with an adulterous woman. In the first case, one supposes the perspective either of the general reader or, more likely, a wisdom perspective such as Murphy's. In the case of the adulterous woman, however, must one readily accept the adulterous woman's own evaluation, that of belittling sexuality? If so, then her absence of wonder is itself a wonder, at least from a wisdom perspective.[23] In other words, to wonder in a positive way about sexuality may be of a piece with wondering at how one could not have sensed the wonder of sexuality.

I would suggest that in both cases the root cause of wonder is precisely the absence of cause. Michel de Montaigne's puzzlement over the enigma of evil has the same origin (see previous chapter). Just as goodness is without cause, for its own sake, so

---

[20]Alternatively and usually, the comparison would be between the two women, both of whom leave no trace, since the adulteress either disguises her deed or, discovered, claims to have done no wrong. It seems, rather, that a contrast is intended here, fully focused on the *man* or youth pedagogically addressed from the very beginning of the book of Proverbs.

[21]Murphy, *Proverbs*, 234.

[22]Ibid., 235–36.

[23]Waltke (*Proverbs: Chapters 15–31,* 490) maintains these opposing senses of wonder through the opposition "awesome" versus "aw(e)ful," both seen as provoking awe or surprise.

too is evil equally beyond the reach of any causality one could imagine. Just as there is love without cause (Cordelia's "no cause, no cause" in *King Lear*), so too the rabbinic concept of *sin'at khinam*, hatred for which no cause can be discovered, hatred for its own sake, as it were.[24]

The connective "so too," implying a comparison, argues in this direction. First of all, we recall that the contrast between opposite kinds of women is an essential theme of the entire opening section of the book of Proverbs, glorifying Lady Wisdom and denigrating the Foreign Woman, also an adulteress.[25] In our riddle in Prov 30, the implied contrast is also accompanied by a comparison: just like that woman, so too the adulteress! Does this mean that the first woman is also an adulteress? If so, then there is no contrast at all! Their commonality, rather, lies in two points: first of all, in their *both* being seductive; secondly, in their *both* being wondrous. How so?

Two aspects are stressed by the commentary within the text. On the one hand, the adulteress's wiping her mouth clean parallels the absence of trace or tell-tale signs, as if by caricature. This mimicry of denial seeks to place her in the same category of innocence as the aforementioned young woman. The adulteress's equation of sex with eating, however, also denies their commonality, the fact that they all provoke wonder. The joke then seems to be on her: for the very denial of wonder ("I have done no wrong, it is all as natural as eating!") itself provokes wonder. People will be astonished both by the immorality itself and by the attempt to pass it off, to assert that no harm has been done and will have no consequences.[26]

---

[24]See Montaigne's essay "On Cruelty," in *The Complete Essays of Montaigne*, 316. Thus, Raymond C. Van Leeuwen: "Perhaps more horrifying than the deed itself is the lack of guilt or remorse, as if the deed might be wiped away and leave neither physical nor moral tracks, like a ship on the seas" (*Proverbs* [*NIB* 5; Nashville: Abingdon: 1997], 254). For "horrifying" read "wondrous." André Gide's *acte gratuit* provides a modern example of a random unprovoked act, also morally unexplainable.

[25]See Prov 6:26; 7:10.

[26]Reacting to the presence of unpunished evil in the world, Rashbam (on Qoh 8:10–14) interprets Qohelet's key word *hebel* as the *tohu* of Gen 1:2 ("and the earth was *tohu*"), since people are astounded (*tohim*) by it. See Fox, *A Time to Tear Down*, 33.

A final note on the central concept or image of *derek,* "path or road." We have moved from notions of movement and trace—the before and after of movement that in fact allows the movement to be perceived, as one views a picture from the outside. At another level altogether is the notion of *derek* as "manner" or "behavior," as in "he has a *way* with women." For here we shift from a movement or behavior that is self-referential and self-contained, to a relationship between the creature and its element or place. Whether the creatures in Prov 30:18–20 have a destination is unclear—the boat probably does, for the others it is not so sure—but it is also irrelevant, since, as we have seen above, they make their appearance in cameo scenes quite removed from "real" life concerns such as having a place to go.[27]

Creation and Its Risks

Jewish liturgy, following Ps 136:6, pictures the Creator-God as performing incredible balancing acts: God the magician, working wonders. Such feats were thought to be wondrous because of God's power but especially in the face of dangers intrinsic to all levels of creation. In biblical times who would have thought of living in rocky places, inhospitable to both grazing and agriculture? Who would have attempted flying?[28]

The sages constantly pointed out the world's dangers. From Job we know that bad things can happen to the best of us, beyond our understanding and seemingly without any provocation. From Qohelet we know that everything under the sun is, if not total vanity (frankly, this reading is overkill, although bad experiences can so easily be generalized) then certainly transient, and accompanied by large doses of tragedy along the way. These books stress that you cannot take any of it with you, and that there is a variable

---

[27]So too with the element or place occupied by the creatures: they are just there, and although *how* they manage to just be there was a concern of Qohelet in chapter 1 (they operate on replacement cycles), that is not at all the case here.

[28]Such risk on a grand scale was allowed only on the seas, and this may explain, in our riddle, its proximity to the fourth element, which deals entirely with human matters.

disconnect between intention and outcome, effort and return. Moreover, you are going to die, no question about it, and probably sooner rather than later. Like injustice, sin crouches at the door, and do you really think you will be able to overcome it? In such a universe, why stick your neck out and expose yourself to failure and unrewarded effort?

And yet, their advice is resolute:

Look at the ant, you lazy slug! (Prov 6:6)

Enjoy your youth! (Qoh 11:9)

Cast your bread upon the waters! [as in boats?] (Qoh 11:1)

Take chances!

In fact, one of the most glorious pieces of positive advice in Scripture flaunts those great ills of human ignorance and the unpredictability of the future by putting them to positive advantage:

Just as you do not know the way of the wind,
like the powers hidden in the pregnant womb,
you do not know the working of God, who makes everything.
In the morning sow your seed,
and do not let up your effort even by evening.
For you have no way of knowing which will succeed, whether this one or that one.
And perhaps both will succeed. (Qoh 11:5–7)

Of course there are dangers and risks to be taken: it is programmed that way! But you must take possession of your transience, of what is given you!

And here we come to our riddle:

Air is pure *hebel,* a mere breath; and yet, does not the heavy bird attempt the sky?

Earth, a slip on its hardest form can lead to sure death; and yet, does not the slippery snake glide across the crag without falling?

Water is completely permeable; and yet, does not the heavy boat tempt the deep?

Young man: fire is insatiable; yet you must jump in and seek out your mate!

But don't be foolish. Accepting risk is one thing, courting sure disaster is quite another. For there are fires and there are fires.[29] The wondrous ones burn but do not consume. The others, also wondrous, *do* consume. Thus, seek out *your* mate (Qoh 9:9–10), but not your neighbor's. Bottom line: the world is transient, flimsy, and in a word risky, like the earth stretched out on water; but the wise know how to survive and deal and go forward. Qohelet would have approved.

Finally, like both the man with a woman and with the adulteress, one has to have a *derek,* meaning both a *way* with things and also a proper path or road to follow.[30] There is nothing more dear to the wisdom tradition than this notion, heavily weighted in the direction of right and wrong, of *tsaddiqim* and *reshaᶜim:*

> The Lord cherishes the way of the righteous,
> But the way of the wicked will perish. (Ps 1:6)

Sexual relations with the adulteress will leave no trace, wiped away as one wipes one's mouth after eating. But—surprise!—it now emerges, from the closing contrast with the adulteress, that the righteous person does have a direction. How? By leaving a "trace." This ironic contrast with the adulteress may well be the most wondrous message of our proverb. And, again, the reading may go in either direction, according to the riches of one's own heart: either as "normal" (as eating) or as, well, miraculous. Again, Whybray:

> Probably the reference is not to the act of copulation itself but to what follows: human gestation and birth—the formation of a child

---

[29]"Sexualized fire is par excellence the connective hyphen of all symbols. It unites matter and spirit, vice and virtue. It idealizes material knowledge and materializes ideal knowledge. It is the principle of an essential ambiguity. . . . The reason for such deep duality is that fire is both in us and outside us, invisible and spectacular, spirit and smoke" (Gaston Bachelard, *La psychanalyse du feu* [Paris: Gallimard, 1938], 111).

[30]This would then be an important instance of *antanaclasis,* of repetition of the same word in close proximity with different meanings. Without explanation, William McKane (*Proverbs, A New Approach* [OTL; London, 1970], 79) lists the two possible meanings as "path" and "sovereignty."

in the womb, which is equally seen as a great mystery in Job 10:10–11.[31]

Whybray's "probably" is crucial, keeping the matter open but also affirming that the responsibilities of human freedom apply as much to the ways of interpretation and attitude as to the roads of action. And here we return to the original wonder, of the bush aflame but not consumed. God's voice arises from that flame, if you only turn aside and see and think upon it. For this *mar³eh* is either merely a strange "sight" or it is a "vision"—the same word can have both meanings in biblical Hebrew. As Henry David Thoreau put it, "it may be in Uranus, or it may be in the shutter." Or perhaps both. And the ongoing wonder—both a risk and an opportunity—is in wisdom's "perhaps."

The indeterminacy of "perhaps" links the vulnerability and "vanity" themes of Qohelet with the need to confront the riskiness of an open future:

> The flux [the equivalence of Qohelet's *hebel* or transience] is simply—for better or worse (it all depends)—the element in which things are inscribed, the space in which they are forged, the indeterminacy that is built into whatever gets built, in virtue of which whatever is constructed is deconstructible, which means not only able to be destroyed, but also able to be remade, reconfigured, and reinvented. The flux thus explains the eventiveness in things. It is not only why things are able to fall apart, but why they are able to have a future, why the work of creation can be continued by humankind in a work of continuous re-creation. The ability of a thing to be reinvented and to surpass itself goes hand in hand with its vulnerability to destruction, which is all part of the risk.[32]

---

[31]Whybray (*Proverbs,* 416), who is in good company here, since Rashi explains the verse "the two became one flesh" (Gen 2:24) as referring not to copulation but rather to the production of a child. A further move in the direction of a theological and miraculous reading would be the notion that God, as per Gen 4:1, is a partner in procreation.

[32]Caputo, *The Weakness of God,* 82.

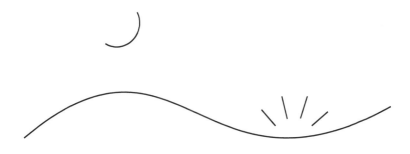

CONCLUSIONS

As explicit divine intervention diminished, so too did clear prophetic communication decline from Moses's face-to-face encounters until prophecy became cloudy and ceased altogether, yielding to what is known as wisdom.[1] Naphtali Tur-Sinai summarizes the matter very well:

> The Deity, which, if it so desired, could state the whole truth clearly, purposely expressed the truth in concealed form and by means of circumlocutions, so that only the intelligent person, the initiated, the expert, might be able to interpret it. Accordingly, prophecy and the interpretation of dreams form for us one of the main sources in the investigation of the riddle.[2]

Between full divine presence and absence arose what we have here called a twilight zone of revelation, where communication remained a possibility, but an unclear one. If God spoke at all, the methods were now the ambiguous and equivocal ones of oracles, dreams, signs, and "chance" happenings (even such things as the sound of a bird), all susceptible to multiple interpretations. In response, wisdom teachers tended to avoid clear religious and holiness interests such as cult and prophecy, turning instead to the

---

[1]This decline cannot be plotted only chronologically, however, since it may still be the case that at any given point in time all levels of contact with God are present and available. For, according to midrashic tradition, did not Abraham, in a world full of idols and violence, discover God on his own and with his own powers?

[2]Tur-Sinai, "The Riddle in the Bible," 140.

normal course of everyday life and its secular meanderings. For example, the author of Proverbs and those who included it in the canon had no problem with inserting secular proverbs of a purely practical nature, nor did the latter-day sages whose words are preserved in such compendia as the *Ethics of the Fathers.*

Works now regarded as standard wisdom creations reacted creatively to God's absence by stressing a skepticism that could lean both ways. Job did everything in his power to achieve a religious understanding of unjustified pain, ending up in a skeptical acceptance of the universe's complexity that paradoxically included God. Qohelet asked whether it is indeed true that after death the body goes downward and the spirit upward. For these authors life goes on and problems are dealt with as they arise. And if God is not always felt to be present, the ambiguity protects such a possibility, for "who knows?" When Qohelet offers his bottom-line conclusion to "fear God and keep his commandments," the message is intellectual, personal, and of course ambivalent: since we just do not know the solution to all of life's problems and how God will judge, it is better to be careful and always do your best. But such fear and caution maintain an openness to deeper religious understanding, where fear can yield to respect and trust, believing that we will continue our human journey upward, accepting what comes and leaving the rest to God.

Wisdom has described the ideal human person as a Tsaddik, as one involved in the creation and sustenance of the world, as outlined in the creation ideology of the book of Genesis. The plot of this book is the creation of the seed of Jacob, the sons that become the tribes of Israel. The etiology given Israel stresses the evolution from the name Jacob-the-devious to that of victor, and with God no less: "For you [Jacob] have struggled with God and won." Whether the patriarch contended with God Himself or an angelic being is hardly crucial, since later the name is confirmed by the deity (Gen 35:9). At this confirmation the blessings awarded are introduced by a command that goes back to the first commandment of the Torah:

> "You shall be called Jacob no more, rather Israel will be your name."
> And he called his name Israel. . . .
> "Be fertile and increase." (Gen 35:10–11)

The repetition marks a particular stress, not only of identity but perhaps also of a second etiology. There is an exegetical tradition of relating Jacob's new name to *yashar,* "straight, upright." Jacob-The-Crooked would thus become straightened out, morally speaking. Israel, in person but also in his seed, would thus fulfill the plot of Genesis, the book of *Yashar.*[3]

The *Pirkei de-Rabbi Eliezer* identifies the first divine being as Israel himself, meaning, I would imagine, that Jacob's struggle was with an *ʾish ʾakher,* "an other person" who was none other than himself! An essential aspect of human creation is thus self creation:

> Within the intimate but teeming space of the ark, Noah becomes, in the midrashic view, a new person—effectively, and retroactively, a person whom the Torah can describe as a tzaddik, "a righteous man."[4]

Other self-creations include Joseph, growing up as a spoiled brat to become the family savior and the sustainer of myriads; Samson, inscribed prenatally by an angel named *peliʾ* ("wonder," Judg 13:18), unsuccessful both at peaceful coexistence and love, but following his signs and evolving from a ladies' man to a liberator; Saul, unable to fit into a job for which he was unqualified, but salvaging remnants of his deeper self through prophetic interludes; Solomon, in his decision to save and not split the baby, a pure practitioner of wisdom creation ideology; an aged *bakhur* glad of having enjoyed his youth and with intimations of things yet unseen but wondrous; a virile man turning away from adultery and, erotically, founding a family.

There is an egalitarian streak among the sages that regarded power as dangerous and to be neutralized. Just as false prophets claimed divine communication (1 Kgs 13), so too unscrupulous people could project authority through another form of power-speak, proverbs and aphorisms. How, for example, does one counsel a youth enticed by the power of the proverb: "stolen waters are sweet" (Prov 9:17)? How can the public misjudge Saul and be allowed to enforce this opinion through a faulty proverb? One important wisdom argument made by the Saul story is that, if

---

[3] For a discussion of Jacob's name see Sarna, *Genesis,* 404–5.
[4] Zornberg, *Genesis,* 58.

proverbs are to be used, then they must be subjected to at least the same criticism as ordinary speech.

Power-speak becomes even more dangerous when the subject is God. The sages had a deep understanding that, of all forms of power, God's was the most beneficent and seductive, thus potentially the most dangerous. If God sometimes seemed absent, the hunger remained, and a critical question became: "How do we talk honestly about God?" In the world of Pharaoh, whose idea of God seems particularlistic, Joseph the Tsaddik talked about nothing else. Modern-day America, where ninety percent of people believe in heaven, presents a different scenario. In such a climate the sages may have preferred reticence, in order not only to achieve social justice but also to protect God. Emmanuel Levinas's formulation is worthy of sustained reflection: "to bear witness to God is precisely not to state this extraordinary word."[5]

Modesty of speech goes hand in hand with intellectual honesty, and for the sages this begins with what Michel de Montaigne (again!) called sincerity. By this he meant dealing with life honestly, as it is and not what we would like it to be. Just as "the Torah speaks in the language of human beings," so too is the world available to our experience, our pains, and our hopes. To be frank, this may amount to simply hanging on or in, come what may, perhaps not what one would like. But the chances are worth taking, for they are entwined with the wildest possibilities:

a) an awareness of unsatisfied thoughts, vast yearnings, and fields of new dreams, now enabled by aging and the accompanying withdrawal from the busy humdrum;

b) twilight thoughts in twilight years, aroused by the sound of a bird and ever-fertile nature;

c) joy with the woman of one's youth; the wonderment aroused by both sexuality and evil;

d) the *puer-senex* conundrum, which includes both the standard moral aversion to being dead while we are alive, and also the tease of being alive even after we are dead;

---

[5]Emmanuel Levinas, quoted in Michael Fagenblat, "Lacking All Interest: Levinas, Leibowitz, and the Pure Practice of Religion," *HTR* 97 (2004): 1.

e) intimations beyond mortality, of something outside the cycle
   and circle of transience.

In the last analysis the appeal is to a human nature still unde-
veloped (or, perhaps, underdeveloped), thoughts yet to be clari-
fied and satisfied, Levinas's "the not yet";[6] to God's very nature as,
in its definitional essence, the futurity of the future (*'ehyeh*);[7] to
yet a fourth day somewhat like the preceding three but of a wondrous nature.[8] In Qohelet's hopeful ambivalence, "all is still before them" (9:1).[9] He refers not to "the world to come" but rather
to "*this* world to come," the eternity of the here and now in this
simple world that remains so far beyond our human understanding, both risky and pregnant with wondrous possibility (Qoh
3:11).[10] Who would want to be anything but a builder of the future, a Tsaddik?

We can now return to our earlier musings on literal representation and interpretation, and ask: Are the possibilities in Qoh
12:1–8 happening in the real world? This would be the case in the
event of a military invasion or general catastrophe such as a
drought: mills would shut down, social activities would cease or
be cut back. The intent of the passage, however, is more that of a
general situation applicable to each and every individual. The
question then becomes: Are the possibilities being taken away (by
disease, old age) or are they being refused? The option offered
here seems actually to occupy the median position between the
two: as the hair turns gray a person may "decide" that certain
things are no longer "interesting," perhaps that these things are

---

[6]"le pas encore," Levinas, *Totality and Infinity,* 247.

[7]Exod 3:14. Not "I am who I am" (NRSV) but rather: "I shall be who I
shall be."

[8]In the original creation narrative the fourth day begins a triad similar to
the previous one, but of a different qualitative level, for now that the environments are in place, the creatures are brought forth that are to inhabit and interact with them: birds in the sky, fish in the sea (but also boats), fertile men and
women. . . . See above, chapter 2, n21.

[9]Many commentators refer this to the past, reinforcing the predestina-
tion argument, although this seems a bit far-fetched. The meaning, rather, is
both spatial, "in front of them," and temporal, "in the future." So too James L.
Crenshaw, Graham Ogden, and Robert Gordis (on Qohelet, ad loc.), who interprets: "the future is uncertain." And thus, we add, the meaning is open.

[10]Neher, *Notes sur Qohélét,* 100.

no longer "appropriate" to this season of life. Thus, again in participation with the Creator-God and nature, balances and adjustments are reached.

Some of us are humanly proactive and, well, just plain heroic. The Talmud puzzles over the verse in Psalms where David claims to "awake the dawn" (57:9[57:8]; 108:3[108:2]), for is not the reverse the case, that the dawn awakens him?[11] At other times life itself seems to take the lead. I wake up to discover that I am no longer young. Nature itself has taken over. How could I not have known? Maybe I should be more thoughtful. Maybe I will be surprised into it, as with the sound of a bird. . . . I had better listen up a bit better. Who knows?

---

[11]See *b. Ber.* 3b–4a. Reclaiming one's active nature in the face of contrary evidence is alive and well in Henry David Thoreau's inversion of dawn, which becomes a figure or symbol of a *spiritual* awakening or state of heightened awareness (*Walden,* "What I Lived For").

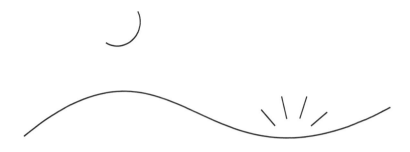

Excursus: Righteousness in the Ethics of the Fathers

In Jewish practice, the liturgical reading of the *Ethics of the Fathers*—the most popular collection of mishnaic sayings—is introduced by the following preamble:

> All Israelites have a portion in the world-to-come, as it is said: "And your people, all of them righteous, shall inherit the land forever: the branch of My plantings, the work of My hands, in order to be glorified" (Isa 60:21). (*b. Sanh.* 10:1)

The righteous, as we shall see, are those who work together as a community or "people" of God to build up the world. Though constantly frustrated and rejected, the righteous will all have their "portion," their reward appointed by the Lord. This hope and promise are designated by both time and place: the world-to-come and the land. Our text in fact offers a definition of the utopian ideal of the world-to-come, Jewish style: the entire people living in the land / Land forever.[1]

Note carefully that the text does not exclude other peoples from the "land"; rather, it reassures Israelites that they will inherit a

---

[1]While the land surely has a concrete reference ("the Torah never entirely departs from its literal sense"), it allows considerable allegorical extension, as can be seen from such a text as Ps 37: "dwell in the land and enjoy security" (v. 3); "those who wait upon the Lord shall inherit the land" (v. 9); "the meek shall inherit the land" (v. 11); also vv. 22, 29, 34.

portion, and that they will do so corporately because of their communal and total dedication to righteousness. This leaves other portions for other peoples of the earth, as Israel is thus *one* branch of God's plantings. Thus, there exists a single standard (righteousness) for all peoples, and there is open admission to its labors and benefits, based on a merit system of righteousness.

The proof-text then specifies these two components in theological terms: the *people* are seen, organically and dynamically, as God's planting that grows and fructifies, while the *land,* the work of God's hands, seems to pre-exist. The two notions come together in the verse in Psalms that speaks of the reward of the world-to-come as "light sown for the righteous" (97:11). These verses seem in fact complementary in their use of developmental imagery: Isa 60:21 views the righteous as planted, while Ps 97 applies the planting imagery to the reward.

This, then, is the allegorical frame of *Abot,* repeated at the start of each chapter in its liturgical or inspirational extension: history is a tree of God's own planting and the righteous are its branches. The final fruit will bring glory, surely to God and just as surely to the righteous.

At the conclusion of the reading, the following epilogue is recited:

> Rabbi Chananya the son of Akashya says: "The Holy One—Blessed be He—desired to increase Israel's worth; therefore He gave them Torah and commandments in abundance. As it is said: 'For the sake of His (his?) righteousness the Lord desires to magnify and glorify the Torah'" (Isa 42:21).

There are two ways to read this mishnah. On the one hand, in His desire to increase Israel's worth God acts out of a sense of His own righteousness as the supreme Sustainer of the universe. Or, on the other, He may wish to vindicate Israel from some accusation or guilt, in which case He would be acting to restore Israel's righteousness, now understood as a declaration of innocence. In both cases, it is Israel's attachment to the Torah—as demonstrated in the learning just performed—that confirms the desired result: the declaration of God's righteousness and of Israel's guiltlessness.

One reason for the selection of this particular proof-text is its resumption of the concept of righteousness as presented in the preamble, thus completing the bracketing of the entire chapter. There it is a question of Israel's righteousness; but the assertion of Israel's creation by God means that Israel's righteousness receives its ultimate motivation and justification from God's own righteous nature. Here the obverse may be implied: that God gives Torah for the sake of his (Israel's), not only His, righteousness. Rabbi Chananya thus implies that God and Israel's righteousness is of one kind and continuous. That, we recall, is also the message of Ps 1.

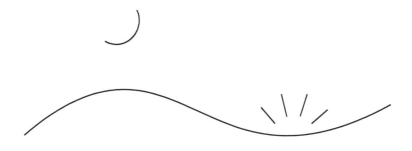

Bibliography

Abarbanel, Don Isaac (1437–1508). *Commentary on the Earlier Prophets*. Jerusalem: Torah ve-Daat, 1955.

Aitken, Kenneth T. *Proverbs: The Daily Study Bible*. Philadelphia: Westminster, 1986.

Aletti, Jean-Noël. "Le jugement de Salomon 1 R 3, 16–28." Pages 313–37 in *Toute la sagesse du monde: Hommage à Maurice Gilbert, S. J.* Edited by François Mies. Namur: Lessius, 1999.

Alter, Robert. *The Art of Biblical Narrative*. New York: Basic, 1981.

———. *The David Story*. New York: Norton, 1999.

———. *Genesis: Translation and Commentary*. New York: Norton, 1996.

Andersen, Francis I., and David Noel Freedman. *Hosea: A New Translation with Introduction and Commentary*. Anchor Bible 24. Garden City, N.Y.: Doubleday, 1980.

Arama, Isaac (1420–1494). *Akedat Yitzak* [Commentary on the Chumash and the Five Megillot]. Pressburg: V. Kittseer, 1849; repr., Jerusalem: Yisraʾel–Ameriqah Tel Aviv, 1960.

Bachelard, Gaston. *La psychanalyse du feu*. Paris: Gallimard, 1938.

Bechtel, Lyn M. "Rethinking the Interpretation of Genesis 2.4B–3.24." Pages 77–117 in *A Feminist Companion to Genesis*. Edited by Athalia Brenner. Sheffield: Sheffield Academic Press, 1993.

Berlin, Adele. *Poetics and Interpretation of Biblical Narrative*. Winona Lake, Indiana: Eisenbrauns, 1984.

Beuken, William A. M. "No Wise King Without a Wise Woman (1 Kings iii 16–28)." Pages 1–10 in *New Avenues in the Study of the Old Testament.* Edited by Adam S. van der Woude. Oud-testamentische Studiën 25. Leiden: Brill, 1989.

Blanchot, Maurice. *Écriture du désastre.* Paris: Gallimard, 1980.

Boling, Robert G. *Judges: Introduction, Translation, and Commentary.* Anchor Bible 6A. Garden City, N.Y.: Doubleday, 1975.

Brettler, Marc Zvi. *The Book of Judges.* New York: Routledge, 2002.

Brown, Francis, S. R. Driver, and C. A. Briggs. *A Hebrew and English Lexicon of the Old Testament, with an Appendix Containing the Biblical Aramaic.* Oxford: Clarendon, 1906.

Brueggemann, Walter. *First and Second Samuel.* Interpretation. Louisville, Ky.: Westminster John Knox, 1990.

Caputo, John D. *The Weakness of God: A Theology of the Event.* Bloomington: Indiana University Press, 2006.

Cassuto, Umberto. *Commentary on the Book of Genesis.* 5th ed. [Hebrew]. Jerusalem: Magnes, 1969.

Cogan, Mordechai. *1 Kings: A New Translation with Introduction and Commentary.* Anchor Bible 10. New York: Doubleday, 2001.

Collins, John J. *The Bible after Babel: Historical Criticism in a Postmodern Age.* Grand Rapids: Eerdmans, 2005.

———. *Jewish Wisdom in the Hellenistic Age.* Louisville, Ky.: Westminster John Knox, 1997.

Crenshaw, James L. *Ecclesiastes: A Commentary.* Old Testament Library. Philadelphia: Westminster, 1987.

———. *Joel: A New Translation with Introduction and Commentary.* Anchor Bible 24C. New York: Doubleday, 1995.

———. "The Samson Saga: Filial Devotion or Erotic Attachment?" *Zeitschrift für die alttestamentliche Wissenschaft* 86 (1974): 470–504.

———. *Samson: A Secret Betrayed, A Vow Ignored.* Atlanta: John Knox, 1978.

———, ed. *Studies in Ancient Israelite Wisdom.* New York: KTAV, 1976.

Curtius, Ernst Robert. *European Literature in the Latin Middle Ages.* New York: Harper, 1953.

Deurloo, K. A. "The King's Wisdom in Judgment: Narration as Example (1 Kings iii)." Pages 11–21 in *New Avenues in the Study of the Old Testament.* Edited by Adam S. van der Woude. Oudtestamentische Studiën 25. Leiden: Brill, 1989.

Di Santo v. Pennsylvania, 273 U.S. 34, 42 (1927).

Elizur, Yehudah. *Judges.* [Hebrew]. Jerusalem: Mossad Harav Kook, n.d.

Emerson, Ralph Waldo. *The Portable Emerson.* Edited by Carl Bode. Rev. ed. The Viking Portable Library. New York: Penguin Books, 1981.

Emmrich, Martin. "The Symbolism of the Lion and the Bees: Another Ironic Twist in the Samson Cycle." *Journal of the Evangelical Theological Society* 44 (2001): 67–74.

Epstein, Isidore, ed. *Babylonian Talmud.* 18 vols. London: Soncino, 1935–1948.

Ethics of the Fathers. See Pirkei Abot.

Fagenblat, Michael. "Lacking All Interest: Levinas, Leibowitz, and the Pure Practice of Religion," *Harvard Theological Review* 97 (2004): 1–32.

Fisch, Harold. *The Holy Scriptures: English Text Revised and Edited.* Jerusalem: Koren, 1992.

———. *Poetry with a Purpose.* Bloomington: Indiana University Press, 1990.

———. *A Remembered Future: A Study in Literary Mythology.* Bloomington: Indiana University Press, 1984.

———. "Ruth and the Structure of Covenant History." *Vetus Testamentum* 32 (1982): 425–37.

Fishbane, Michael. *Text and Texture.* New York: Schocken, 1979.

Fokkelman, J. P. *Narrative Art and Poetry in the Books of Samuel.* Assen: Van Gorcum, 1981–1990.

Fontaine, Carol. "The Bearing of Wisdom on the Shape of 2 Samuel 11–12 and 1 Kings 3." *Journal for the Study of the Old Testament* 34 (1986): 61–77.

———. *Traditional Sayings in the Old Testament.* Sheffield: Almond, 1982.

Foucault, Michel. *Les mots et les choses.* Paris: Gallimard, 1966.

Fox, Everett. *The Five Books of Moses.* New York: Schocken, 1995.

Fox, Michael V. *Qohelet and His Contradictions.* Sheffield: Almond, 1989.

———. *A Time to Tear Down and a Time to Build Up: A Rereading of Ecclesiastes.* Grand Rapids: Eerdmans, 1999.

Freedman, Amelia Devin. *God as an Absent Character in Biblical Hebrew Narrative: A Literary-Historical Study.* New York: Lang, 2005.

Gammie, John G. and Leo G. Perdue, eds. *The Sage in Israel and the Ancient Near East*. Winona Lake, Ind.: Eisenbrauns, 1990.

Ginzberg, Louis. *The Legends of the Jews*. 6 vols. Philadelphia: Jewish Publication Society, 1968.

Goldin, Judah. "The Youngest Son or Where Does Genesis 38 Belong?" *Journal of Biblical Literature* 96 (1977): 27–44.

Gordis, Robert. *Koheleth, The Man and His World: A Study of Ecclesiastes*. 3d ed. New York: Schocken, 1968.

Greenstein, Edward L. "The Riddle of Samson." *Prooftexts* 1 (1981): 237–60.

Grossman, David. *Lion's Honey*. Translated by Stuart Schoffman. Edinburgh: Canongate, 2006.

Harper, William Rainey. *Amos and Hosea*. International Critical Commentary. Edinburgh: T&T Clark, 1966.

Hélias, Pierre-Jakez. *The Horse of Pride*. Translated by June Guicharnaud. New Haven: Yale University Press, 1978.

Heschel, Abraham J. *The Prophets*. New York: Jewish Publication Society, 1955.

Hurvitz, Avi. *Wisdom Language in Biblical Psalmody* [Hebrew]. Jerusalem: Magnes, 1991.

———. "Wisdom Vocabulary in the Hebrew Psalter: A Contribution to the Study of 'Wisdom Psalms.'" *Vetus Testamentum* 38 (1988): 41–51.

Isaiah da Trani (ca. 1180–1250). *Commentary*. Edited by A. J. Würtheimer. 3 vols. Jerusalem: Ketav Yad va-Sefer, 1978.

Jacob, Benno. *The First Book of the Bible: Genesis*. Translated by Ernest I. Jacob and Walter Jacob. New York: Ktav, 1974.

Japhet, Sara, and Robert B. Salters. *The Commentary of R. Samuel Ben Meir Rashbam on Qoheleth*. Jerusalem: Magnes, 1985.

Keil, Yehudah. *The Book of Proverbs* [Hebrew]. Jerusalem: Mossad Harav Kook, 1983.

———. *Commentary on the Book of Kings* [Hebrew]. Jerusalem: Mossad Harav Kook, 1989.

———. *1 Samuel* [Hebrew]. Jerusalem: Mossad Harav Kook, 1981.

Krüger, Thomas. *Qoheleth*. Minneapolis: Fortress, 2004.

Landy, Francis, "Are We in the Place of Averroes? Response to the Articles of Exum and Whedbee, Buss, Gottwald, and Good." *Semeia* 32 (1984): 131–48.

Lasine, Stuart. "The Riddle of Solomon's Judgment and the Riddle of Human Nature in the Hebrew Bible." *Journal for the Study of the Old Testament* 45 (1989): 61–86.

Leibowitz, Nehama. *Studies in Bereshit (Genesis) in the Context of Ancient and Modern Jewish Bible Commentary* [Hebrew]. Translated by Aryeh Newman. 4th rev. ed. Jerusalem: World Zionist Organization, 1981.

Leone Ebreo. *Dialoghi d'amore.* Edited by Santino Caramella. Bari: Laterza, 1929.

Levinas, Emmanuel. *Dieu, la mort et le temps.* Paris: Grasset, 1993.

———. *Totality and Infinity.* Translated by Alfonso Lingis. Pittsburgh: Duquesne University Press, 1969.

Levine, Baruch. *Numbers 21–36: A New Translation with Introduction and Commentary.* Anchor Bible 44. New York: Doubleday, 2000.

Lohfink, Norbert. *Qoheleth: A Continental Commentary.* Minneapolis: Fortress, 2003.

Long, Burke O. *I Kings, with an Introduction to Historical Literature.* Forms of Old Testament Literature 9. Grand Rapids: Eerdmans, 1984.

Maimonides [Moses ben Maimon]. "Laws of Kings." *The Code of Maimonides: Book XIV, The Book of Judges.* Translated by Abraham M. Hershman. New Haven: Yale University Press, 1949.

———. "Laws of Repentance." *Book of Knowledge [Mishneh Torah, Book I].* Translated by Moses Hyamson. New York: Bloch, 1937.

Malbim (Meir Loeb ben Jehiel Michael, 1809–1879). *Commentary on the Torah* [Hebrew]. Printed in standard editions of the Hebrew Bible with commentaries.

Marks, Herbert. "Biblical Naming and Poetic Etymology." *Journal of Biblical Literature* 114 (1995): 21–42.

Mathewson, Steven D. "An Exegetical Study of Genesis 38." *Bibliotheca Sacra* 146 (1989): 373–92.

McCarter, P. Kyle, Jr. *I Samuel: A New Translation.* Anchor Bible 8. Garden City, N.Y.: Doubleday, 1980.

McKane, William. *Proverbs: A New Approach.* Old Testament Library. London: SCM, 1970.

Meiri; Ha-Meiri. *See* Menahem Ha-Meiri.

Menahem Ha-Meiri (1249–ca. 1310). *Perush 'al Sefer Mishlei* [Commentary on the Book of Proverbs]. Edited by Menachem Mendel Zahav. Jerusalem: Otsar ha-Poskim, 1969.

———. *Perush 'al Sefer Tehilim* [Commentary on the Book of Psalms]. Edited by Menachem Mendel Zahav. Jerusalem: Otsar ha-Poskim, 1971.

Mishnah: Danby, Herbert, ed. and trans. *The Mishnah: Translated from the Hebrew, with Introduction and Brief Explanatory Notes.* London: Oxford University Press, 1933.

Mishnah: Neusner, Jacob, ed. and trans. *The Mishnah: A New Translation.* New Haven: Yale University Press, 1988.

Müller, Hans-Peter. "Der Begriff Rätsel im Alten Testament." *Vetus Testamentum* 20 (1970): 465–89.

Montaigne, Michel de. *The Complete Essays of Montaigne.* Translated by Donald Frame. Stanford, Calif.: Stanford University Press, 1976.

Murphy, Roland E. *Ecclesiastes.* Word Biblical Commentary 23A. Dallas: Word Books, 1992.

———. *Proverbs.* Word Biblical Commentary 22. Nashville: Thomas Nelson, 1998.

———. *The Tree of Life: An Exploration of Biblical Wisdom Literature.* New York: Doubleday, 1990.

———. *Wisdom Literature.* The Forms of Old Testament Literature 13. Grand Rapids: Eerdmans, 1981.

Neher, André. *Notes sur Qohélét.* Paris: Éditions de Minuit, 1951.

Niditch, Susan. "Samson as Culture Hero, Trickster, and Bandit: The Empowerment of the Weak." *Catholic Biblical Quarterly* 52 (1990): 608–24.

———. "The Wrong Woman Righted: An Analysis of Genesis 38." *Harvard Theological Review* 72 (1979): 143–49.

O'Connell, Robert H. *The Rhetoric of the Book of Judges.* Leiden: Brill, 1996.

Ogden, Graham. *Qoheleth.* Readings: A New Biblical Commentary. Sheffield: JSOT Press, 1987.

The New Oxford Annotated Bible: Revised Standard Version. New York: Oxford University Press, 1977.

Pardes, Ilana. *Countertraditions in the Bible.* Cambridge, Mass.: Harvard University Press, 1992.

Parker, Alexander A. *The Allegorical Drama of Calderón: An Intro-duction to the Autos Sacramentales.* Oxford: Dolphin, 1968.

Perdue, Leo G. "Cosmology and Social Order in the Wisdom Tra-dition." Pages 457–78 in *The Sage in Israel and the Ancient Near East.* Edited by John G. Gammie and Leo G. Perdue. Winona Lake, Ind.: Eisenbrauns, 1990.

———. *Wisdom and Cult.* Society of Biblical Literature Disserta-tion Series 30. Missoula: Scholars Press, 1977.

Perry, T. A. "Cain's Sin in Genesis 4:1–7: Oracular Ambiguity and How to Avoid It." *Prooftexts* 25 (2006): 259–76.

———. "The Coordination of *ky / 'l kn* in Cant. i 1–3 and Related Texts." *Vetus Testamentum* 54 (2005): 528–41.

———. *Dialogues with Kohelet: The Book of Ecclesiastes: Transla-tion and Commentary.* University Park: Pennsylvania State University Press, 1993.

———. *Erotic Spirituality: The Integrative Tradition from Leone Ebreo to John Donne.* University: University of Alabama Press, 1980.

———. *The Honeymoon Is Over—Jonah's Argument with God.* Peabody, Mass.: Hendrickson, 2006.

———. "Metaphors of Sacrifice in the Zohar." *Studies in Com-parative Religion* 16/2 (n. d.): 188–97.

———. *The Moral Proverbs of Santob de Carrión: Jewish Wisdom in Christian Spain.* Princeton: Princeton University Press, 1987.

———. "A Poetics of Absence: The Structure and Meaning of Chaos in Genesis 1:2." *Journal for the Study of the Old Testa-ment* 58 (1993): 3–11.

———. *Wisdom Literature and the Structure of Proverbs.* Univer-sity Park: Pennsylvania State University Press, 1993.

Petersen, David L. "Genesis and Family Values." *Journal of Biblical Literature* 124 (2005): 5–23.

Pirkei Abot (Ethics of the Fathers). Pages 446–61 in *The Mishnah: Translated from the Hebrew, with Introduction and Brief Ex-planatory Notes.* Edited and translated by Herbert Danby. London: Oxford University Press, 1933.

Pope, Marvin. *Job: Introduction, Translation, and Notes.* 3d ed. Anchor Bible 15. Garden City, N.Y.: Doubleday, 1973.

Rad, Gerhard von. *Genesis, A Commentary.* Translated by John H. Marks. Rev. ed. Philadelphia: Westminster, 1972.

———. *Wisdom in Israel.* London: SCM, 1972.

Ramban (Rabbi Moshe ben Nachman, 1194–1270). *Commentary on the Torah.* 5 vols. Translated and annotated by Charles B. Chavel. New York: Shilo, 1971.

Rashbam (Samuel ben Meir, ca. 1085–ca. 1158). *See* Japhet, Sara, and Robert B. Salters.

Rashi (Rabbi Shlomo Yitzhak, 1140–1105). *See Torat Hayyim.*

Rendsburg, Gary A. "David and His Circle in Genesis xxxviii." *Vetus Testamentum* 36 (1986): 438–46.

———. "The Guilty Party in 1 Kings III 16–28." *Vetus Testamentum* 48 (1998): 534–41.

Ross, Allen P. "Genesis." Pages 15–101 in *The Bible Knowledge Commentary: An Exposition of the Scriptures.* Edited by John F. Walvoord and Roy B. Zuck. 2 vols. Dallas: Victor, 1985.

Roth, Philip. *American Pastoral.* Boston: Houghton Mifflin, 1997.

Roth, Wolfgang M. *Numerical Sayings in the Old Testament: A Form Critical Study.* Supplements to Vetus Testamentum 13. Leiden: Brill, 1965.

La Sainte Bible. L'École Biblique de Jérusalem. Paris: Cerf, 1956.

Sarna, Nahum M. *Exodus: The Traditional Hebrew Text with the New JPS Translation.* Philadelphia: Jewish Publication Society, 1991.

———. *Genesis: The Traditional Hebrew Text with the JPS Translation.* Philadelphia: Jewish Publication Society, 1989.

———. *Songs of the Heart: An Introduction to the Book of Psalms.* New York: Schocken, 1993.

Schipper, Jeremy. "Narrative Obscurity of Samson's *hidah* in Judges 14:14 and 18." *Journal for the Study of the Old Testament* 27 (2003): 339–53.

Segert, Stanislav. "Paronomasia in the Samson Narrative in Judges XIII–XVI." *Vetus Testamentum* 34 (1984): 454–61.

Seow, Choon-Leong. *Ecclesiastes: A New Translation with Introduction and Commentary.* Anchor Bible 18C. New York: Doubleday, 1997.

Sforno (Obadiah ben Yaakov, 1475–1550). *See Torat Hayyim.*

Soggin, J. Alberto. *Joshua: A Commentary.* Translated by R. A. Wilson. Old Testament Library. Philadelphia: Westminster, 1972.

———. *Judges: A Commentary.* Translated by John Bowden. Old Testament Library. Philadelphia: Westminster, 1981.

Soncino Books of the Bible: The Psalms. Translated by A. Cohen. London: Soncino, 1945.

Sternberg, Meir. *The Poetics of Biblical Narrative: Ideological Narrative and the Drama of Reading.* Bloomington: Indiana University Press, 1985.

Sweeney, Marvin A. *The Twelve Prophets.* 2 vols. *Berit Olam.* Collegeville, Minn.: Liturgical, 2000.

Tanakh: The Holy Scriptures: The New JPS Translation According to the Traditional Hebrew Text. Philadelphia: Jewish Publication Society, 1988.

Targum Onkelos. See Torat Hayyim.

Taylor, Archer. *The Proverb and an Index to the Proverb.* Hatboro, Pa.: Folklore Associates, 1931.

Theroux, Paul. "America the Overfull." *New York Times* Op-Ed, Sunday Dec. 31, 2006.

Thoreau, Henry David. *Walden, or Life in the Woods; and "On the Duty of Civil Disobedience."* Introduction by W. S. Mervin with an afterward by Perry Miller. Revised and updated bibliography. New York: New American Library, 1999.

Torat Hayyim: Chumash [the Five Books of Moses], *with Classical Commentaries.* Edited by Mordechai Breuer et al. 7 vols. Jerusalem: Mossad Harav Kook, 1986–93.

Tosefta Berakhot. Edited by Saul Lieberman. New York: Jewish Theological Seminary of America, 1955.

Tur-Sinai, Naphtali. "The Riddle in the Bible." *Hebrew Union College Annual* 1 (1924): 125–49.

Van Leeuwen, Raymond C. *Proverbs.* New Interpreter's Bible 5. Nashville: Abingdon, 1997.

Waltke, Bruce K. *The Book of Proverbs: Chapters 1–15.* New International Commentary on the Old Testament. Grand Rapids: Eerdmans, 2004.

———. *The Book of Proverbs: Chapters 15–31.* New International Commentary on the Old Testament. Grand Rapids: Eerdmans, 2005.

Weinfeld, Moshe. *Deuteronomy and the Deuteronomistic School.* Oxford: Clarendon, 1972.

Weitzman, Steven. "The Samson Story as Border Fiction." *Biblical Interpretation* 10 (2002): 158–74.

Westermann, Claus. *Genesis: An Introduction.* Translated by John Scullion. Minneapolis: Fortress, 1992.

Whybray, Roger N. *Ecclesiastes: Based on the Revised Standard Version.* New Century Bible Commentary. Grand Rapids: Eerdmans, 1989.

———. *Proverbs: Based on the Revised Standard Version.* New Century Bible Commentary. Grand Rapids: Eerdmans, 1994.

Wildavsky, Aaron. "Survival Must Not Be Gained through Sin: The Moral of the Joseph Stories Prefigured through Judah and Tamar." *Journal for the Study of the Old Testament* 62 (1994): 37–48.

Wolde, Ellen van. "Who Guides Whom? Embeddedness and Perspective in Biblical Hebrew and 1 Kings 3:16–28." *Journal of Biblical Literature* 114 (1995): 623–42.

Yadin, Azzan. "Samson's *hidah.*" *Vetus Testamentum* 52 (2002): 407–26.

Zakovitch, Yair. *The Song of Songs: Introduction and Commentary* [Hebrew]. Jerusalem: Magnes, 1992.

Zornberg, Aviva Gottlieb. *Genesis: The Beginning of Desire.* Philadelphia: Jewish Publication Society, 1995.

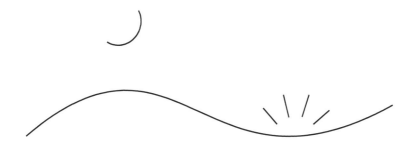

INDEX OF NAMES AND SUBJECTS

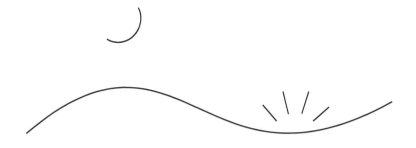

INDEX OF ANCIENT SOURCES

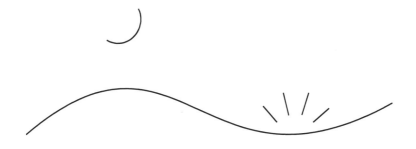

INDEX OF HEBREW WORDS